BELOVED CHEF AND BEST-SELLING AUTHOR LIDIA BASTIANICH shares, for the first time, the timeless recipes that have made her flagship restaurant, Felidia, a New York City dining legend for almost four decades.

Ever since it opened its doors on Manhattan's Upper East Side in 1981, Felidia has been revered as one of the best Italian restaurants in the country. In these pages, Lidia and longtime Executive Chef Fortunato Nicotra share 115 of the recipes that capture the spirit of the Felidia menu past and present. From pastas and primi to appetizers and meats, and from breads and spreads to sides and soups, these are some of Lidia's absolute favorite dishes, lovingly adapted for home cooks to re-create in their own kitchens.

Here are recipes for old-school classics such as Pasta Primavera and Linguine with White Clam Sauce and Broccoli. Contemporary favorites include Pear and Pecorino Ravioli, Chicken Pizzaiola, Short Ribs Braised in Barolo, and Eggplant Flan with Tomato Coulis. Exquisite dessert recipes include Warm Chocolate-Hazelnut Flan, Open Cannolo, and Limoncello Tiramisù, while Passion Fruit Spritz and Frozen Peach Bellini come from the restaurant's lively bar. *Felidia* is a beautifully illustrated, full-color cookbook that takes readers behind the scenes of the restaurant's storied history and is filled with the same warmth and hospitality that are the hallmarks of all of Lidia's books. It's the next-best thing to enjoying an evening out at this award-winning eatery

Fortunato

ALSO BY LIDIA MATTICCHIO BASTIANICH

My American Dream: A Life of Love, Family, and Food

Lidia's Celebrate Like an Italian

Lidia's Mastering the Art of Italian Cuisine

Lidia's Egg-citing Farm Adventure

Lidia's Commonsense Italian Cooking

Lidia's Family Kitchen: Nonna's Birthday Surprise

Lidia's Favorite Recipes

Lidia's Italy in America

Nonna Tell Me a Story: Lidia's Christmas Kitchen

Lidia Cooks from the Heart of Italy

Lidia's Italy

Lidia's Family Table

Lidia's Italian-American Kitchen

Lidia's Italian Table

La Cucina di Lidia

FELIDIA

Felidia
FELIDIA

FELIDIA

Recipes from My Flagship Restaurant

Lidia Matticchio Bastianich

WITH CHEF FORTUNATO NICOTRA
AND TANYA BASTIANICH MANUALI

PHOTOGRAPHS BY JENNIFER MAY

Alfred A. Knopf New York 2020

THIS IS A BORZOI BOOK PUBLISHED BY ALFRED A. KNOPF

www.aaknopf.com

Library of Congress Cataloging-in-Publication Data
Names: Bastianich, Lidia, author. | Nicotra, Fortunato, author. |
Manuali, Tanya Bastianich, author. | May, Jennifer, photographer.
Title: Felidia : recipes from my flagship restaurant / Lidia Matticchio Bastianich with
Chef Fortunato Nicotra and Tanya Bastianich Manuali ; photographs by Jennifer May.
Description: First edition. | New York : Alfred A. Knopf, 2019.
Identifiers: LCCN 2018060923 (print) | LCCN 2019000910 (ebook) |
ISBN 9781524733094 (eBook) | ISBN 9781524733087 (hardcover : alk. paper)
Subjects: LCSH: Cooking, Italian. | Felidia (Restaurant) | LCGFT: Cookbooks.
Classification: LCC TX723 (ebook) | LCC TX723 .B3156 2019 (print) | DDC 641.5945—dc23
LC record available at https://lccn.loc.gov/2018060923

Interior photography by Jennifer May
Jacket design by Kelly Blair

Manufactured in the United States of America
Published October 29, 2019
Second Printing, June 2020

This book is dedicated to all the talented and hardworking people that through the years have made Felidia the great restaurant that it is; this is a tribute to all of you.

Grazie Mille

—LIDIA BASTIANICH

Contents

APPETIZERS

SOUPS

PASTAS AND PRIMI

Dried Pastas and Sauces

Fresh Pastas and Gnudi

Risottos

SEAFOOD

MEAT AND POULTRY

SIDES

Acknowledgments

I have been writing cookbooks for thirty years, and it was time to sit down and create a collection of recipes that span the history of what customers and viewers know as my flagship restaurant, Felidia. Restaurant recipes are not always easy to replicate in the typical home kitchen. But together with Felidia's longtime Executive Chef Fortunato Nicotra, my co-author and daughter, Tanya, and a team of very gifted individuals, we have done just that.

I would like to first thank all of the employees of Felidia, whose collaborative efforts have kept the restaurant open for almost forty years. I give a big thank-you to kitchen and front-of-house management and staff. It takes a village, and our many years of success would not have been possible without a dedicated team of hardworking people who make Felidia's hospitality and dining experiences happen every day. Some of my dear friends who worked the front and back of the house are no longer with us, but they helped to give this place its energy and history.

I must thank my mother, Erminia, who helped raise my two children during the early years when we were opening Felidia, our first Manhattan endeavor. She stayed at home with Joe and Tanya during many late nights and eventually worked as a receptionist and even in the coat room when the situation demanded it. I thank my son, Joseph, for working his paper route as a small kid in Queens to help finance the opening and my daughter, Tanya, for working here as a teenager in the summers, and also now, as she manages not only Felidia but many other restaurants.

Chef Fortunato Nicotra arrived in 1996 when I began to expand the family business and has been behind the range ever since. He brought with him authentic Italian tradition, coupled with a persistent search for the best of both Italian and local ingredients, as well as a flair for artistic and contemporary presentation. I thank him for his long years of dedication and inspiration to the many chefs and cooks who have worked in the Felidia kitchen.

Amy Stevenson has been testing recipes and heading my Public Television show kitchen for many years, and she was with us testing each of these recipes to make sure that home cooks will be able to easily create these delicious classics. Thank you to Liz Crabtree in the recipe kitchen as well!

I thank Peter Gethers and Tom Pold for pushing us to work harder and write better; it was a pleasure working on the book with both of you, and your rounds of edits are always welcome! Thank you to Janna Devinsky for her utmost professionalism and organization; it is much appreciated. I send a heartfelt thank-you to Paul Bogaards for years of friendship and support and for always being enthusiastic about our books. You are a believer and we love that. To our Knopf promotional mavens, Emily Reardon and Sara Eagle, we are so thankful for your work in promoting. Thank you, Anna Knighton, Kristen Bearse, Kelly Blair, and Carol Carson, for designing the book—inside and out—and making it all look so good. It is a tough job to pull everything together and thank goodness we have you to do it for us. You made it all so easy. And for capturing it all with a wonderful eye, thank you to Jennifer May. Your work in photography is gorgeous, and it is an absolute pleasure to work with you. Thanks also to Barb Fritz for styling the photos and Liam Canning for lighting it all up.

Thank you to our office and restaurant staff who provide us with support so we can be creative and make books. Thank you to the American Public Television team for the fabulous work done in the distribution of the show and to Laurie Donnelly, the late Anne Adams, Bara Levin, Matt Midura, and Jeffrey Elias at WGBH. Our years together have been great ones. I also would like to thank the many sponsors of our Public Television show who help me to continue sharing recipes with my fans and restaurant customers: Cento, Consorzio del Grana Padano, Loacker, Rovagnati, Fabbri USA, Auricchio Provolone, Locatelli Pecorino, Olitalia, Regione Puglia, and FESR. Thank you also to Juliska for the gorgeous tableware and linens and to the wonderful showroom consultants at Clarke, who provide the gorgeous kitchen in which the show is filmed.

Introduction

I am proud to say that Felidia has stood as one of the preeminent restaurants on Manhattan's East Side since April 15, 1981. But thirty-seven years ago, we weren't so sure this would be the case. New York has one of the most challenging restaurant climates in the nation. And even though classics like Delmonico's, Old Homestead, Peter Luger's, Keens, and Katz's Delicatessen have found ongoing success and continue to thrive, the vast majority of the establishments that open in the country's most competitive food market will close their doors within the first five years, according to Hudson Riehl of the National Restaurant Association.

I knew the odds, but I had a vision, and I was determined to make it work.

In 1981, with two young children and two successful restaurants under our belts, my husband, Felix, and I took on what would prove to be the most daunting and risky project of our lives, the building of Felidia on East Fifty-eighth Street in New York City. Our two Queens eateries, Buonavia in Forest Hills and Villa Secondo in Fresh Meadows, were drawing crowds, but we aspired to open a new, more elegant establishment in Manhattan, where we could showcase the regional Italian food we had both grown up on—a cuisine that few restaurants were serving at the time.

During the 1970s and early '80s, most Italian restaurants were serving the simplest of Italian American dishes—spaghetti and meatballs, chicken Parmigiana, baked ziti, lasagna—all smothered in marinara sauce. That's because most Italian food in America originated with the Italian immigrants who had come to the United States from the southern part of Italy, mainly Calabria, Campania, and Sicily. In order to cook their traditional foods, they needed Italian products such as Aceto Balsamico, Prosciutto di Parma, and Grana Padano. However, these ingredients were not readily available to them here in the States, so they had to improvise, using what they could find. That meant, for example, substituting U.S.-grown beefsteak tomatoes for the sweet, thin-skinned San Marzano tomatoes of Italy. Pasta was precooked and then just reheated in boiling water, sauced, and served. Not to cook pasta *al minute* and al dente was and still is sacrilege in Italy. Veal cutlet topped with mounds of oozing mozzarella is unheard of there, where a parmigiana is a cutlet sprinkled with grated cheese and baked in the oven until crisp and served on a thin layer of tomato sauce. At the time, meat was far more expensive in Italy, and the good cuts were hard to find, whereas in America beautiful cuts of meat were readily available, so chefs here were able to load their Sunday sauces with plenty of meatballs, sausages, and braciole. American garlic was the one ingredient that was close to the Italian version, so they used a lot of it—it reminded them of home.

When we opened our very first restaurant, Felix and I knew we had to include these Italian American favorites on our menu, too, so we hired the best Italian American chef we could find to run the kitchen. But we wanted to offer our customers something more. Over time, slowly, we began to incorporate some of the recipes we had known from our childhoods in our native Istria, an area that once belonged to Italy and is now part of Croatia. We had both come to the United States from Communist Yugoslavia—Felix at the age of eighteen, and I when I was just twelve years old.

My passion in the kitchen is deeply rooted in my childhood in Istria. Food—growing it, preparing it, and eating it—was constantly intertwined with my daily life, and it is those early memories, and my time spent in the kitchen with my grandmother, that continue to drive me today, as I seek to re-create these simple yet unforgettable culinary pleasures, one dish at a time.

At Buonavia, our first restaurant, which my husband and I opened in 1971, I started as a hostess, but slowly moved to the role of sous-chef in the kitchen, working alongside the chef and introducing him to the flavors I recalled from my youth.

I was not sure how such dishes would be accepted by our clientele, and most of the time I would not list them on the menu. Instead, I would offer them to customers in a small tasting dish alongside the meals they had ordered. I enjoyed coming out of the kitchen, walking through the restaurant, and chatting with guests at their tables. I'd tell them about the dish and its origin, and solicit feedback. There were winners, including fresh-pasta dishes such as pappardelle and mushrooms (page 100) and fuzi with braised duck (page 110)—in which the duck is simmered in broth with tomatoes to concentrate its flavor—and other dishes that weren't met with the same level of enthusiasm.

Meanwhile, Felix enjoyed the many hours he spent working the front of the house, greeting customers and playing the showman as he prepared special tableside dishes with a flourish. The consummate restaurant man, he labored long and hard behind the scenes, paying close attention to sourcing the best-quality meat, seafood, and other supplies at the best price. The family station wagon often reeked of fish after a run to the fish market, to the dismay of our children, Tanya and Joe. It wasn't just the stench of fish that had the kids complaining. We used the car to transport all of the meat and poultry from the markets to the restaurant, so the odor of the juice of chicken guts was frequently intermingled with the fishy smells. The children were embarrassed to invite their friends to drive with us in the station wagon and avoided offering our services as carpool drivers as much as they could.

In 1977, when we decided to open Villa Secondo, I had no reservations about running it on my own, while Felix remained at Buonavia. Although I still served as sous-chef, my role in the kitchen became increasingly prominent, and I began to take even more risks with the menu. As the owner, I had to manage both the front and the back of house.

At the time, diners were skeptical of dishes like fegato alla Veneziana (calves' liver and onions), and tripa d'muncalè (Venetian-style tripe). But tastes have changed over the years, and now those are big favorites. Although, even today, tripe isn't an American favorite—but it's still on the menu at Felidia for those who like it (including me). Polenta, a dish not typically found in Italian American restaurants, was another hit. I also introduced patrons to cozze alla Triestina, mussels in a white-wine-and-breadcrumb sauce (page 34), a regional recipe that differed from the commonly prepared mussels marinara with lots of red sauce.

Word of the flavorful dishes we were serving began to spread, and soon journalists and food critics were turning up at Villa Secondo to sample my regional fare. It wasn't long before people started making the short trip from Manhattan to Queens to try it for themselves. The consensus was that I needed to bring my special Istrian and northern Italian dishes to Manhattan. I knew I'd be breaking new ground if I moved ahead. Back then, there were very few women chefs. It was a role that was almost always held by a man.

Ultimately, the positive feedback I received from patrons and food critics convinced me I was ready to move up to the role of first chef and demonstrate my well-honed talents in the kitchen when we opened Felidia in Manhattan.

Although I'd never been formally trained in a chefs' school, I had extensive experience in the kitchen. I'd spent my early years working alongside my beloved grandmother Rosa, helping out with chores and preparing meals on the small farm she and my grandfather Giovanni owned in Busoler, a tiny Istrian village on the outskirts of the city of Pola. My mornings included feeding the pigs, milking the goats, and collecting the eggs from the chickens that roamed the courtyard in front of their house, where a fig tree, like a big umbrella, provided much-needed shade and plenty of juicy figs for homemade jam for the breakfast toast. Afternoons had me out in the garden, picking tomatoes, beans, herbs, and potatoes for the next meal. In season, I enjoyed foraging for asparagus in the sprawling pine forest behind the house. The dishes were simple in their preparation but were made with the freshest ingredients.

When my family left Yugoslavia, it was my great-aunt, a personal chef in Trieste, Italy, who took me into the kitchen and taught me the art of food preparation and presentation. Later, when we immigrated to the United States and both of my parents had to go to work, it was me in the kitchen in the afternoons after school, preparing the family dinners with ingredients my mother had left for me.

I was sixteen when I met Felix, who was seven years my senior and shared my passion for food. Much of our courtship involved visiting new restaurants, sampling different cuisines, and even taking notes on the interior décor of the places we ate at—all in preparation for opening our own establishment at some point in the future.

At the time, Felix was working as a captain at the highly regarded Romeo Salta, an Italian restaurant on West Fifty-sixth Street in Manhattan. It was one of the first restaurants in Manhattan to serve fine Italian cuisine, and Felix savored his role as a front-of-house man. Even when we had friends over for dinner at home, he would end up making a flambé dessert at the table, and everyone loved it. I was fascinated by this kind of showmanship, and when Felix took me to Romeo Salta to celebrate a birthday, I got to see where and how he had learned his tricks of the trade. It was an extraordinary experience, and one I fondly remember even today.

The elegant décor, the crisply pressed white linen tablecloths—nothing was lost on me. I delighted in the changes of china and silverware with each course, and the swapping out of the wineglasses, from champagne glass to white wine glass to red wine glass. I especially loved the servers' attention to detail—the waiter artfully unfolding the napkin in my lap or grating fresh cheese on my pasta, the flaming dessert made tableside and served deliciously warm. I marveled, too, at all the little extras—the cookies, biscotti, and chocolates that came as surprises after the dessert was served. To think that maybe I was sitting in the seat that Sophia Loren had occupied!

I had valuable culinary experience of my own. When I was fifteen, I had an after-school job at Walken's Bakery, a family-run business in Astoria owned by Paul Walken, the father of the actor Christopher Walken, whom I still count among my special friends. Most days, I'd sell cakes and other baked goods to customers, stock the shelves, and help keep the place clean and tidy. On Sundays, I got to perfect my cake-decorating skills. It was the one day of the week when the bakers would go home early to be with their families—and leave undecorated cakes to be finished by the staff. The job fell to me.

Later, I waitressed at various pizzerias and restaurants in Manhattan, where I stayed just long enough to learn what I could about each new business before moving on to another. I changed jobs so frequently that my mother fretted that I couldn't hold down a position for more than a few months. But I told her not to worry: I was deliberately moving from place to place, picking up new skills as I went.

After opening two restaurants in Queens, Felix and I had loads of experience between us when, in 1979, we set out in search of a site to build Felidia—a combination of our two first names. We found a turn-of-the-century brownstone at 243 East Fifty-eighth Street, between Second and Third Avenues. Back then, the New York dining scene was wholly different from today. Fine dining belonged to French restaurants like Lutèce and La Grenouille. There were a handful of restaurants serving northern Italian cuisine, but few had polenta or risotto on their menus. At the time, Fifty-eighth Street was buzzing with great Italian restaurants—Tre Scalini, La Girafe, Altri Tempi, Gian Marino, Bruno's, Anche Vivolo, and La Camelia—all fine-dining establishments, but their menus were unlike what we were going to offer.

There was already a restaurant operating at 243 East Fifty-eighth Street, San Martin, which served Spanish cuisine out of a simple storefront with a white stucco façade. We knew the façade and the interior could all be redone. We were

drawn to the brownstone because of its location, its size, and the fact that it was a mixed-use building with apartments on the upper floors. It reminded us of similar structures in Italy, where many restaurants operate from the houses where the owners live—*casa e bottega,* as they say in Italian. We didn't intend to live on the premises, however; we would need the money from the upstairs rental to help offset the mortgage cost.

We also liked that there was a parking lot just a few steps away, at the corner of Fifty-eighth Street and Second Avenue. We were hoping that some of our regulars from Queens would drive into Manhattan to eat at our new restaurant, and figured that the lot would make parking easy for them. But that was not to be. Just a year after our restaurant opened, the parking lot was sold, and workmen flooded the site to begin work on a new apartment building.

The owner of the brownstone knew that we were going to be hard-pressed to pull together financing for the massive undertaking, so he agreed to accept a down payment, the remainder to be paid once we sold our two Queens locations. Everything seemed to be falling into place when we sat down with the architects we had hired to help us with the renovations. This would be our first time doing a major building overhaul, and we were determined to give it an upscale look and feel. This was Manhattan, after all, and we needed to be competitive. We brought in Antonio Morello and Donato Savoie of Studio MORSA on Centre Street in New York's Little Italy to draw up the plans for the interior, a step that we hadn't taken with either of our Queens restaurants. We had been very frugal before, spending only what was necessary to give them a fresh look inside.

There were forty feet of empty property behind the building. The architect's plan was to dig out the vacant portion of the parcel and construct a basement there that could be used for storage. A two-story structure would then be erected on top

of that storage space—the first floor to be used as a kitchen, and the second floor to house another dining room.

We planned to add a skylight atop that new second floor to create a "*giardino,*" an enclosed patio, like those found in Italy. When completed, the building would hold two dining areas and a bar—enough to seat ninety-five to a hundred patrons. The architects also found elaborate, antique mahogany panels at an estate sale in upstate New York, salvaged from a Hudson River mansion. They would be restored and installed inside the restaurant to create a warm and upscale space for diners, with their rich patina and shine, which reminded me of maple syrup. To be sure, the wood panels were an added cost, but everyone felt they were a worthwhile investment.

Throughout the construction process, Felix and I spent our daylight hours worrying over each detail. In the evening, we would go through the budgetary projections and cost estimates, trying our best to ensure that the numbers worked. We assumed the role of general contractors for the project and continued to press ahead as the work became ever more ambitious—and costly. We were about a month away from our anticipated December 1980 opening date when we were informed that the foundation under the structure was unstable and needed to be reinforced—a major expense we hadn't planned on. Correcting the problem meant delaying the opening and going well over budget. But we knew we didn't have a choice in the matter, and so we green-lit the project and postponed the opening.

We had projected an initial budget of seven hundred thousand dollars. But the additional work on the foundation pushed us over a million dollars, or the equivalent of more than three million today. Though that's not a lot of money when compared with the costs for opening a high-end restaurant nowadays, we were doing this all on our own, without any partners. We cut costs where we could. Financing was solely our responsibility, and finding adequate funds to bring the project to fruition was becoming a serious problem. My parents, Erminia and Vittorio Matticchio, pulled money from their personal retirement account to help, but even that wasn't enough.

The tremendous financial pressure weighed heavily on both of us, and we dealt with it in our own ways. Felix grew quiet and withdrawn, while I struggled to stay positive. I didn't know much about depression at the time—no one in our circle talked openly about mental health in those days—but in retrospect I realize that Felix had fallen into a depression amid all the stress. He would not call or talk to his friends, and he could not sleep at night. He was anxious and no longer seemed interested in the project. Desperate to make sure that the restaurant got done, I took on a leading role, securing a bank loan and becoming general contractor all by myself.

I had purchased Queen Anne–style chairs in Italy for the restaurant and had them shipped back to New York. My plan had been to have them professionally stained and upholstered here. But, with the bills piling up, I realized we had to find another, much less expensive way of getting the chairs done. My mother, our then nine-year-old daughter, Tanya, and I hopped into a car and drove to a fabric shop, where we selected a beautiful brocade of roses, a pattern you might find on couches in Renaissance Italy. Now all we had to do was figure out how to do the actual work. Because the restaurant accommodated up to a hundred guests, upholstering the chairs would be an enormous task. I visited an upholsterer and asked for tips.

I brought the chairs home from Manhattan a few at a time and placed them in the garage behind our house. There my father, Vittorio, methodically sanded each one before applying multiple layers of stain and a satin finish. Each one took hours. When the woodwork was done, he would move to the upholstery, carefully covering the seat and rear cushion. He repeated this process over and over again, literally dozens of times, happy to lend a hand when it was needed the most.

But my father suffered a stroke and passed away before the restaurant could be completed. His unexpected death added to the stress that everyone was feeling. Still, we had no choice but to move ahead. Tanya and others pitched in and finished the remaining chairs. But I was sorrowful, exhausted, and terrified that we might lose everything.

By early December, it was clear the restaurant would not be ready to open for the Christmas holiday, which meant we would miss the lucrative holiday-season business. We were seriously behind schedule, and running out of money. Some months, we couldn't make our mortgage payment plus pay the additional loan we had with the building's former owner, who knew how cash-strapped we were and agreed to let us pay late—with interest.

We were determined to spend money where it made sense while being frugal on other costs. Rather than buying expensive new pots and pans for the kitchen, we visited restaurant supply stores and picked up used ones at a fraction of the cost. I was quite familiar with those supply companies, after dealing with them for both of the Queens restaurants. We spent hours cleaning and shining all the pots and pans. Little Tanya would help to scrub and clean whatever she could. Though it was difficult and time-consuming work, it had to get done, and there was no one else to do it. Everything hinged on getting the restaurant open so that we'd finally have a source of revenue.

There were times when we barely had enough money to feed the family. Our teenage son, Joe, even took a job making bagels at a bagel store in Bay Terrace in the early mornings, before school, and continued with his paper route, too. He chipped in everything he made toward household finances so that the family could eat; Joe was our "secret financier" at the time.

Near the end, there was absolutely no money left to pay the workers who were still putting in long hours to complete the project. I was cooking every day, well into the evening, to test various recipes for the menu. To encourage the workers to stay and continue laboring beyond the regular workday, my mother and I started cooking for them at the restaurant, and even cleaned up after them at the end of each day, so they could concentrate on efficiently continuing construction on the restaurant.

Somewhat surprisingly, some of the owners of other restaurants on Fifty-eighth Street reached out to help, too. The chef from Bruno's, across the street, and the owners of Tre Scalini, a few doors away, brought food and drinks and visited with us late in the evenings, encouraging us not to give up.

The work continued through the cold, harsh winter months. By April 1981, we were out of funds and owed money not just to the bank and the building's former owner but also to contractors. Though Felidia still wasn't finished, it was close. We decided we had no choice but to open. We would finish all the areas that diners could see but leave some of the smaller projects, like painting a few corners and finishing the wine racks behind the bar, until later. To be sure, we made certain that all the utility connections had been properly made and that all the major equipment, including refrigerators, the stove, and other appliances, was in working order.

The opening-night event would be invitation-only. Since most of the invitations were to family, friends, and longtime customers from our two Queens restaurants, I decided to keep their design simple and easy to reproduce. I used a standard-sized, eight-and-a-half-by-eleven-inch sheet of paper folded in half. One half of the page featured an image and became the front of the invitation; the actual invitation was handwritten inside. I quickly dashed something out on a piece of paper. I wanted to telegraph that Felidia was going to use nothing but the best ingredients and everything was going to be farm-fresh. For the cover image, I found an old black-and-white photo of my beloved Nonna Rosa and cropped it to add emphasis to the basket full of fresh eggs by her side, and the apron she wore over her black dress. Inside was my handwritten invitation.

We cordially invite you to celebrate
the opening of

Felidia

243 East 58th ST. New York City
our new restaurant

Wednesday April 15, 1981

5:00 P.M – 11:00 P.M.

Please come Felice & Lidia

R.S.V.P. 758-1479

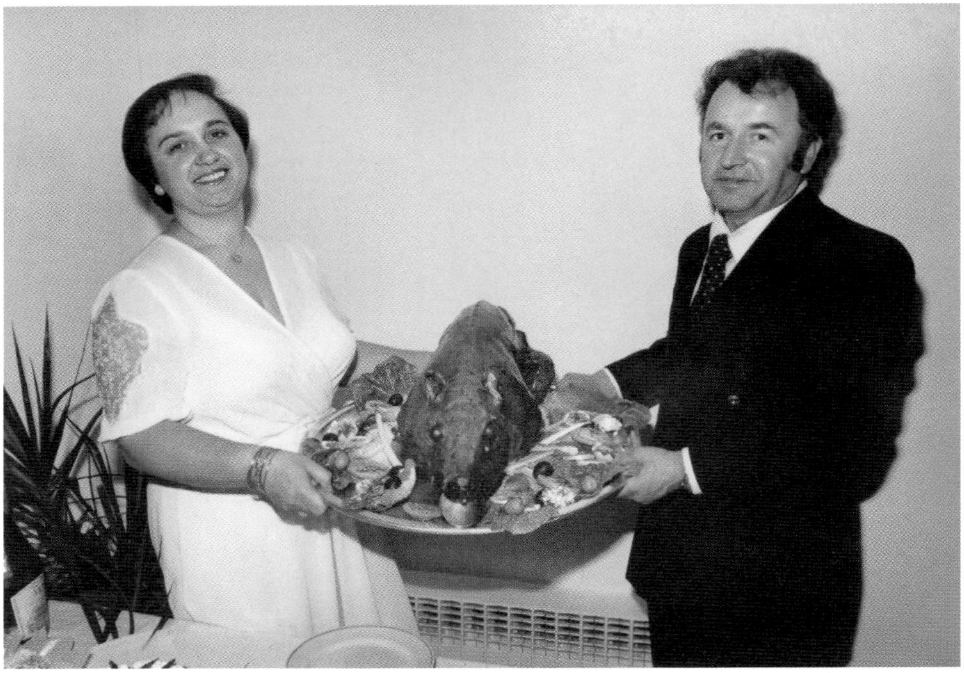

The day of the opening party, the front of the restaurant was decorated with magnums of wine and a huge spray of flowers. The dark, rich mahogany walls that had been brought in from upstate New York gave the space a warm feeling and served as a gorgeous backdrop for the blossom-filled arrangements. We set out an elaborate assortment of antipasti on a buffet table with a green marble top and brass legs that had been set up next to the bar. There were some ten to twenty different dishes on the table, including marinated fish, vegetables, octopus salad, seafood salad, and grilled eggplant. An elaborate dinner followed the antipasti. In keeping with our Istrian roots, we served a whole suckling pig, and its entrance into the dining room on a platter was met with oohs and aahs and loads of applause.

There were a few mishaps on that opening night, of course, but nothing that the diners would have noticed. One of the refrigerators didn't chill down as fast as it should have, and the staff had some anxious moments in the kitchen. Nevertheless, it was a momentous night for us all, and Felidia was finally open to the public. The opening meant that money began flowing in, and we were able to start tackling the frightening stack of unpaid bills.

My early signature main courses included ossobuco alla Milanese (page 163), whole roasted branzino (page 135), and even fegato alla Veneziana, or seared calves' liver. I also introduced regional dishes, such as pasutice all'Istriana (fresh pasta with seafood sauce), krafi (Istrian wedding ravioli, stuffed with rum, raisins, and three different Italian cheeses), frico (Montasio-cheese crisp), polenta e cacciagione (polenta with wild game), and insalata di polpo e patate (warm octopus-and-potato salad, page 47). Homemade risotto, polenta, fresh pasta, stuffed pasta, and gnocchi were all on the menu. I also served lots of wild game and many regional recipes from Trieste, such as mussels Triestina (page 34), fuzi (in other parts of Italy called garganelli) with mixed seafood sauce, or hen guazzetto, dishes that had been popular when I had served them at my restaurants back in Queens.

To my utmost delight, Felidia, with its regional Italian menu and female chef, was an instant hit. Still, I worried about filling tables, prompting my mother, Erminia, to commence a one-woman advertising campaign. For months after the opening, she stationed herself on the corner of Third Avenue and Fifty-eighth Street, where she handed out flyers and pointed people down the block to our restaurant. Her efforts were laudable, but it was a *New York Times* review that really put Felidia on the map. Almost immediately, the phone began ringing off the hook with people calling to make reservations. Soon prominent personalities and even celebrities began stopping in to sample the fare. Julia Child and James Beard were among the early famous diners, and their visits to the restaurant eventually led to a friendship and the creation of my cooking show for Public Television.

In the years that followed, Felidia served such notable guests as Roberto Benigni, Robert De Niro, Paul Newman, Robert Redford, Pierce Brosnan, Mark Rylance, Steve Martin, Sean Connery, Leo DiCaprio, Mario Cantone, Danny DeVito, James Spader, Mike Piazza, Jodie Foster, Isabella Rossellini, Vanessa Williams, Carole Bouquet, Glenn Close, Maria Grazia Cucinotta, Antonella Clerici, Kathie Lee Gifford, Sophia Loren, Phil Collins, Mick Jagger, Carlos Santana, Michael Jordan, Mike D'Antoni, Gualtiero Marchesi, Thomas Keller, Cesare Giaccone,

Massimo Bottura, Daniel Boulud, Barbara Bush, Maria Bartiromo, Pino Cuttaia, Billy Joel, Il Volo, Alan Alda, prime ministers, presidents, and countless others.

I received many accolades during my tenure in the kitchen, including the prestigious James Beard Award for Best Chef: New York City in 1999 and Outstanding Chef in 2002. But I didn't do it alone. Everything I do involves teamwork, and I strive to surround myself with people who support my drive and vision. We were lucky to have the brothers Dante and Nino Laurenti on our team. With some gentle coaxing, they agreed to leave their posts at Brussels Restaurant—a fine northern Italian establishment that was owned by Albert Giambelli, the brother of Francesco Giambelli of the iconic Giambelli's Ristorante on Fiftieth Street—and join the staff at Felidia. Dante was an extraordinary cook, but at Felidia he took on the role of maître d' par excellence. He loved working in the dining room—finishing pasta, boning pheasants, chicken, and fish—and the customers adored him. He also made a big show for diners who ordered our dessert crêpes or palacinke, which we served tableside and flambéed with some Grand Marnier. His brother Nino was a sommelier, great with wine; together, they made a terrific team. Sam Peros was a fixture at the bar, and his convex martini—a martini poured to the brim of the glass so that the drink appears higher in the center than on the sides—became famous and earned Felidia a feature article in *Cosmopolitan,* with Sam as the star.

I had been executive chef of Felidia for almost fifteen years when I began hav-

ing trouble with my knees. By then, the restaurant was running like a fine-tuned machine, but the thought of turning over the reins to someone new overwhelmed me. But I was nearing fifty and knew the time had come, so I put out feelers with friends and colleagues, hoping to find an executive chef who could step into my shoes. It was not a decision I took lightly. I was possessive of my "child"—Felidia. Who would love it as much as I did?

After about a year of research and the trial of three new possible chefs, I was still at square one. I decided to call my friend and fellow chef Luigi Caputo from Torino to see if he might be able to recommend someone up to the task. Within a few days, he called me back. He had found a person he thought was the perfect fit for me, a young chef named Fortunato Nicotra. Chef Fortunato had been born in Sicily but raised and schooled in Torino, in the heart of northern Italy's Piemonte region, where his parents had immigrated to work in the factories. He attended culinary school in Torino and worked in restaurants in Germany and France before returning to Sicily, where he ran two restaurants, each with a Michelin star, in the seaside town of Milazzo. He had the cuisine of Piedmont and northwestern Italy under his belt, and at home, with his mother, he cooked Sicilian food. I had northeastern Italy covered myself, and the rest of Italy we could share; at least, that was my vision.

After a few telephone interviews, I asked him to come to New York, so he could see Felidia, we could get in the kitchen together, and I could taste his food. He was eager to showcase all the fancy foods he had learned to prepare in France. I tasted his dishes, and I liked what I sampled. But it wasn't quite what I was seeking for Felidia. I asked him if he could prepare some of the dishes his mother had cooked for him in Sicily. It was then I knew I had a winner. His cooking was authentic, regional, and full of flavor, and I immediately felt comfortable with him in my kitchen. He was enthusiastic and passionate, and he jumped behind the line. I had a lot to tell him about me and my food, and I wanted to know more about his style. But, in my mind, there was no doubt that we could make good "food music" together.

I slowly relinquished my kitchen to Fortunato, and he took it over with all his might. Now, twenty-five years later, I feel he still leads one of the best Italian kitchens in New York. Not to say the arrangement didn't take some getting used to. Fortunato was accustomed to cooking for fifty people a night in Sicily, and he walked into Felidia and began cooking for two hundred. It resulted in an almost addictive kind of energy that made him constantly feel the need and desire to taste, learn, cook, and evolve. Slowly, we fell into a rhythm, sharing our culinary secrets, trading recipes, and blending our respective ideas and talents, with award-winning results. Just three months after his arrival, Ruth Reichl of *The New York Times* awarded Felidia three stars. And, in 2006, the *Times*' Frank Bruni gave it a second three-star review.

Needless to say, it quickly became apparent that there was no need for me to change Fortunato or his food. He was, and still is, cooking what I love—innovative Italian regional cuisine made with great respect for traditional and seasonal products. We travel to Italy together on a regular basis, sometimes with other chefs from our group, to refresh and catch up on what is happening with food in the different regions of the country. I think I brought him closer to the cuisine of Istria and Friuli–Venezia Giulia, and I love when he teaches me one of his mother's special Sicilian dishes.

In 1998, Felidia was named one of the "Top Ten Italian Restaurants in the United States" by *Wine Spectator,* followed in 2008 with a Number 2 designation by Jerry Shiver of *USA Today* in his year-end roundup of restaurants around the world.

The kitchen at Felidia is Fortunato's domain now, but I continue to pay regular visits to share with him some new dish I have found or some new product I have tasted. Usually, he ends up creating his own rendition of the idea. It still excites me when he comes up with a new dish and, if I am in the office, he brings me up a tasting. I have great respect and admiration for this talented chef who had the courage to push me slowly out of my own kitchen. Often, when I am traveling through Italy and I make a new discovery, I send him photos right away. Then, when I return to New York, we get together in the kitchen and test these new ideas; inevitably, some end up on our menus.

Today the menus at Felidia reflect the meeting of two Italians from very different areas of the peninsula with similar connections to food. My formative years were spent with my grandmother on a farm in bucolic Busoler, collecting freshly laid eggs and picking plump red cherries and juicy ripe figs from the family's fruit trees. Fortunato's early days were spent with his Sicilian mother, who prepared home-cooked meals every day and tried to re-create Sicilian flavors in their home in Torino. He spent summers in a rural town in Sicily where bread was made by one of his aunts and tomato paste was left out to dry in the sun by others. But

he also watched and cooked alongside his beloved neighbor Signora Delfina, in a courtyard similar to the one in Busoler that I so fondly recall, and he learned some of Piedmont's oldest and most prized culinary traditions.

Felidia
Ristorante
243 East 58th Street New York, N Y 10022 (212) 758 1479

The more than one hundred recipes in this cookbook include signature dishes or parts of signature dishes that you can find on the Felidia menu today, such as Fortunato's ever-evolving beet salad (page 43), the popular candele pasta with spicy tomato and rosemary (page 83), and the Berkshire pork chops Milanese (page 158). Also included are dishes that were popular a decade or even two or three decades ago, when I was still in the kitchen—recipes such as the always sold-out ossobuco alla Milanese (page 163) and the Rigatoni Woodsman Style (page 96), a favorite of Tanya's.

Though I am no longer at the helm in the kitchen, Felidia is still my home. It is here that I maintain a simply furnished office full of cookbooks and photos, and a small staff who work on it all—restaurants, marketing, cookbooks, television, and specialty foods. Today I am behind an empire of restaurants and eateries including Becco, Del Posto, Lidia's Kansas City, Lidia's Pittsburgh, and Eataly in New York, Chicago, Boston, Los Angeles, Las Vegas, and Brazil. I have authored fourteen cookbooks, three children's books, and my own memoir. I also have my own television production company and a line of specialty pastas and sauces. But my heart belongs to Felidia.

So—come on in. Odds are, I'll be there to greet you and make sure that everything is perfect.

FELIDIA

FELIDIA

COCKTAILS

Food is the heart of a restaurant, but a comfortable, friendly bar with great drinks and a smiling, welcoming bartender is like a prelude to a great symphony or opera. The Felidia bar is an intimate and welcoming part of the restaurant, known for its warmth, hospitality, and delicious classic Italian cocktails, wines by the glass, and many craft-made Italian drinks with an American twist (or even vice versa). Every time I walk in, it feels like coming home. I often sit at the edge of the bar and watch the dining room, even to this day. The selection of drinks at the bar is contemporary, refreshing, and playful; a number of regular guests come in just for the unique cocktails and to eat a quick, casual dinner.

The big mahogany bar is immediately visible upon entering the brownstone building that Felidia occupies. Italian mosaic-tile floors and deep-honey-patina woodwork all add to the atmosphere: you know it is going to be good when you cozy on up to the large slab of white Carrara marble and grab a stool covered in fine Italian leather. I purchased the old woodwork in the 1980s from a mansion on the Hudson River that was being torn down. Its history has added warmth to the space over the years of Felidia's history. From when we first opened with our bartender, Sam Peros, who was famous for his handsome mustache and convex martini—poured to the brim so that the drink seems to be higher in the center than the sides—up until today, when the staff know all the regulars and their preferences and newcomers are made to feel right at home, Felidia's bar is the place where you meet friends and relax with a drink; if you get hungry, the bartender will set you up with a delicious appetizer or a steaming hot plate of pasta.

PANZANELLA BLOODY MARY

Panzanella is a traditional Tuscan tomato-and-bread soup or salad I have often enjoyed on trips to Italy, and an American Bloody Mary with an Italian twist is the fun way we serve it at Felidia. This drink uses all the panzanella ingredients except the bread, but you can serve a thin slice of toasted bread on the side as part of the garnish. I like the crunch the toast adds.

MAKES 4 DRINKS

1 tablespoon extra-virgin olive oil
½ teaspoon ground peperoncino
4 very thin slices country bread
Kosher salt
1 Persian cucumber, coarsely chopped
1½ cups very ripe red cherry tomatoes
3 tablespoons chopped pickled onions (or chopped red onion if pickled onions aren't available)
6 ounces vodka
2 ounces freshly squeezed lime juice
1½ teaspoons Worcestershire sauce
1 teaspoon hot sauce, or to taste
Freshly grated horseradish, to taste
Maldon smoked sea salt, for rimming the glasses
Celery sticks, for garnish
Tomolives (pickled green cherry tomatoes), for garnish

Preheat the oven to 350 degrees F.

Combine olive oil and ground peperoncino in a small bowl. Put the bread on a baking sheet, and bake until crisp, about 8 to 10 minutes, depending on thickness. Immediately brush lightly with the peperoncino oil. Season lightly with salt, and let cool.

Combine the cucumber, tomatoes, and pickled onions in a blender, and blend until smooth. Strain into a pitcher through a fine-mesh strainer, pressing on the solids. Stir in the vodka, lime juice, Worcestershire sauce, hot sauce, and horseradish.

Rim four rocks-glasses with the Maldon smoked salt, and fill them with ice. Pour the mixture over the ice, and add a celery stick and tomolive to each. Serve the spicy toasts on the side (not in the drink).

STOCKING A HOME BAR

Felidia's bar is well stocked with multiple brands of alcohol, as well as sodas, bitters, and fruits and pickled vegetables for garnishes. This setup isn't easy to replicate outside of a restaurant, but that doesn't mean you can't serve great drinks at home. When you're stocking a home bar, it is best to use a side counter or table and have one ice bucket to put bottles in and another for ice. As for wines, a white sparkling, a red, and a white are sufficient. You will need the basic liquors: vodka, rum, gin, tequila, and Scotch. Select two or three fruit juices—orange, grapefruit, and cranberry will do—and a few small bottles of club soda and Coke. Add a small selection of garnishes, such as orange and lemon slices and olives, and you have yourself a full-fledged bar.

RESERVE DU DOMAINE
OVER 15 YEARS OLD
RHUM
Barbancourt
DISTILLE ET MIS EN BOUTEILLE PAR
J. P. GARDERE & Cie
PORT AU PRINCE
HAITI
DON BAIRO
elisir amaro
ANNO DOMINI 1452
DON BAIRO
AMARO TONICO DIGESTIVO
APERITIVO A BASE DI VINO
Preparato con infusi naturali, estratti da erbe e sostanze aromatiche vegetali.
Prodotto imbottigliato da ROSSO ANTICO S.p.A. PONTI SUL MINCIO (MN) Lic. Min. 744
Per conto della
ANTICA CASA BAIRO
della Gio. BUTON & C. S.p.A. (BO). CONT. ml 750
ALCOOL 20,05% in vol.
ZUCCH. g 20,50% in vol.
RICETTA ORIGINALE OLANDESE
Petrus Boonekamp
L'AMARO
Petrus BK.
MAAGBITTER
IDIT QUI NON
SERVAT OCCIDIT
QUI NON SERVAT OC
CIDIT QUI NON SERVAT
OCCIDIT QUI NON SERVAT
MARCA DEPOSITATA
CHERRY
BUTON
LIQUORE
GRAND PRIX PARIGI 1900
HERRY BRAND

FRAGONCELLO

In Istria, I remember, my grandmother would always infuse our homemade grappa with herbs and the fresh fruits of the season, such as cherries, blackberries, or strawberries. This cocktail was a favorite at Felidia several years ago; the sweetness of the strawberries and simple syrup creates a refreshing drink for the late spring and summer months. I prefer cocktails that are not too sweet. This recipe is easily multiplied for a group.

MAKES 1 DRINK

1 cup sugar
1½ cups chopped very ripe strawberries, plus 1 strawberry, finely diced, for garnish
2 ounces vodka
1 tablespoon freshly squeezed lime juice
Sprigs of mint

Combine the sugar with 1 cup water in a small saucepan, and bring to a simmer to dissolve the sugar. Add the strawberries, and simmer until they're very soft and the syrup is bright red, about 10 minutes. Let steep 15 minutes. The sugar syrup keeps well in the refrigerator for the next party.

Strain through a fine-mesh strainer without pressing on the solids. (You can keep the cooked strawberry solids to stir into plain yogurt or to top ice cream.) Chill until cold, at least 1 hour.

Chill a martini glass. Fill a cocktail shaker with ice. Add 1½ ounces of the strawberry syrup, as well as the vodka and the lime juice. Shake. Strain into the chilled glass, add the finely diced strawberry, and serve immediately. You can alternate some fresh strawberries and sprigs of mint on a stirrer or toothpick for added garnish.

BASIL MARTINI

Martinis ruled in the 1980s, when Felidia opened, and remain popular at the bar today. The basil martini is a welcome variation in the summer months, when this herb, which both Chef Nicotra and I love, is in season. We both like fresh herbs in our food, so why not in our martinis?

The recipe for the syrup makes about 1 cup, more than you need for one drink, but this recipe is easily multiplied for a group. The syrup also keeps for several days in the refrigerator and is good stirred into iced tea or as a base for sorbet.

MAKES 1 DRINK

1 cup sugar
2 cups loosely packed fresh basil leaves
2 ounces gin
Micro-basil, for garnish
Basil seeds, for garnish, if desired
Strip of lime peel, removed with a vegetable peeler, for garnish

Combine the sugar with 1 cup water in a small saucepan. Bring to a simmer to dissolve the sugar. Set aside, and let cool completely.

Bring a medium saucepan of water to a boil. Plunge the basil into the boiling water, and cook until wilted and bright green, about 10 to 15 seconds. Transfer immediately to an ice bath to cool. Drain, and pat dry.

Combine the simple syrup and blanched basil in a blender, and blend until smooth. Strain through a fine-mesh strainer. Chill until cold, at least 1 hour.

Chill a martini glass. Fill a cocktail shaker with ice. Add 1 ounce of the basil syrup as well as the gin. Shake. Strain into the chilled glass, and garnish with the micro-basil, basil seeds (if using), and lime peel. Serve immediately.

PASSION FRUIT SPRITZ

I like fruit cocktails with some bubbles, and passion fruit is one of Chef Nicotra's favorite dessert flavors. Here he combines it with prosecco for a light, easy, and delicious fruity drink.

MAKES 1 DRINK

4 ounces chilled prosecco
2 ounces passion fruit juice
1 ounce Aperol
Passion fruit seeds, for garnish

Combine the prosecco, passion fruit juice, and Aperol in a white-wine glass, and stir. Add ice, and garnish with passion fruit seeds. You can also garnish with a slice of almost any fresh fruit, according to season. A slice of orange or peach would be good. Serve immediately.

GREEN GIMLET

This drink is for the vegetable lover, and it's wonderfully refreshing. The kale and cucumber balance beautifully with the green apple.

The simple syrup can be used to sweeten other cocktails, as well as iced tea or iced coffee. This recipe makes about 1 to 1½ cups of green juice, but can easily be multiplied as needed. The syrup will also keep for several days in the fridge; just shake before using.

MAKES 1 DRINK

1 cup sugar
1 Persian cucumber, chopped, plus slices, for garnish
2 stalks celery, chopped
2 cups coarsely chopped cavolo nero (Tuscan or black kale)
1 small green apple, unpeeled, chopped
2 ounces gin
¾ ounce freshly squeezed lime juice
Sliced lime, for garnish

To make 1 cup simple syrup, combine 1 cup water and 1 cup sugar and simmer until the sugar dissolves. Cool.

Combine the simple syrup, chopped cucumber, celery, cavolo nero, and apple in a blender, and blend until smooth. Strain through a fine-mesh strainer.

Chill a coupe glass. Fill a cocktail shaker with ice. Add 1 ounce green juice, the gin, and the lime juice. Shake. Strain into the coupe glass, and garnish with cucumber and lime slices. Serve immediately.

CUCUMBER GIN *and* TONIC

This drink is a celebration of simplicity. The rosemary is not something you expect to find in a drink, but it gives just the right kick to a delicious classic.

—Chef Nicotra

MAKES 1 DRINK

½ Persian cucumber, thinly sliced
2 thin slices lime
2 ounces gin
4 ounces chilled tonic water
Fresh rosemary sprig, for garnish

Combine the cucumber, lime, and gin in a highball glass, and refrigerate, to let the flavors infuse, for 15 to 30 minutes.

To serve, add the tonic to the glass, and stir. Add ice to the glass, along with the rosemary sprig, and stir to distribute the rosemary flavor. Serve immediately.

RHUBARB NEGRONI

Everyone likes a classic, myself included. A Negroni is an iconic Italian cocktail that is typically served as an apéritif. This American twist on the Italian original adds rhubarb, which is almost never used in Italy.

This recipe makes about 1 cup syrup, which is more than you need, but it will keep for up to 2 weeks in the fridge to make more cocktails or sweeten other beverages. The rhubarb can be stirred into yogurt or added to a smoothie.

MAKES 1 DRINK

1 cup sugar
2 cups chopped fresh rhubarb
1 ounce Campari
1 ounce gin
1 ounce sweet vermouth
Orange slice or poached rhubarb, for garnish

Combine the sugar with 1 cup water in a small saucepan. Bring to a simmer to dissolve the sugar. Add the rhubarb, and simmer until it is falling apart, about 15 minutes. Let cool slightly, then strain through a cheesecloth-lined strainer, pressing gently on the solids so the syrup doesn't become cloudy. Chill until cold, at least 1 hour.

Fill a cocktail shaker with ice. Add 2 ounces of the rhubarb syrup, the Campari, gin, and vermouth. Shake, strain into a highball glass, and add ice. If you wish, garnish with poached rhubarb or a slice of orange. Serve immediately.

RUM *and* CHINOTTO

Chinotto is an Italian drink made from the extracts of sun-ripened chinotto oranges, a particular specialty from the south of the country. For this cocktail, Felidia's bar takes an Italian classic and adds a liquor that is loved by many Americans—rum. It is like an Italian riff on a rum-and-Coke.

MAKES 1 DRINK

2 thin slices lime
1½ ounces dark rum
4 ounces chilled Chinotto
Citrus slice, for garnish

Drop the lime slices into the bottom of a highball glass. Add the rum and Chinotto and stir. Add ice, and serve immediately, garnished with a citrus slice.

BUTTERNUT SQUASH DAIQUIRI

When in season, butternut squash is used in Italy in soups, pastas, and desserts, and as a vegetable side dish. Very much part of Italian cuisine, it is a seasonal ingredient used throughout the Felidia menu in the fall and winter months, so it's natural to include it at the bar as well, for a unique take on a guest favorite—the daiquiri.

This recipe makes about 1 cup butternut-squash syrup. Leftover syrup will keep for about 2 weeks in the refrigerator and is also good in hot or iced tea or for poaching fall fruit.

MAKES 1 DRINK

1 cup sugar
1 cup coarsely grated peeled butternut squash
2 ounces dark rum
1 ounce freshly squeezed lime juice

Combine the sugar with 1 cup water in a small saucepan, and bring to a simmer to dissolve the sugar. Add the grated squash, and simmer until tender but not falling apart, about 10 to 15 minutes. Let cool. Strain through a fine-mesh strainer. Reserve and refrigerate the butternut-squash syrup and solids separately. Chill until cold, at least 1 hour.

Chill a martini glass. Fill a cocktail shaker with ice. Add 1 ounce of the syrup, as well as the rum and lime juice. Shake. Strain into the martini glass, and garnish with a dollop of the reserved grated squash. Serve immediately.

SGROPPIN

This is a much-loved drink often served in the Friuli–Venezia Giulia region. Sgroppin or Sgroppino is an alcoholic mixed drink from Venice, made of lemon sorbet with vodka or grappa, and optionally topped with the sparkling wine prosecco. It's been on the menu at Felidia since we opened, and I often serve it at home, at the close of a meal on special occasions.

MAKES 1 DRINK

½ cup lemon sorbet
3 ounces chilled prosecco
1 ounce grappa
Lemon twist

Chill a champagne flute.

Combine the sorbet, prosecco, and grappa in a blender, and blend until smooth. Pour into the chilled flute, and serve immediately with a lemon twist for garnish.

FROZEN PEACH BELLINI

The peach Bellini is a classic drink that you cannot miss when in Venice. It's simply prosecco with the addition of peach purée. This version is a twist on the original recipe: at Felidia, we use peach sorbet to make an ice-cold drink that is welcome at any time of the year.

MAKES 1 DRINK

½ cup peach sorbet
4 ounces chilled prosecco

Chill a champagne flute.

Combine the sorbet and prosecco in a blender, and blend until smooth. Pour into the chilled flute, and serve immediately.

BREADS

Focaccias, Crackers, and Spreads

Focaccias can be found all over Italy. The seasonings and herbs vary, as does the flour used to make the dough. At Felidia, we have been making focaccia since opening day, and Chef Nicotra continues the tradition. He makes a wonderful focaccia with *grano arso* or burnt wheat, which is dark in color and has a smoky, nutty flavor. He also makes a selection of different gluten-free breads for guests with dietary restrictions.

When dining at Felidia, guests are welcomed to the table and served a selection of house-made breads and delicious vegetarian spreads prepared fresh daily in the kitchen. These are presented like a bouquet, with the breads arranged so that it is easy to pick the one that catches your eye.

I remember making bread with my grandmother; in the early morning at Felidia, when the bread is being made, the same smell permeates the restaurant.

I prefer to serve healthy bean-based spreads instead of butter. In Italy, traditionally, bread is served plain at the table. Butter is never served, and the newer trend of dipping bread in olive oil is more of an American thing than an Italian one, although some restaurants in Italy are doing it as well. Over the years, the spread selections at Felidia have changed, and seasons play a part in what guests will find. Chef Nicotra likes to present Italian flat crackers in a short, cylindrical vase. We put a napkin or piece of parchment paper inside, then stack the crackers so they are upright. This makes it easy to grab them individually to eat, and they look beautiful.

POLENTA CRACKERS

Crostini di Polenta

Everybody likes to nibble on crispy thin crackers. Chef Nicotra came up with this recipe after I shared my childhood stories of how I would pick at the crispy layers of polenta left in the pot when my grandmother cooked it. The remaining heat of the cast-iron pot dried the polenta that remained into polenta chips. I loved to peel them off and munch on them like corn chips.

I ate them plain, but they can also be served with toppings as a small bite. They can be topped with cured meats, such as prosciutto, or pâté; or add Grana Padano and put them in the oven to get the cheese melted and crispy. They also work great at home as finger food. The corn-based polenta is a good option for those who follow a gluten-free diet.

MAKES ABOUT 42 CRACKERS

½ cup heavy cream
1½ teaspoons kosher salt
2 bay leaves
1 cup polenta
2 tablespoons unsalted butter
2 tablespoons freshly grated Grana Padano

Preheat the oven to 300 degrees.

Bring 2½ cups water, the cream, salt, and bay leaves to a simmer in a small saucepan. Simmer 5 minutes, to infuse the bay flavor into the water; discard the bay leaves.

Whisk in the polenta in a slow, steady stream until all is incorporated and no lumps remain. Adjust the heat so the polenta is just simmering (a few bubbles will pop and burst to the surface). Cook, stirring often, until the polenta is creamy and thick but still thin enough that you will be able to spread it, about 12 to 15 minutes. Then beat in the butter and grated Grana Padano.

While the polenta is still hot, spread it on a piece of parchment paper the size of a baking sheet (about 15 by 12 inches). Lay another sheet of parchment paper over the top. Roll lightly with a rolling pin to a thin, even layer, about ⅛ inch thick. Remove the top paper and let the polenta cool.

Cut the polenta into 1½-inch squares. Divide between two parchment-paper-lined baking sheets. Bake until crispy, rotating the trays once halfway through, about 35 to 40 minutes in all.

ITALIAN FLAT BREAD

Schiacciata

This dish was once referred to as pane povero *or poor bread, but it's actually like a thin focaccia and close to what the Tuscans call schiacciata. No matter what you call it, it's delicious. It pairs very well with a salumi-and-cheese board for an aperitivo or quick bite. Chef Nicotra's mother uses Marsala, a Sicilian cooking wine, in her cannoli, which inspired him to use it in this flat bread. It "bubbles" the dough when you cook it. Since the bread is baked in a half sheet pan, it is all in one piece. To serve any of the flat breads and focaccias, I like to cut them into long rectangular pieces and place them in a cylindrical bread-serving bowl.*

SERVES 6 TO 8 OR MORE

1 teaspoon active dry yeast
Pinch of sugar
2 tablespoons extra-virgin olive oil, plus more for oiling the bowl and baking sheet
4 cups bread flour, plus more if needed
1½ teaspoons kosher salt
¼ cup dry Marsala
1 large egg
Coarse salt, for sprinkling

The day before you want to make the bread, stir the yeast and sugar into 1½ cups warm (90 to 110 degrees) water. Let sit until bubbly, about 3 minutes; then stir in the olive oil. Refrigerate.

Combine the flour and salt in the bowl of an electric mixer fitted with the dough hook. Add the yeast mixture and the Marsala. Beat at low speed until combined. The dough should come together in a loose mass and be somewhat sticky. Increase speed to medium, and knead until the dough is smooth and forms a very loose ball around the hook, adding a little more flour or water if necessary, about 4 minutes.

Oil a large bowl with olive oil, and scrape the dough into the bowl, turning it to coat it thoroughly in the oil. Cover with plastic wrap, and let rise in the refrigerator, at least 8 hours or up to overnight.

Stretch the dough so that it reaches almost to the edges of an oiled half sheet pan. Cover loosely with plastic wrap, and let rise 30 minutes while you preheat the oven to 450 degrees. Beat the egg in a small bowl with a pinch of salt. Brush this lightly over the dough, and sprinkle lightly with coarse salt. Bake on the bottom rack of the oven until cooked through and golden brown on top and bottom, about 20 minutes. Cool on a rack, and serve warm or at room temperature.

WHOLE-WHEAT WALNUT FOCACCIA

Focaccia Integrale alle Noci

Chefs like to bake with different flours, and especially in recent years have returned to some forgotten grains, such as amaranth. Many types of flour are also now accessible to the home cook. Whole-wheat flour is readily available, and mixing it with all-purpose flour, as I do here, makes the focaccia lighter. And adding walnuts, as Chef Nicotra does at Felidia, renders it more flavorful and nutritious. This earthy focaccia makes any bread basket special. It is also great split in half and made into sandwiches, such as prosciutto and cheese toasted in a panino press. Its hearty flavor pairs well with a robust cheese course as well.

SERVES 6 TO 8

1 packet (2¼ teaspoons) active dry yeast
Pinch of sugar
2½ cups all-purpose flour, plus more as needed
1 cup whole-wheat flour
2 teaspoons kosher salt
1 cup chopped walnuts
Extra-virgin olive oil, for the bowl and for brushing
Coarse salt, for sprinkling

Stir the yeast and sugar into 1½ cups warm water (between 90 and 110 degrees). Let sit until bubbly, about 3 minutes. Combine the flours and salt in an electric mixer fitted with the paddle attachment. Add the yeast mixture, and beat at low speed to make a sticky dough. Switch to the dough hook, and knead at medium speed. The dough should be slightly wet, but not too liquid. If it's too dry, add another tablespoon or so of water. If it is still very loose, add a few more tablespoons of flour. Knead the dough in the mixer at medium speed until it forms a soft, springy ball around the dough hook, about 4 minutes. Add the walnuts and mix, just to incorporate them.

Oil a large bowl with olive oil and scrape the dough into the bowl, turning it to coat it thoroughly in the oil. Cover with plastic wrap, and let rise at room temperature until doubled in size, about 1½ hours.

Preheat the oven to 425 degrees. Lightly brush a quarter sheet pan with olive oil. Punch the dough down, and spread it with your fingers onto the oiled pan. Cover completely but loosely with oiled plastic wrap, and let rise until puffed, about 30 to 45 minutes. Once the dough has risen, lightly dimple it in places with your fingers. Bake until golden on the top and bottom, about 20 minutes. Remove from the oven, and immediately brush lightly with olive oil and sprinkle with coarse salt. Cut into squares to serve.

GLUTEN-FREE FOCACCIA

Focaccia Senza Glutine

There are many different types of gluten-free flour blends on the market. This recipe works best with one that contains rice flour and potato starch. Felidia has become well known for its selection of gluten-free items—including this delicious focaccia and our gluten-free pastas. As chefs, we feel responsible for our guests. We want to make sure they eat well, enjoying great flavors, but we also feel responsible for meeting their dietary needs.

MAKES ONE 9-BY-13-INCH FOCACCIA

1 packet (2¼ teaspoons) active dry yeast
½ teaspoon sugar
¼ cup extra-virgin olive oil, plus more for the bowl
2 to 2¼ cups gluten-free flour blend
1½ teaspoons kosher salt
1 teaspoon xanthan gum
Coarse salt, for sprinkling

Sprinkle the yeast and sugar over 1¼ cups warm (90 to 110 degrees) water. Stir to combine, and let sit until bubbly, about 3 minutes. Stir in 2 tablespoons of the olive oil.

Combine 2 cups of flour, salt, and xanthan gum in the bowl of an electric mixer fitted with the paddle attachment. With the mixer at low speed, pour in the yeast mixture, and beat to make a sticky dough. The dough will be wet but should stick to the paddle; if not, add more flour, a tablespoon at a time, up to another ¼ cup. Knead about 30 seconds at high speed to bring the dough together.

Scrape out the dough, and form it into a loose ball. Oil a large bowl with olive oil, and scrape the dough into the bowl, turning it to coat it thoroughly in the oil. Cover with plastic wrap, and let the dough rise in a warm place until doubled in size, about 1 hour.

Punch the dough down, and spread with your fingers into a 9-by-13-inch rectangle on a parchment-paper-lined baking sheet. Cover the dough with an oiled sheet of plastic wrap, and let it rise until puffed, about 30 minutes.

Meanwhile, preheat the oven to 425 degrees. Once the dough has risen a second time, gently make dimples in it with your finger. Brush gently with the remaining 2 tablespoons olive oil. Sprinkle with coarse salt. Bake until cooked through and crisp, about 25 minutes. (Depending on the brand of flour used and how brown you like your focaccia, you can move it to the top rack halfway through baking time to encourage the top to brown.)

FELIDIA SPREADS

The bread at Felidia is served with spreads instead of the extra-virgin olive oil or butter often seen in other restaurants. The flavors are seasonal and have evolved over time, but the technique and base are virtually the same as on the day we opened. The recipes included here are typical of what has been served at Felidia over the years, but the legumes are interchangeable. These spreads work well with both regular and toasted country bread, flat bread, breadsticks, and even crudités. You can also toast some country bread, drizzle it with extra-virgin olive oil, add the spread, and use this as a delicious base for a shrimp salad or even grilled calamari. Small, simple white 4-to-6-ounce ramekins are great vessels for the spreads. You can also top with small whole pieces of the ingredient each spread is made from—basil on the basil spread, etc.—to indicate what you are serving. At home, I often serve these spreads with cocktails as well, with some crackers.

BASIL SPREAD

Purea di Fagioli al Basilico

SERVES 4 TO 6

Kosher salt
4 cups packed fresh basil leaves
1 cup packed fresh Italian parsley leaves
¼ cup pine nuts, toasted
1 large clove garlic, crushed and peeled
½ cup extra-virgin olive oil
One 15½-ounce can cannellini beans, rinsed and drained
⅓ cup freshly grated Grana Padano

Bring a large saucepan of salted water to a boil. Add the basil, and blanch until bright green and wilted, about a minute. Cool in an ice bath, drain, and wring very dry.

Place the basil, parsley, pine nuts, garlic, and a large pinch of salt in the work bowl of a food processor. Pulse to make a chunky paste. With the processor running, add the oil in a steady stream to make a thick sauce. Add the beans, and process to make a smooth bright-green purée. Sprinkle in the grated Grana Padano, and pulse to incorporate. Serve at room temperature.

CARROT SPREAD

Purea di Ceci alla Carote

Carrots, a much-loved vegetable, are always available, and turning them into a delicious spread is another way to introduce them to your table. This carrot spread is also a fantastic alternative sandwich spread, replacing mayo.

SERVES 4 TO 6

Kosher salt
1 cup coarsely chopped carrots
One 15½-ounce can chickpeas, rinsed and drained
1 teaspoon grated orange zest
½ cup extra-virgin olive oil

Bring a medium saucepan of salted water to a boil. Add the carrots, and simmer until tender, 8 to 10 minutes. Drain, and cool under running water.

Put the carrots, chickpeas, orange zest, and a large pinch of salt in the work bowl of a food processor. Process to make a coarse purée. With the processor running, add the olive oil in a steady stream to make a smooth, orange purée. Serve at room temperature.

COCO NANO BEAN SPREAD

Purea di Fagioli

Coco nano is a small, inexpensive, medium-waxy white bean that is tender when cooked and and does not have a strong flavor. It's perfect for a purée, since you need a bean that will absorb flavors, such as onions, pine nuts, and citrus zest.

SERVES 6 TO 8

2 cups dried coco nano beans, soaked overnight
2 fresh bay leaves
2 cloves garlic, crushed and peeled
¾ cup extra-virgin olive oil
Kosher salt
Freshly ground black pepper
1 plum tomato, finely diced
¼ cup finely chopped red onion
Juice and grated zest of 1 lemon
2 tablespoons pine nuts, toasted

Drain the beans, and place them in a large saucepan with cold water to cover by 2 inches. Add the bay leaves, garlic, and 2 tablespoons of the olive oil. Bring to a simmer, and cook until the beans are tender but not falling apart, about 40 to 50 minutes. Let cool in the cooking liquid, then drain, reserving about ½ cup cooking liquid. Discard the bay leaves but not the garlic. Set aside about ¾ cup cooked beans.

Place the remaining beans in the work bowl of a food processor. With the processor running, slowly add ½ cup of the olive oil to make a smooth purée. If the purée is too thick (and not spreadable), add some of the reserved cooking liquid, a tablespoon at a time, to adjust the consistency. Season well with salt and pepper.

Put the remaining whole beans in a medium bowl. Add the tomato, red onion, lemon zest, and pine nuts. Drizzle with the lemon juice and remaining 2 tablespoons olive oil. Season with salt and pepper, and toss well. Serve the dip in a wide bowl topped with the whole beans.

APPETIZERS

Appetizers—or antipasti, as they are called in Italy—are an important part of the restaurant menu. An appetizer should be a tantalizing entry to what is to be a great and balanced meal. Chef Nicotra's antipasto selections at Felidia are very much in line with Italian tradition. Italians love antipasti that include not only cured meats and cheeses but also pickled vegetables and light salads that showcase the bounty of the season. In a restaurant, the antipasto is an introduction to the kitchen in small bites that let you enjoy a wide breadth of flavors and experience the chef's talent.

A traditional meal starts with an antipasto, then a pasta, and then the main course or secondo, followed by dessert, of course. Oftentimes, though, people choose to order an antipasto followed by either a pasta or a main course, opting for a two-course meal, and then dessert. Since I really like my guests to get a full Italian experience, we often serve some antipasto family-style in the middle of the table for guests to share, and do the same with the pasta course; then guests enjoy their own main courses. This allows everyone to taste a bit of everything without ordering too much.

At Felidia, appetizers are mostly light dishes, often using seasonal ingredients. Many guests enjoy starting with a salad, and not just a mixed green salad. A favorite appetizer salad at Felidia is broccoli rabe, squash, and ricotta with toasted almonds (page 41). In the spring, salads with string beans and asparagus abound. Octopus has been a part of the appetizer section at Felidia since I opened the place. It has undergone many iterations, first appearing as part of a seafood salad that was on the antipasto table on our first night. We serve antipasti individually today, but back in 1981, there was a large table placed right after the bar, laden with huge platters, ranging from seafood salad to cima alla genovese to caprese salad. Guests would let the captain know what they wanted from the antipasto table, picking one or many things; the plate would be delivered to the table. This is impossible nowadays, mainly because of health-code restrictions. It's a shame: the buffet table was a gorgeous cornucopia of antipasti. Today the octopus served by Chef Nicotra is grilled and served with pickled onions. It is absolutely delicious.

BEEF CARPACCIO *and* ARUGULA SALAD *with* SHAVINGS *of* PORCINI MUSHROOMS *and* GRANA PADANO RESERVE

Carpaccio di Manzo, e Rucola, Porcini e Grana Padano Riserva

In this refreshing appetizer, all the ingredients are raw, so they need to be at their best. Fresh seasonal porcini mushrooms are best, but shiitake and trumpet mushrooms also work beautifully in this recipe and are often easier to find. If pressed for time, you can also use cremini mushrooms. Whichever type of mushroom you choose, make sure they are firm and free of blemishes. Before slicing, trim any tough parts from the stems—if using shiitakes, cut the stems off completely—and wipe the caps clean with a damp paper towel.

If mushrooms are not in season, asparagus and artichokes also work very well here. A light, delicate pecorino can also be used in place of the Grana Padano.

SERVES 6

10 ounces beef filet mignon, trimmed
One 4-ounce piece Grana Padano Riserva (aged at least 20 months), plus ½ cup freshly grated
6 tablespoons extra-virgin olive oil
3 tablespoons freshly squeezed lemon juice
Kosher salt
4 ounces baby arugula, cleaned and spun dry
2 ounces fresh porcini or seasonal mushrooms, wiped clean, trimmed, thinly sliced
Freshly ground black pepper

Place the beef in the freezer and leave it there for 30 minutes or so, to firm it up. With a very sharp knife, slice it as thinly as possible. (Alternatively, ask your butcher to slice the meat for you when you buy it, and package it between slices of butcher paper—use it the very same day to avoid discoloration.) Place the sliced beef on a platter as your base, fanned out with a slight overlap between the pieces. Shave the piece of Grana Padano with a vegetable peeler to make long shards and set these aside.

In a large bowl, whisk the olive oil and lemon juice with a large pinch of salt until blended. Drizzle half the dressing over the beef filet. Add the arugula and mushrooms to the remaining dressing in the bowl, and sprinkle with salt and pepper. Toss until the salad is coated with the remaining dressing. Fold the shaved Grana Padano into the salad, and place this mixture over the carpaccio.

In a blender, combine the grated Grana Padano and ¼ cup water. Blend, adding a tablespoon more water at a time (up to 1 cup total, at the very most) to make a smooth sauce that coats the back of a spoon. Drizzle this over the salad, and serve immediately.

MUSSELS TRIESTINA

Cozze alla Triestina

I remember eating this dish as a child with a hunk of Grandma Rosa's bread next to the mussels. When I had finished, all that was left was a pile of mussel shells and a happy little Lidia. This is my favorite way to eat mussels, and it was one of the dishes served on opening night at Felidia—April 15, 1981. The best part is dunking crusty bread in the sauce, as I did as a child. If there are any leftovers, remove the mussels from the shells and return them to the sauce; tomorrow you can warm the sauce and toss with hot cooked pasta.

SERVES 4 TO 6

6 tablespoons extra-virgin olive oil
6 cloves garlic, crushed and peeled
1 large onion, sliced ½ inch thick
3 fresh bay leaves, or 4 dried bay leaves
Kosher salt
¼ teaspoon peperoncino flakes
2 cups dry white wine
3 pounds mussels, soaked, debearded if necessary, and scrubbed clean
1 bunch scallions, chopped
½ cup chopped fresh parsley
2 to 4 tablespoons dried breadcrumbs
Crusty bread, for serving

In a large Dutch oven, heat 4 tablespoons of the olive oil over medium-high heat. When the oil is hot, add the garlic, and cook until it is sizzling and just golden around the edges, about 2 minutes. Add the onion, and cook, stirring occasionally, until softened, about 5 minutes. Sprinkle in the bay leaves and ½ teaspoon salt. Push the vegetables aside, and make a hot spot in the bottom of the pan. Add the peperoncino to this spot, and let it toast for a minute. Pour the white wine into the pot. Bring to a boil, and cook until the wine is reduced by half, about 3 to 4 minutes.

Once the wine has reduced, add the mussels and scallions. Stir, and adjust the heat so the sauce is simmering. Cover, and simmer until the mussels open, about 5 minutes. Most of the mussels should have opened (discard any that have not). Sprinkle with the parsley. Stir in enough breadcrumbs to thicken the bubbling sauce slightly. Drizzle with the remaining 2 tablespoons olive oil, and toss well. Remove the bay leaves. Transfer the mussels to a serving bowl, and pour the juices over the top. Serve immediately with crusty bread.

QUINOA *with* SPRING VEGETABLES

Quinoa "Quinotto" Primavera

I started introducing guests to the nutritious quinoa grain years ago. Quinoa is not an Italian grain, but I really like it, and it has been on the menu in some recipes ever since. Initially, it was something for our gluten-free patrons and those avoiding dairy. I served it in a simple salad of seasonal vegetables and extra-virgin olive oil, but it is now used in other dishes as well. Our guests love it, and Lidia does, too.

You can also make the one-side-grilled tuna (semi carpaccio) (page 138) with quinoa, if you want to avoid breadcrumbs or seeds.

—Chef Nicotra

SERVES 4 TO 6

4 cups chicken or vegetable broth, or water
½ cup fresh peas
6 asparagus spears, cut into ½-inch lengths
3 tablespoons unsalted butter
2 tablespoons extra-virgin olive oil
1 large shallot, finely chopped
1 cup quinoa, rinsed well
1 cup finely chopped baby spinach leaves
Kosher salt
Freshly ground black pepper
½ cup freshly grated Grana Padano

Put the stock in a medium saucepan, and bring to a bare simmer over low heat. Bring a separate medium saucepan of salted water to a boil. Once the water is boiling, add the peas. After 2 minutes, add the asparagus. Cook until just crisp and tender, about 2 to 3 minutes. Drain, cool in an ice bath, and pat dry.

Melt 1 tablespoon of the butter in the olive oil in a large skillet over medium heat. When the butter is melted, add the shallot and cook until softened but not browned, about 4 minutes. Add the quinoa, and stir to coat in the oil. Let the quinoa toast for a minute or two, then ladle in enough stock just to cover. Bring to a simmer, cooking and stirring until the liquid is almost absorbed; then ladle in more stock. Continue to stir and add stock, as you would for risotto, until the quinoa is just tender, adding the peas and asparagus, as well as the spinach, with the last few ladles of stock. Season with salt and pepper to taste. (You will need between 3 and 4 cups stock to finish; don't worry if you don't use it all.)

Once the quinoa is tender, remove the skillet from the heat, cut the remaining 2 tablespoons butter into bits, and sprinkle them into the skillet with the Grana Padano. Beat vigorously to incorporate. Serve immediately.

VARIATION: Instead of using raw baby spinach, start the recipe by blanching 4 cups packed baby spinach leaves in boiling water until tender, about 2 minutes. Cool in an ice bath, and squeeze out all of the excess liquid. Purée in a blender with a few tablespoons of water until smooth. Add to the quinoa with the last addition of stock.

LEMON GULF SHRIMP *in* SALTED BAKED VIDALIA ONIONS

Gamberi al Limone con Cipolle al Sale

This is Chef Nicotra's take on the "shrimp scampi" dish that was so popular in Italian American restaurants in New York back when I first opened Felidia, in 1981. I often served a version in my first two restaurants, in Queens. They were butterflied, cooked in a sauce of white wine, garlic, and lemon with some parsley, and served with their tails sticking up. Chef Nicotra's flavors are much more delicate, and the presentation is far more sophisticated, but everyone who loves shrimp scampi will certainly be reminded of it with this dish.

SERVES 4

For the Shrimp

4 medium-sized sweet onions, such as Vidalia or Maui
Rock salt, to cover onions
2 tablespoons extra-virgin olive oil, plus more for pan-frying
Kosher salt
12 ounces large shrimp, peeled, deveined, and butterflied
Cornstarch, for dusting the shrimp

For the Sauce

1 cup heavy cream
3 tablespoons chopped garlic
2 to 3 tablespoons freshly squeezed lemon juice
Kosher salt
Freshly ground black pepper
2 tablespoons chopped fresh chives
2 tablespoons pine nuts, toasted

Preheat the oven to 350 degrees.

Wash and dry the onions. Spread a layer of rock salt in an 8-by-8-inch baking dish (or other dish in which the onions will fit snugly but without touching), add the onions, and then cover completely with more rock salt. Bake until the onions are soft but still firm enough to hold their shape (test one or two with a skewer), about 1 hour to 1 hour and 15 minutes. Remove from the rock salt, reserving some of the salt for serving. Let the onions cool until you can handle them; then slice off the tops and reserve them. Scoop out all but two layers of each onion.

Slice the scooped-out insides of the onions. Heat a medium skillet over medium-low heat. Add 2 tablespoons of the olive oil. When the oil is hot, add the sliced onions and season with salt. Cook, adjusting the heat so the onions don't burn, and stirring often, until they're deeply caramelized, about 25 to 30 minutes. Keep warm.

Meanwhile, make the sauce. Heat a medium skillet over medium heat. Add the cream and garlic, and bring to a simmer. Simmer until garlic is softened, about 7 to 8 minutes. Pour the cream mixture into a blender, and blend until smooth. Return it to the skillet, and add 2 tablespoons lemon juice. Simmer until slightly thickened, about 2 minutes. Season with salt and pepper and the additional lemon juice, if needed.

For the shrimp, season the shrimp with salt and pepper. Spread some cornstarch on a plate, for dredging. Heat about ¼ inch of olive oil in a large skillet over medium-high heat. Lightly dredge the shrimp in the cornstarch, tapping off the excess. Fry the shrimp until cooked through and crisp, about 3 to 4 minutes. Drain on paper towels, and season with salt.

To serve, add the shrimp to the simmering sauce, and turn to coat until glazed. Fill the bottoms of the onion shells with the caramelized onions. Top with the shrimp and sauce. Serve the onions on a bed of reserved salt, sprinkle with the chives and pine nuts, and top each with an onion top. Serve immediately.

SCALLOPS SALTIMBOCCA

Capesante Saltimbocca

Saltimbocca is a traditional Roman recipe made of thin slices of prosciutto pounded over scaloppine of veal, which gives the veal a savory complexity. In this recipe, Chef Nicotra uses speck to bring the same complexity to sea scallops. Scallops have a similar texture to veal, so it makes sense. Seafood and speck together create a wonderful sweet-and-salty combination. Serve with sautéed spinach (page 180), drizzled with good balsamic vinegar.

SERVES 4

1½ pounds Yukon Gold potatoes
12 dry sea scallops, "foot" or side muscle removed (about 12 ounces to 1 pound)
Kosher salt
12 small fresh sage leaves
12 thin slices speck
Vegetable oil, for frying
2 ears corn, shucked
2 tablespoons unsalted butter
½ to ¾ cup heavy cream
2 tablespoons chopped fresh chives
1 tablespoon extra-virgin olive oil

Peel ½ pound of the potatoes, and cut them into matchsticks. Soak them in a bowl of ice water for 1 hour.

Season the scallops lightly with salt. Press a sage leaf onto the top of each scallop, then wrap each scallop in a slice of speck, trimming to fit if necessary.

Pour about 3 inches of vegetable oil into a medium pot and heat to 360 degrees. Bring a medium pot of water to a boil, add the corn, and simmer until the kernels are tender, about 5 minutes. Drain, and rinse to cool. Cut the kernels from the cobs, and reserve. Put the remaining 1 pound potatoes in the same pot with water to cover, bring to a simmer, and cook until tender, about 15 to 18 minutes.

Drain the potatoes, and peel while still hot. Press through a ricer or food mill back into the pot, adding butter to melt over low heat. Add enough cream to make a smooth purée. Stir in the corn kernels and chives, and season with salt. Cover and keep warm.

Drain the potato matchsticks well and fry, in two batches, in the heated oil until crisp, 2 to 3 minutes per batch. Drain on paper towels and season with salt.

Heat a large nonstick skillet over medium-high heat. Add the olive oil. When the oil is hot, add the scallops and sear on both sides until the speck is crisp and the scallops are just cooked through, about 2 minutes per side.

Serve the scallops on top of the corn purée and garnish with the fried potato sticks.

THINLY SLICED VEAL *with* "TONNATO" SAUCE

Vitello Tonnato

I was born in Sicily, but I grew up and completed my culinary education in Piedmont. I love cooking the traditional foods of that region. Vitello tonnato is a classic summer dish from Piedmont. However, in Sicily, tuna and capers reign, so I added capers to the traditional sauce to add freshness and some Sicilian flavors.

—Chef Nicotra

SERVES 6

For the Veal

2 small carrots, cut into large chunks
2 stalks celery, cut into large chunks
1 small onion, quartered
2 fresh bay leaves
6 whole black peppercorns
One 2-pound piece boneless veal eye round, trimmed of all fat and tied
1 cup dry white wine
1 teaspoon kosher salt

For the Sauce

One 5½-ounce can oil-packed white tuna, drained
1 tablespoon drained capers, plus more for garnish
2 anchovy fillets
2 tablespoons freshly squeezed lemon juice
2 tablespoons extra-virgin olive oil
3 tablespoons mayonnaise
Kosher salt
Freshly ground black pepper
Optional garnishes: crispy capers, chopped parsley, celery leaves, roasted yellow and red peppers
Lemon slices

Scatter the carrots, celery, onion, bay leaves, and peppercorns over the bottom of a medium Dutch oven. Set the veal on top. Pour the wine over, and sprinkle with the salt. Add enough cold water just to cover the veal, about 6 cups. Bring to a simmer, and cook over low heat until the veal reaches an internal temperature of 135 degrees. Remove from the heat, and let the veal cool in the poaching liquid. Refrigerate until chilled, at least 4 hours or overnight, reserving the poaching liquid and vegetables.

For the sauce, combine the tuna, 1 tablespoon of the cooked carrots, the capers, anchovies, ½ cup poaching liquid, and lemon juice in a food processor, and process until smooth. Add the olive oil and mayonnaise, and process again until smooth. Season with salt and pepper. Chill 1 hour or up to overnight.

Untie and thinly slice the chilled meat against the grain, arrange it on a serving platter in a petal-like pattern, and spread the sauce over it. If desired sprinkle with crispy capers, parsley, and celery leaves. Add the lemon slices and serve. Small slivers of roasted yellow and red peppers also complement this dish, adding color, if used as a garnish.

BROCCOLI RABE *with* ROASTED BUTTERNUT SQUASH *and* FRESH RICOTTA

Broccoli di Rape, Zucca e Ricotta

Chef Nicotra added this dish to the menu a decade ago, and it remains a favorite that changes slightly according to the season. The bitterness of broccoli rabe is not to everyone's liking, so the sweet butternut squash was introduced to add balance, and the ricotta adds some creaminess (you can also use a fresh Italian cheese such as mozzarella or burrata). I often like to eat a bigger portion of this as a vegetarian main course.

SERVES 4 TO 6

For the Butternut Squash
One 3-pound butternut squash, peeled, seeded, and cut into ½-inch-thick slices
2 tablespoons extra-virgin olive oil
Kosher salt
Freshly ground black pepper

For the Broccoli Rabe
1 bunch broccoli rabe
3 tablespoons extra-virgin olive oil
2 cloves garlic, crushed and peeled
Kosher salt
Freshly ground black pepper

For Assembly
½ cup homemade ricotta (see page 44) or fresh or store-bought
¼ cup sliced almonds, toasted

For the squash, preheat the oven to 400 degrees. Toss butternut squash with the olive oil in a large bowl. Season with ½ teaspoon salt and freshly ground black pepper. Spread the squash on a baking sheet. Roast until tender and lightly browned, turning once, about 20 minutes in total.

For the broccoli rabe, trim by first cutting off the tough ends of the stems; then, holding a stem with the florets in your hand, nick a little piece of the end of the stem with a paring knife and pull the little piece of the stem toward you, peeling the stem partially. Continue working your way around the stem until the stem is peeled. As you peel, some of the large, tough outer leaves will also be removed; discard those as well. Repeat with the remaining stems. Wash and drain.

Heat the olive oil in a large skillet over medium heat. Add the garlic, and cook until golden brown, about 1 minute. Lay the broccoli rabe into the oil, and season lightly with salt and pepper. Stir and toss.

Pour ¼ cup water into the skillet, and bring to a simmer. Cover the skillet tightly, and cook, turning the stalks occasionally, until the broccoli rabe is tender, about 10 minutes. Taste, and season with additional salt if necessary.

To assemble, place a layer of broccoli rabe on a platter, followed by a layer of butternut squash, and repeat. Top with the ricotta, and sprinkle on the sliced almonds. Serve.

ROASTED BEET *and* BEET GREEN SALAD *with* APPLE *and* GOAT CHEESE

Insalata di Barbabietole, Mele e Caprino

My daughter, Tanya, and I have always loved beets—we often serve them at home—and so have been pleased to see beet salad gain such popularity in restaurants everywhere in the last few years. Felidia is no exception. Although we generally incorporate apples into this recipe, peaches and apricots also work beautifully during the summer months.

SERVES 6

3 bunches small or baby (about 1 to 1½ inches in diameter) yellow and red beets with greens attached (about 3 pounds total)
Kosher salt
Freshly ground black pepper
¼ cup extra-virgin olive oil
2 tablespoons good-quality balsamic vinegar
1 medium-sized tart, crisp apple, such as Granny Smith, cut into matchsticks
4 ounces slightly aged goat cheese

Preheat the oven to 400 degrees.

Remove the greens from the beets, leaving about ½ inch of stem. Scrub the beets, and poke each with a fork a few times. Rinse the beet greens well, trimming off the tough parts of the stems, and cut the softer stem pieces into 2-inch lengths. Set the stem pieces and leaves aside. Put the beets in a shallow baking dish with about ¼ inch of water and cover with foil. Roast until beets are slightly shriveled and tender all the way through, about 1 hour. Remove from the baking dish, and let cool completely.

While the beets are roasting, bring a large pot of salted water to a boil. When the water is boiling, add the beet greens and stems, and cook until tender, about 8 minutes. Remove to an ice bath to cool. Drain, and press very dry.

Peel the cooled beets, cut into wedges or slices, and add to a large bowl with the greens. Season with salt and black pepper. Drizzle with the olive oil and vinegar, and toss well. Gently toss in the apple, and arrange the salad on a platter. Crumble the goat cheese over the top, and serve.

HOMEMADE RICOTTA

La Nostra Ricotta

Ricotta is one of my favorite fresh cheeses. I remember making it with my grandmother on her small farm. She would spread it on a piece of her bread and drizzle it with honey; that was my breakfast. It's very satisfying to eat the fruit of your labors.

House-made ricotta is prepared daily at Felidia, and it's really not that difficult for the home cook to do as well. It can be served on toasted bread, to add freshness to our penne "al brucio" (page 83), and also works well in a green spring soup (page 68). I often have it today as a snack on toasted bread with a small anchovy laid on top.

MAKES 2 TO 3 CUPS

2 quarts whole milk, preferably organic
1 cup heavy cream, preferably organic
½ cup buttermilk
½ teaspoon kosher salt
3 tablespoons freshly squeezed lemon juice

Line a large sieve with a double layer of damp cheesecloth and set this over a bowl. Combine the milk, cream, buttermilk, and salt in a medium heavy-bottomed saucepan, and slowly bring to a boil.

Add the lemon juice, and reduce the heat to the lowest setting. Stir gently until the mixture begins to curdle, about 2 minutes. Remove from heat, and let sit without stirring for 5 minutes. Pour the mixture through the cheesecloth, and let drain about 20 to 30 minutes. What's left in the cloth is the ricotta. Chill until ready to use.

NOTE: If you don't get at least a heaping cup of ricotta, you can reheat the liquid and repeat the process, using more lemon juice to recurdle it.

SMOKED SALMON, EGG WHITE FRITTATA, *and* AVOCADO SANDWICH

Panino con Salmone Affumicato, Frittata di Bianchi d'Uovo, Avocado

Felidia opened in 1981, so we are now in our third generation, and my grandchildren all have their favorite dishes; that's a lot of favorite dishes. This is my grandson Lorenzo Manuali's. Our smoked-salmon sandwich is a fun party food for the home cook and can often be found on the bar menu.

MAKES 4 SMALL PANINI, SERVING 1 OR 2

1 tablespoon extra-virgin olive oil, plus more for brushing the bread
2 large slices good-quality whole-wheat bread (or 4 small slices)
2 large egg whites
Kosher salt
3 tablespoons chopped fresh chives
2 scallions, finely chopped
2 slices good-quality smoked salmon
2 thin slices ripe tomato
Handful of arugula leaves
½ ripe avocado, peeled and sliced

Heat a small nonstick skillet over medium-low heat. Brush the skillet with olive oil, and add the bread, pressing, to toast it on both sides, about 2 minutes per side. Remove from skillet and reserve.

Whisk the egg whites in a medium bowl with a generous pinch of salt. Whisk in the chives and scallions. Return the skillet to medium-low heat, then pour in the egg-white mixture and turn the heat down very low. Cook gently for approximately 2 minutes. Lift a corner of the frittata with a spatula and check to see if the bottom has started to brown. When it has, flip it by giving the pan a quick, firm shake up and over toward you, so that the frittata dislodges and flips over in one piece. (Or you can turn it over gently with a spatula.) Cook the second side for 1 to 2 minutes, again checking to see if the bottom has browned to your liking. Slide the frittata out of the pan and onto a plate or cutting board.

Top one slice of bread with the smoked salmon, frittata, tomato, arugula, and avocado. Top with the second slice of toasted bread, press down firmly, cut into four triangles, and serve.

ROBIOLA *and* SPECK "AUTOGRILL" PANINO

Panino "Autogrill"

Speck and robiola sandwiches are often found in the bars along the Autostrada (the highway) in Italy. It is my daughter Tanya's favorite sandwich when she stops in an Autogrill. It is more often found in the north of Italy, because the speck in the sandwich comes from that region. The smoky flavor of the speck and the creamy robiola are a perfect combination. Feel free to add a handful of baby spinach, arugula, or a few radicchio leaves for crunch. When I am working in the Felidia office, I often ask Chef Nicotra to send one of these sandwiches up for lunch.

MAKES 1 SANDWICH

¼ cup robiola cheese, at room temperature
2 slices good-quality whole-wheat bread
3 slices speck
1 tablespoon extra-virgin olive oil, plus more for brushing the bread

Spread the robiola on both pieces of bread. Layer the speck over the robiola on one slice. Top with the other slice of bread, robiola side down.

Heat a medium skillet over medium-low heat. Brush the outside of the sandwich lightly with olive oil, and add 1 tablespoon oil to the skillet. When the skillet is hot, add the sandwich, pressing it down. Cook until golden on one side, pressing occasionally, about 3 minutes. Flip, and repeat on the other side. Remove to a cutting board, cut into quarters, and serve.

OCTOPUS *and* POTATO SALAD

Insalata di Polpo e Patate

Octopus has been an Italian staple forever, but only in the last 10 years has it become fashionable in American restaurants. I used to make octopus for my customers in the 1970s, using an old family recipe. When it was made at home, Grandma would toss it with warm boiled potatoes to extend the portions so there was enough for everyone. I still love it this way. Chef Nicotra now serves it a bit differently. He grills the legs and tentacles, which creates a wonderful play of textures

SERVES 6

2½ pounds cleaned octopus
4 cloves garlic, crushed and peeled
2 teaspoons dried oregano, preferably Sicilian, on the branch
¼ teaspoon peperoncino flakes
¼ cup red-wine vinegar
1 medium red onion, sliced ¼ inch thick
1½ pounds russet potatoes (about 3 potatoes)
1 cup coarsely chopped marinated artichoke hearts
Juice of 1 large lemon
3 tablespoons extra-virgin olive oil
Kosher salt
¼ cup chopped fresh Italian parsley

Put the octopus in a pot where it will fit snugly. Scatter in the garlic, oregano, and peperoncino. Add a cup of water, and bring to a bare simmer. Cover tightly, and cook until octopus is very tender when pierced with a fork, about 1½ hours. (Add more water, as necessary, throughout the cooking time, to keep an inch of liquid in the bottom of the pan.)

While the octopus cooks, combine 2 cups water and the vinegar and bring to a boil in a medium saucepan. Add the red onion, and simmer until it droops but still has some bite to it, about 5 minutes. Drain. In the meantime, in another saucepan, simmer the potatoes whole until fork-tender, about 25 minutes or more, depending on size. Drain. When they're cool enough to handle, peel and cut them into 1-inch chunks.

When the octopus is done, rinse to cool slightly and cut into 1-to-2-inch pieces. In a large serving bowl, combine the octopus, red onion, potatoes, and artichoke hearts. Drizzle with the lemon juice and olive oil, and toss. Season with salt, and sprinkle with the parsley. Toss and serve.

TOMATO *and* BREAD SALAD

Panzanella

Today every chef has his or her own rendition of panzanella. The idea is to use leftover bread to soak up the delicious juices of seasonal summer tomatoes. We finish our summer panzanella salad with a traditional Italian cheese, such as thin slices of Grana Padano, fresh slices of ricotta salata or mozzarella, or even a spoonful of burrata, which has become a popular choice over the last few years. If you use a variety of different heirloom tomatoes, the salad becomes a colorful sight to behold. It is perfect as an appetizer or as a side with grilled fish or meat.

SERVES 6

8 ounces 2-day-old country-style bread, crusts removed, cut into ½-inch cubes (about 8 cups)
2 pounds ripe tomatoes, preferably a mix of heirloom, cored, seeded, and cut into chunks (about 4 cups)
1 cup chopped red onion
2 Persian cucumbers, sliced
½ cup extra-virgin olive oil
¼ cup red-wine vinegar
Kosher salt
Freshly ground black pepper
½ cup fresh basil leaves, coarsely shredded, a few whole leaves reserved
One 3-ounce piece ricotta salata, or 1 small ball fresh mozzarella or burrata (optional)

Toss the bread, tomatoes, onion, and cucumbers in a large bowl until well mixed. Drizzle the olive oil and vinegar over the salad, and toss to mix thoroughly. Season with ½ teaspoon salt and several grinds of black pepper. Let sit until the dressing moistens the bread, about 15 to 30 minutes, depending on how dry the bread was. If the bread isn't soaked after 30 minutes, you can drizzle it with a few tablespoons of water and toss again.

When ready to serve, sprinkle with the basil, and, if using, shave the ricotta salata over the salad with a vegetable peeler. Season again with salt and pepper, toss gently, and serve. A sprig of basil placed in the center of the bowl makes for a great presentation.

LOBSTER CAPRESE

Insalata di Astice con Pomodori e Mozzarella

Caprese salad, tomatoes and mozzarella, is a typical Italian dish found throughout the peninsula. It was a constant in all my earlier restaurants and during the early years of Felidia as well. Adding lobster gives it a bit of Sardinian flair. Sardinia is known for its spiny lobsters, although they are different from the New England lobsters we are used to here. I first came up with a version of this dish in 2006, when doing research for my book Lidia's Italy. *As we always do, Chef Nicotra and I shared ideas and food experiences, and it didn't take long for this rendition to appear on the Felidia menu. We even served it at a dinner for Pope Francis. Scallops or large shrimp can be substituted for the lobster. If using scallops, sear them first and then slice them.*

SERVES 4 AS A MAIN COURSE,
6 AS AN APPETIZER

Kosher salt
2 live lobsters (about 1¼ pounds each)
1½ pounds ripe tomatoes, cut into wedges (an assortment of colors is nice)
⅓ cup extra-virgin olive oil
1 small ball fresh mozzarella, preferably buffalo mozzarella (about 8 to 10 ounces)
½ cup loosely packed fresh basil leaves, coarsely chopped, or a few small sprigs of thyme

---

Fill a large stock pot with salted water, and bring to a rolling boil. Add the lobsters and cover; when the water returns to a boil, cook for 10 minutes for 1¼-pound lobsters (add a minute or two if they are closer to 1½ pounds). Then drain and rinse the lobsters and let them cool.

When the lobsters are cool enough to handle, twist and pull off the claws and knuckle segments where the knuckles attach to the front of the body. Lay the lobsters flat on a cutting board, and split them in half lengthwise with a heavy chef's knife. Remove the digestive sac, found right behind the eyes, and pull out the vein running along the back of the body and the tail. You can leave the tomalley and roe in the body pieces, or you can remove them and discard, if not to your liking. Separate the meaty tail piece from the carcass of the four split halves. Remove the shell from the upper half of the lobsters, pluck the feathered attachments and any extra skin, and cut the lobster body with small legs attached into three pieces, putting the pieces in a large mixing bowl as you work.

Separate the knuckles from the claws, and crack open the shells of both knuckles and hard claw pincers with the thick edge of the knife blade, or kitchen shears; pull the meat out. Get the meat out of the knuckles as well. Cut the tail sections, shell on, crosswise into three pieces each and set in a bowl, after removing the shell.

To serve, add the tomatoes to the bowl of lobster pieces, drizzle with the olive oil and ½ teaspoon salt, and toss well. Arrange the tomatoes and mozzarella on a serving platter. Sprinkle them with the basil or thyme, then mound the remaining lobster on top and serve.

EGGPLANT FLAN *with* TOMATO COULIS

Sformato di Melanzane con "Colatura" di Pomodoro

A chef's flavor profile is an accumulation of his or her experiences. This eggplant flan was popular with guests at both of the Michelin-starred restaurants I worked at in the 1980s in Milazzo, Sicily. The dish combines flavors from the popular "alla Norma" sauce of Catania, Sicily—eggplant, ricotta salata, basil, tomatoes. I brought it with me to Felidia in the 1990s, and Lidia immediately fell in love with it.

—Chef Nicotra

SERVES 6

For the Flan

Cooking spray, for the ramekins
1 medium eggplant (about 1 pound)
3 tablespoons extra-virgin olive oil
1 small onion, chopped
¼ cup fresh basil leaves, plus sprigs for optional garnish
Kosher salt
Freshly ground black pepper
¼ cup freshly grated Grana Padano
3 large eggs
1 cup heavy cream

For the Coulis

4 ripe plum tomatoes
2 tablespoons extra-virgin olive oil
Kosher salt
Freshly ground black pepper
Slices of ricotta salata (for serving)
Eggplant chips (optional)

Preheat the oven to 350 degrees. Spray six 5-ounce ramekins with cooking spray.

Place the eggplant on a baking sheet, and bake until it collapses and is tender throughout, about 30 to 40 minutes. Let cool. Reduce oven temperature to 325 degrees.

Cut open the eggplant, and pick out the large groups of seeds (or press flesh through a strainer, leaving the seeds behind).

Heat a small skillet over medium heat. Add the olive oil. When the oil is hot, add the onion, and cook until tender, 8 to 10 minutes. Let cool.

Heat a kettle of water on the stove. Put the eggplant flesh, onion, and basil leaves in a blender. Season with salt and several grinds of black pepper. Blend until smooth. Add the grated Grana Padano and eggs, and blend again. Add the cream, and blend until smooth.

Divide the mixture among the ramekins, and place all six in a 9-by-13-inch baking dish. Pour the hot water from the kettle into the dish to come halfway up the sides of the ramekins. Bake until the custards are set, with just a small amount of jiggle in the very center, about 25 to 30 minutes. Remove from the oven, and let cool slightly in the baking dish.

Meanwhile, for the coulis, bring a large saucepan of water to a boil. With a paring knife, cut an "X" in the base of each tomato. Drop the tomatoes into the boiling water, and cook just until

(recipe continues)

the peel begins to come away from the flesh at the "X," about 1 to 2 minutes. Put the tomatoes in an ice bath and let cool. Peel and discard the skin of the tomatoes. Halve the tomatoes, removing and discarding the core and seeds. Chop the tomatoes (you should have about 1½ cups). Put the tomatoes in a blender, and, with the blender running, add the olive oil. Process until smooth. Pass through a strainer, and season with salt and pepper.

To serve, spoon some of the coulis onto each serving plate. Invert and unmold a warm flan and place in the center of each plate. The plating of this dish could be enhanced with a thin slice of ricotta salata placed on top of the flan, and with a fresh sprig of basil placed on top. Some thin eggplant chips (fried eggplant skin) also make for a wonderful garnish to accompany the flan.

STUFFED CALAMARI

Calamari Ripieni

This dish is delicious served over mashed potatoes or polenta, or simply with a mixed salad. At Felidia, we often serve it on top of braised beans and escarole. The dish began as something I cooked for my family, and I carried it over to the Felidia menu when we first opened. Of course, it has undergone several variations since.

SERVES 4 TO 6

Twelve 5-to-6-inch calamari with tentacles, cleaned
6 tablespoons extra-virgin olive oil
1 small onion, finely chopped
2 teaspoons chopped fresh thyme
Kosher salt
Pinch of crushed peperoncino
1 cup dry white wine
1 bunch scallions, trimmed and finely chopped
¼ cup dried breadcrumbs, plus more as needed
3 tablespoons chopped fresh Italian parsley

Preheat the oven to 400 degrees.

Finely chop the calamari tentacles, but not the bodies, with a sharp knife (or pulse in a food processor), and set aside. In a large skillet over medium-high heat, heat 3 tablespoons of the olive oil. Add the chopped onion, and cook until softened, about 5 minutes. Add the chopped tentacles, thyme, 1 teaspoon salt, and the peperoncino. Cook and stir until the tentacles are cooked through, about 2 to 3 minutes. Pour in ½ cup white wine, and cook to reduce by half. Stir in the scallions, and remove from the heat. Scrape the mixture into a large bowl, and stir in the breadcrumbs and chopped parsley. The filling should be slightly wet, not sandy. If needed to adjust consistency, add more wine or breadcrumbs a tablespoon at a time to reach the right consistency. Let cool.

When the filling is cool, lay the calamari bodies out on your work surface. Fill each body with about 2 to 3 tablespoons filling. Do not overfill the calamari or they will burst during baking; it is okay if there is a little stuffing left. Seal the calamari closed by sticking a toothpick in a weaving motion through the opening of each body.

Oil a 9-by-13-inch glass or ceramic baking pan with 3 tablespoons olive oil. Lay the calamari in the baking pan in one layer. Sprinkle any remaining stuffing over the calamari. Pour in ½ cup water, the remaining ½ cup wine, and season with salt. Cover tightly with foil, and bake until the calamari are tender and the liquid is simmering, about 25 to 30 minutes. Uncover, and continue to bake until the calamari are golden on top, about 10 minutes. If the calamari are done and there is still too much liquid in the pan, remove the calamari to a platter and transfer the sauce to a skillet; reduce over high heat until slightly thickened. If plating on a platter, family-style, line the calamari neatly down the center and drizzle over them the remaining sauce. Remind guests to be careful of the toothpicks, or gently remove them prior to serving.

GRILLED CALAMARI

Calamari alla Griglia

Depending on the season, you can serve this simple grilled calamari over a baby-arugula-and-tomato salad, as below, or atop braised cannellini beans. If you find large calamari, they should be cut into rings after cooking, about ¼ inch in width. If you are able to find the smaller calamari (about 3 inches), they can be left whole.

In the restaurant we grill the calamari, but at home you can also use a cast-iron pot.

SERVES 4

For the Calamari

1½ pounds medium calamari, tubes and tentacles, cleaned
¼ cup extra-virgin olive oil, plus more for drizzling
6 cloves garlic, peeled and sliced
1 tablespoon fresh thyme leaves
½ teaspoon crushed peperoncino
Kosher salt

For the Tomato Salad

1 pound ripe tomatoes
2 tablespoons chopped fresh Italian parsley, or ½ cup leaves
3 tablespoons extra-virgin olive oil
1 tablespoon red-wine vinegar
Kosher salt
Freshly ground black pepper
4 cups loosely packed baby arugula (optional)

Toss the calamari in a large bowl with the olive oil, garlic, thyme, peperoncino, and ½ teaspoon salt. Cover, and let marinate at room temperature for 1 hour, or refrigerate up to overnight.

Preheat a grill or grill pan to medium-high heat. (The calamari can also be cooked in a preheated cast-iron skillet.)

When the grill is hot, lay the calamari on the grill in one layer. Set a heavy skillet over the calamari to weight it down. Cook until charred, about 2 minutes. Flip the calamari, weight with the skillet again, and continue to cook until the calamari is just cooked through but still tender, about 1 to 2 minutes. Transfer the calamari to a cutting board, and cut into thick rings (or leave whole, if small).

Toss the tomatoes and parsley with the oil and vinegar in a large bowl. Season with salt and pepper. Add the arugula, if using, and the calamari, toss gently, and serve immediately.

POACHED SEAFOOD SALAD

Insalata di Frutti di Mare

This dish truly tastes of Italy. It was on the first menu at Felidia, and can often be found in many classic Italian restaurants today. Every region of Italy that is on the sea has some version of this seafood salad. It's one of those recipes you can take in any direction you like. You can use whatever seafood is available—scungilli (sea conch), crabmeat, scallops, or any firm fish fillets. You can use lemon juice in place of part or all of the vinegar, and dress the salad up with capers, black olives, roasted peppers, or diced tomatoes, as you see fit. However you make it, it's best prepared about ½ hour before serving, to give the flavors a chance to develop. You can refrigerate the salad, but not for too long. And be sure to bring it to room temperature and check the seasonings before you serve it. When I have family over, this is always well received, served in a large bowl on the table, so everyone can dig in.

SERVES 4 TO 6

½ cup dry white wine
1 stalk celery, chopped
1 medium carrot, chopped
4 fresh bay leaves
1 teaspoon black peppercorns
2 teaspoons kosher salt, plus more for seasoning
1 pound medium shrimp, peeled and deveined
1 pound small calamari (bodies 4 to 6 inches long), cleaned, bodies cut into ½-inch rings, tentacles reserved
2 pounds mussels, scrubbed and debearded if necessary
4 inner stalks celery, thinly sliced (about 1½ cups), plus ½ cup inner celery leaves
4 cloves garlic, crushed and peeled
¼ cup freshly squeezed lemon juice
6 tablespoons extra-virgin olive oil
Peperoncino flakes
2 tablespoons chopped fresh Italian parsley

Bring 2 quarts cold water, the wine, celery, carrot, bay leaves, peppercorns, and 2 teaspoons salt to a boil in a medium Dutch oven. Adjust the heat to a simmer, cover, and cook for 15 minutes, to blend the flavors. This is the court bouillon.

Add the shrimp to the court bouillon, and cook until just opaque, about 3 to 4 minutes. Fish the shrimp out with a spider, and spread them on a baking sheet. (Don't worry if they aren't completely drained—you'll use some of the liquid to finish the salad.)

Add the calamari to the court bouillon, and poach just until they are firm and tender, about 3 minutes. Fish out the calamari, and add them to the shrimp.

Return the court bouillon to a boil. Stir in the mussels, cover the pot, and cook until the shells open and the mussels are firm but not tough, about 4 minutes. Remove with a spider, discarding any that haven't opened, and add to the other poached seafood. When the mussels are cool enough, pluck the meat from the shells directly into a large serving bowl.

To make the salad, transfer the cooled shrimp and calamari to the bowl with the shelled mussels. Add the sliced celery and the garlic, and toss. Drizzle with the lemon juice and oil, and toss. Moisten with some of the reserved cooking liquid, if needed, to keep the salad juicy but not wet. Season with salt and peperoncino. Sprinkle with the parsley and celery leaves, toss, and serve.

SOUPS

Restaurants do not usually have a lot of soups on the menu, but I feel one or two should always be offered, reflecting the season. On a traditional Italian menu, soups are served as primi or the course in between the appetizer and the main course. The soups in this chapter range from the early menus at Felidia—such as the pork, sauerkraut, and bean soup, or yota (page 76), which I recall from my childhood—to the present-day seafood minestra (recipe follows), which is a favorite of mine now.

There is always a soup or minestra bubbling on my kitchen stove at home. I love using vegetables from my garden to make a light soup in summer months; for the winter holidays, I always make a capon broth with passatelli (page 66) at home, and Chef Nicotra does the same at Felidia. For me, soups are a great opener to a meal and can easily be turned into a main course by the addition of proteins, like fish or meat. The beauty of making soups at home is that you can make enough to freeze some for future meals. As a working mother, when the kids were small, I always made sure to have frozen soup on hand for a quick lunch or dinner. Now that my ninety-eight-year-old mother lives with me, I keep a stash of different soups in the freezer for when I am traveling, so she can have an easy meal ready.

Good soups or minestras take time, and my Felidia guests appreciate the effort that goes into making them. They're a fabulous way to highlight seasonal ingredients: a wonderful spring pea soup with a dollop of fresh house-made ricotta in the middle to add a bit of creaminess; a Tuscan ribollita, with kale lacinato and bread (page 72), to warm the bones during the cold winter. There is a soup for every season.

SEAFOOD MINESTRA

Minestra di Pesce con Pasta Mista

Chef Nicotra's seafood minestra is so beloved that we can't take it off the menu. I often enjoy it for a quick lunch in my office, tucked away at the top of Felidia after getting back from a book tour or business trip during the fall and winter months. It's a true comfort food that welcomes me back home, and will certainly have the same effect on you.

For the pasta mista, take whatever leftover uncooked pasta you have, combine it in a plastic bag, and crush it into small pieces. This is a great way to use up any half-empty boxes of pasta you have lying around—a lesson I am sure Chef Nicotra picked up from his mother!

SERVES 6 TO 8

1 live lobster (2 pounds)
One 28-ounce can whole Italian plum tomatoes, preferably San Marzano, crushed by hand
1½ cups dry white wine
1 bunch leeks, white parts sliced, tender pale-green parts washed and coarsely chopped
1 large carrot, thickly sliced
1 large onion, thickly sliced, and 1 large onion, thinly sliced
10 sprigs fresh thyme
Zest of ½ lemon, removed in wide strips with a vegetable peeler
Kosher salt
¼ cup extra-virgin olive oil, plus more for drizzling
¼ teaspoon crushed peperoncino flakes
8 cloves garlic, crushed and peeled
2 pounds mussels, scrubbed and debearded if necessary
1½ cups broken-up raw pasta (pasta mista)
8 ounces large shrimp, deveined
8 ounces sea scallops, side muscle or "foot" removed, halved if large
8 ounces calamari, tubes cut into ½-inch rings, tentacles left whole
¼ cup chopped fresh Italian parsley

Bring a large pot of water to a boil. Add the lobster, and boil until just cooked through, about 13 to 15 minutes. Cool under running water. Remove the lobster meat from the shell, reserving the head and large pieces of shell/claws. Cut the meat into bite-sized pieces and reserve.

For the soup base, combine the tomatoes, wine, leek greens, carrot, thickly sliced onion, thyme, lemon zest, reserved lobster head and shells, and 2½ quarts water in a large Dutch oven. Simmer until reduced by a third, about 30 minutes, skimming and discarding any foam that rises to the surface. Strain into a medium saucepan, pressing on the solids, season with salt, and return to a simmer. (You should have about 8 to 10 cups soup base.)

Wipe the Dutch oven clean with a paper towel, and add the olive oil over medium heat. Add the

(recipe continues)

leek whites and thinly sliced onion. Cook until softened, about 7 minutes. Add the peperoncino and garlic, and cook until garlic is sizzling, about 1 minute. Add about a cup of the soup base, and bring to a simmer.

Add the mussels to the Dutch oven. Cover, and cook until the mussels just begin to open, 2 to 3 minutes. Meanwhile, add the broken-up pasta to the soup base in the medium saucepan, and return to a simmer. Cook until al dente (the pasta should finish cooking about the same time as the seafood).

Once the mussels have begun to open, add the shrimp and scallops. Cover, and simmer until they're almost cooked through, 2 to 3 minutes. Add the calamari, cover, and simmer until the pieces turn white and are just cooked through, about 2 minutes. Add the soup base with pasta and the parsley to the pot, and stir to combine. Remove the garlic, if desired. Serve in wide soup bowls.

CAPON BROTH *with* PASSATELLI

Brodo di Cappone con Passatelli

Food waste is a big problem today. This is one delicious way to recycle the leftover bread we have in our kitchen. Passatelli is a type of pasta traditionally from Emilia-Romagna. It is sometimes served without soup, topped with Bolognese sauce or butter and cheese. At Felidia, we serve it with capon broth—especially during the cold winter months—but chicken broth can be used instead. It's something that I always serve at home for special meals, and it's a staple of the holiday menus at the restaurant.

If you don't have a passatelli maker, you can use a meat grinder without the cutting blade (the passatelli will be extruded through the holes of the grinder). Cut the strands of dough into 1-inch pieces with a knife as they are extruded. You can even freeze the dough in pieces for about 30 to 45 minutes, and then grate on the large holes of a box grater.

MAKES ABOUT 3 QUARTS, SERVING 12

For the Broth
1 whole capon (about 4 pounds)
1 large onion, halved
2 carrots, cut into 1-inch chunks
3 stalks celery, cut into 1-inch chunks
6 sprigs fresh Italian parsley
6 whole black peppercorns
Kosher salt

For the Passatelli
3 large eggs
1 cup freshly grated Grana Padano
Kosher salt
¾ to 1 cup fine dried breadcrumbs
All-purpose flour, for the baking sheet

To Finish
3 cups packed baby spinach
2 tablespoons truffle butter
Freshly grated Grana Padano, for serving

For the broth, wash the capon thoroughly under cold running water and drain well. Put the capon in a Dutch oven large enough to hold it without crowding. Add water to cover by 2 inches, about 5 quarts. Bring to a boil over high heat. Adjust the level of heat to a simmer, and continue to cook for 1 hour, skimming the foam and fat from the surface occasionally.

Meanwhile, with a pair of tongs, place the onion, cut sides down, directly over an open flame, and cook until the cut surface is well browned, about 3 minutes. Move the onion halves as necessary to brown them evenly. (Alternatively, the onion may be browned, cut sides down, in a heavy skillet over medium heat.)

Add the onion, carrots, celery, parsley, and peppercorns to the broth in the pot, and salt to taste. Simmer, partially covered, until the capon is very tender and the stock is very flavorful, about 2 hours.

Strain the broth through a colander lined with a dampened kitchen towel or cheesecloth, reserving both the broth and the capon. If you want to use the stock immediately, you can remove much of the liquid fat floating on the surface by lightly dragging a folded paper towel across it. It will be easier to degrease the stock if you have time to chill it completely in the refrigerator. The fat will then rise to the surface and solidify, so it can be easily skimmed off.

When the capon is cool, remove the breast meat and shred it, discarding the skin and fat.

For the passatelli, beat the eggs in a large bowl. Stir in the cheese and 1 teaspoon salt; then stir in enough breadcrumbs, a bit at a time, to make a dough that is firm but still malleable.

Meanwhile, bring the capon stock to a simmer on the stove. Line a baking sheet with a kitchen towel, and dust with flour. Press pieces of dough through the passatelli maker (or meat grinder with the widest holes), one piece at a time, and as extruded cut into 1-inch pieces and set on the baking sheet. Dust with flour, and repeat with the remaining dough.

Add the passatelli and spinach to the simmering stock, and cook until they rise to the surface. Stir in the truffle butter, and serve immediately, passing grated cheese at the table.

SPRING SOUP

Zuppa di Primavera

This easy-to-make soup sings of spring. Vegetable broth adds more flavor, but the soup can be made with plain water instead. Sorrel can be substituted for all or some of the watercress. The dollop of fresh ricotta adds even more freshness to an already beautiful celebration of spring. Both Chef Nicotra and I love to make this soup when I harvest what has been growing in the garden. Using in-season local products is a hallmark of Felidia's food, and Italian cuisine in general.

SERVES 4 TO 6

3 tablespoons extra-virgin olive oil
3 medium leeks, white and pale-green parts only, halved lengthwise, washed, and sliced
1 large russet potato (about 10 ounces), peeled and cut into chunks
2 cups vegetable broth
1 cup shelled fresh or thawed frozen peas
4 cups packed watercress
⅓ cup sour cream
Juice of ½ lemon, plus more to taste
Kosher salt
Freshly ground black pepper
Fresh ricotta, for optional garnish (see page 44)

Heat the olive oil in a large saucepan over medium heat. When the oil is hot, add the leeks. Cook until tender but not browned, about 7 minutes. Add the potato, broth, and 4 cups water. Bring to a simmer, and cook until potato is just beginning to become tender, about 8 to 10 minutes.

Add the peas, and simmer until peas and potatoes are tender, about 8 to 10 minutes more.

Purée the soup in batches in a blender, adding the watercress and sour cream as you do, to get a completely smooth bright-green soup. Stir in the lemon juice, and season with salt and pepper. Add more lemon juice to taste, if needed. Cover, and chill the soup until it's cold, at least 2 hours. Serve with a dollop of fresh ricotta, if desired.

FRESH CHESTNUT *and* WINTER SQUASH SOUP

Zuppa di Castagne e Zucca

This is a current favorite at Felidia during the late-fall and winter months. The soffritto that Chef Nicotra adds gives the soup a sophisticated and complex taste. To turn it into a main course at home, you can add shrimp or chicken. You can also serve it with barley, farro, or any other grains. Even quinoa will work beautifully. This soup is like velvet—comforting and satisfying.

SERVES 6

For the Soffritto
1 tablespoon extra-virgin olive oil
2 slices bacon, chopped
1 clove garlic, crushed and peeled
1 sprig fresh rosemary
1 cup tomato purée

For the Soup
2 tablespoons extra-virgin olive oil, plus more for drizzling
2 medium leeks, white and pale-green parts only, washed and thinly sliced
1 small butternut squash, peeled and cubed (about 4 cups)
6 cups low-sodium chicken broth, or water
1½ cups peeled, coarsely chopped chestnuts
Kosher salt
Freshly ground black pepper
Freshly grated Grana Padano, for serving

For the soffritto, heat the olive oil in a small skillet over medium heat. Add the bacon, and cook until the fat is rendered, about 3 minutes. Add the garlic and rosemary, and let sizzle a minute. Add the tomato purée, and cook until it's thick and flavorful, about 5 minutes. Strain and reserve.

For the soup, heat the olive oil in a large saucepan over medium heat. When the oil is hot, add the leeks, and cook until softened, about 4 minutes. Add the butternut squash, and cook until golden on the edges, about 3 minutes. Add the stock (or water), the soffritto, and the chestnuts, and season with salt and pepper. Bring to a simmer, stirring frequently, until the squash and chestnuts break down and thicken the soup, about 45 minutes. Season again with salt and pepper. Serve hot in warm bowls, with freshly grated Grana Padano and a drizzle of olive oil.

RICE *and* PEA SOUP

Risi e Bisi

One of my favorite soups from my childhood, this dish can often be found on my table at home. It was one of the first soups on the menu at Felidia, and Chef Nicotra continues the tradition. Either long- or short-grain rice can be used here. Traditionally, the soup was made with short-grain Carnaroli or Arborio rice, and I still think this produces the most authentic flavor and texture. If you need to cook the soup longer or to reheat it, long-grain rice stays more intact when cooked, but you can use short-grain rice as well, it just must be served as soon as it is cooked. When on the Felidia menu now as a special, it's served with a spoon of fresh ricotta (page 44) at the end.

SERVES 6

- 3 tablespoons extra-virgin olive oil, plus more for serving
- ¼ pound bacon (about 3 thick-cut strips), cut crosswise into ⅓-inch pieces
- 1 bunch leeks, white and pale-green parts, washed and thinly sliced (about 2 cups)
- Kosher salt
- 1½ cups Arborio rice
- 3 cups fresh peas, or 1-pound bag frozen peas
- ¼ cup chopped fresh Italian parsley
- ½ cup freshly grated Grana Padano, plus more for serving
- Freshly ground black pepper, to taste

Heat the olive oil in a large Dutch oven over medium heat. Stir in the bacon pieces and cook for several minutes, to render the fat. When the bacon starts to crisp, stir in the leeks. Cook, stirring frequently, until the leeks are wilted and the bacon is caramelized, about 6 minutes.

Add 2½ quarts water and 1 teaspoon salt. Rapidly bring to a boil; then adjust the heat to maintain active bubbling. Cook for an hour, uncovered, to build flavor in the soup base and reduce it by about a third.

Add the rice, and stir. If using fresh peas, add now (add frozen peas halfway through the rice's cooking time). Simmer until the rice is al dente, about 16 to 17 minutes. Stir in the parsley and Grana Padano. Serve in bowls, with a final sprinkle of grated Grana Padano and a drizzle of olive oil. Add freshly ground black pepper to taste.

TUSCAN KALE *and* BREAD SOUP

Ribollita

Ribollita is a hearty Tuscan winter dish that is often served with a piece of toasted crusty bread. When traveling through Tuscany, you can find versions of ribollita with consistencies ranging from soupy to thick, according to the cook's preference. Chef Nicotra tasted this thick version of ribollita during a chef research trip in Altopascio, Tuscany. I tasted ribollita many moons ago, on one of my first food research trips to Italy, and I prefer a ribolitta with a bit more liquid. You can add 2 ounces of diced pancetta when you sauté the vegetables if you'd like a slightly richer and more complex dish. Baked in a baking dish or skillet, topped with Grana Padano for a crispy crust, at 300 degrees until heated through, leftover ribollitta becomes like a torta.

SERVES 6

3 tablespoons extra-virgin olive oil, plus more for drizzling
1 medium onion, chopped
2 leeks, white and pale-green parts, halved lengthwise, washed, and sliced
2 teaspoons chopped fresh rosemary leaves
Pinch of peperoncino flakes
1 cup dried cannellini or borlotti beans, soaked overnight
2 fresh bay leaves
Kosher salt
1 cup tomato purée
1 large bunch black kale (cavolo nero), stemmed and chopped
4 cups crustless day-old bread cubes
Freshly grated Grana Padano, for serving

Heat the olive oil in a medium Dutch oven over medium heat. When the oil is hot, add the onion and leeks and cook until they begin to wilt, about 5 minutes. Add the rosemary and peperoncino, and cook until sizzling, about 1 minute. Drain the beans, and add them to the pot with the bay leaves and 3 quarts water. Bring to a simmer, and cook until the beans are almost tender, about 40 to 45 minutes.

Season the beans with salt, and add the tomato purée. Adjust the heat to a simmer, and stir in the kale. Cook until tender, about 15 to 20 minutes, adding a little more water if it becomes too thick.

Stir in the bread cubes. Cook, stirring and breaking them up with a wooden spoon, until everything is thick but still slightly soupy, about 15 minutes. Season with salt, discard the bay leaves, and serve in soup bowls, drizzled with olive oil and sprinkled with grated Grana Padano.

MUSHROOM SOUP

Zuppa di Funghi

This dish was on the Felidia menu in the 1990s, and Chef Nicotra also prepared it for my daughter Tanya's wedding at the Plaza. We served it with orzo, but you can also use toasted or grilled bread brushed with olive oil.

SERVES 8

2½ quarts good-quality vegetable stock or chicken stock
1 ounce dried porcini
3 tablespoons extra-virgin olive oil
1 medium onion, chopped
2 cups shredded carrots
1 pound fresh porcini (or a mix of seasonal mushrooms), cleaned, trimmed, and cut into ½-inch chunks
Kosher salt
2 tablespoons tomato paste
Peperoncino flakes
½ cup orzo
Freshly grated Grana Padano, for serving

In a small saucepan, bring 4 cups stock just to a simmer. Remove from heat, add the dried porcini, and let steep until softened, about 15 minutes. Remove the porcini from the stock, squeezing back in any liquid they have absorbed. Finely chop the porcini, and reserve the soaking liquid.

Heat the olive oil in a medium Dutch oven over medium heat. When the oil is hot, add the onion, and cook until softened but not browned, about 5 minutes. Add the carrots, fresh mushrooms, and chopped dried porcini, and season with salt. Cook, stirring occasionally, until the mushrooms release their liquid, 6 to 7 minutes. Increase heat to reduce the liquid, about 5 minutes.

Clear a space in the pan, and add the tomato paste. Cook and stir the tomato paste in that spot for a minute, then stir into the mushrooms. Add a pinch of peperoncino and the remaining 1½ quarts stock. Pour in the soaking liquid, leaving any grit that remains in the bottom. Bring the soup to a simmer, and cook until the mushrooms are very tender and the soup is very flavorful, about 40 minutes.

When the soup is almost done, bring a medium saucepan of salted water to a boil. Add the orzo, and cook until it's still quite al dente, or about half the cooking time listed on the package (it will vary by brand). Drain, stir the orzo into the soup, and let the soup simmer until the orzo is fully cooked. (If you want to keep some of the soup for later, remove it to another container, and add the orzo only to the soup you will be serving right away.) Serve in soup bowls with a sprinkle of grated Grana Padano.

TUSCAN FRESH TOMATO *and* BREAD SOUP *with* COD

Pappa al Pomodoro con Baccalà

I have always enjoyed a tomato-based fish soup, and this one is no exception. Pappa al pomodoro is a Tuscan tradition, and although tomato soup is often enjoyed during the summer months, at Felidia this dish is typically popular in the winter, when fresh cod is at its best. However, this soup is a great base any time of year for any roasted fish, such as cod, bass, snapper, or even monkfish.

SERVES 6

5 tablespoons extra-virgin olive oil, plus more for finishing
1 small onion, finely chopped
6 cloves garlic, crushed and peeled
Two 28-ounce cans whole San Marzano tomatoes, crushed by hand
2 large sprigs fresh basil, plus shredded basil for garnish
Kosher salt
Crushed peperoncino flakes
4 cups crustless day-old country bread cubes
1¼ pounds skinless monkfish or cod fillets, cut into 1-inch chunks
Quick-mixing flour, such as Wondra, for dredging
Freshly grated Grana Padano, for serving

Heat 3 tablespoons of the olive oil over medium heat in a large Dutch oven. Add the onion, and cook until wilted, about 3 minutes. Add the garlic, and cook until golden, about 3 minutes.

Add the tomatoes and basil sprigs. Rinse the cans with 3 cups water, and add that as well. Season with 1 teaspoon salt and a generous pinch of peperoncino. Bring to a simmer, and cook until thickened, about 20 minutes.

Once the soup has thickened, stir in the bread cubes. Simmer, breaking up and mashing the bread cubes with a whisk to thicken. Remove and discard the garlic and basil sprigs.

Meanwhile, season the fish with ½ teaspoon salt. Spread the flour on a plate. Heat a large nonstick skillet over medium-high heat, and add the remaining 2 tablespoons olive oil. Dredge the fish chunks in the flour, dusting off the excess. When the oil is hot, add the fish, and brown on all sides until just cooked through, about 2 minutes.

Serve the soup in shallow bowls, sprinkle with Grana Padano, and place the fish in the center. Garnish with the shredded basil and a final drizzle of olive oil.

CRAB *and* LEEK SOUP

Minestra di Granchi e Porri

We originally served this delicately flavored soup without the crabmeat. Chef Nicotra sometimes substitutes cooked lobster pieces or shrimp as a variation, and you can also use vegetable stock and omit the seafood altogether for a vegetarian version.

SERVES 6

¼ cup extra-virgin olive oil, plus more for drizzling
2 small leeks, white and pale-green parts, halved lengthwise, washed, and sliced (about 2 cups)
1 bunch scallions, chopped
3 large russet potatoes (about 2 pounds), peeled and diced
Kosher salt
Pinch of peperoncino flakes
2½ quarts light chicken stock
2 bay leaves
1 pound jumbo lump crabmeat, picked through for shells
Freshly ground black pepper (optional)

Heat 2 tablespoons of the olive oil in a medium Dutch oven. When the oil is hot, add the leeks and scallions, and cook until they're wilted but not browned, about 4 minutes. Add the remaining 2 tablespoons of oil and the potatoes. Season with salt and peperoncino. Cook and stir until the potatoes are lightly golden on the edges, about 6 minutes.

Add the stock and bay leaves. Bring to a simmer, and cook, uncovered, until the potatoes are very tender and the soup has reduced slightly, about 25 minutes.

Remove the bay leaves. Scatter in the crab, and bring to a simmer. Cook until the crab is heated through, 3 to 4 minutes. In the restaurant, this soup is served in a copper pot and ladled out tableside into individual soup bowls. If desired, you can add a drizzle of extra-virgin olive oil and freshly ground black pepper to serve.

PORK, SAUERKRAUT, *and* BEAN SOUP

Yota

Yota or jota is a classic Istrian dish that goes back to my childhood. It has been served on the Felidia menu during many winter months since the restaurant opened in 1981; it's popular when it's cold outside and people crave comfort foods. When I was a child, sauerkraut was something I particularly enjoyed. In Sicily, sauerkraut is not used much in cooking, but the base for this soup is not too different from pasta e fagioli, so Chef Nicotra jumped right into making this traditional soup when he first arrived at Felidia.

SERVES 8 OR MORE

2 tablespoons extra-virgin olive oil, plus more for drizzling
One 1-pound chunk fresh pork butt, cut into 2-inch chunks
Kosher salt
Freshly ground black pepper
8 ounces dried red kidney beans, soaked overnight
3 fresh bay leaves
2 big sprigs fresh thyme
2 big sprigs fresh sage
6 cloves garlic, peeled and finely chopped
2 large russet potatoes, peeled but left whole
2 pounds sauerkraut (preferably the bagged, refrigerated variety), rinsed and drained
1 pound smoked pork sausage, such as kielbasa, cut into 2-inch lengths
1 pound fresh pork sausage, Eastern European–style or sweet Italian

Heat the olive oil in a large Dutch oven over medium heat. Season the pork butt with salt and pepper. Brown the pork on all sides, about 6 minutes in all. Drain the beans, and add to the pot, along with the bay leaves, thyme sprigs, sage sprigs, and garlic. Stir to combine all with the beans. Add 4 quarts cold water. Bring to a simmer over medium-low heat, set the lid ajar, and continue to simmer until the beans just begin to become tender, about 40 to 45 minutes.

Add the potatoes, sauerkraut, and sausages. Return to a simmer, and cook, uncovered, until the potatoes are cooked through and the beans and pork are tender, about 40 to 45 minutes more.

Move potatoes to a medium bowl, and coarsely mash. Stir back into the soup. Season with salt and pepper. Bring to a simmer over medium heat, and cook until thick and flavorful, about 15 to 20 minutes more. Remove the herb sprigs and bay leaves and discard. Serve in soup bowls, drizzled with olive oil.

PASTAS AND PRIMI

The progression of an Italian meal traditionally goes from an appetizer to a primo, then a secondo with vegetables or a contorno, and lastly dessert. The primo can be a pasta, risotto, polenta, or even soup. At Felidia, we make fresh pastas every day. On any given day, there might be a choice of ten or more seasonal pastas on the menu. Our pastas have kept guests coming back for more since the restaurant opened.

Some of the first fresh pastas I served at Felidia included fuzi, pasutice, krafi, and gnocchi—all pastas I made at home, and all pastas taken from the Istrian cooking tradition. Chef Nicotra still cooks the original pastas and has added many more of his own, new classics such as pear and pecorino ravioli (page 103) and chocolate ravioli (page 107).

Risotto is particularly close to my heart. New Yorkers were still unfamiliar with this dish in the 1980s, when I first put it on our menu, with mushrooms in the fall and peas and asparagus in the spring.

In this chapter, you will also find a selection of dried pastas that have graced Felidia's menus over the years, with sauces and the suggested pasta shapes that work well with them. There are also some of our most popular current fresh-pasta recipes, along with some other primi that can be prepared easily at home.

DRIED PASTAS AND SAUCES

100% DURUM WHEAT SEMOLINA
NET WT 16 OZ (1 LB) 454G

PENNE *with* SPICY TOMATO SAUCE, ROSEMARY, *and* RICOTTA

Penne "al Brucio"

This dried-pasta dish is super easy to make. It's called "al brucio" because of the spicy flavor. It originally did not include ricotta, but that helps balance the spiciness of the sauce. You can also top it with a spoon of burrata at the very end, or even a slice of buffalo mozzarella. At Felidia, we make it with candele pasta, an extra-long, smooth pasta that is tubular, hollow, and wide, like a rigatoni, and looks like a long candle (which is also called a candele *in Italian). Chef Nicotra's mother used to make this pasta for him when he was young, and she still does when he goes home to Sicily.*

SERVES 6

Kosher salt
6 tablespoons extra-virgin olive oil
4 cloves garlic, crushed and peeled
3 sprigs fresh rosemary
2 cups cherry tomatoes
Pinch of sugar
¼ teaspoon peperoncino flakes, or to taste
1 pound dried penne rigate
½ cup fresh basil leaves, shredded
½ cup freshly grated Grana Padano, plus more for serving
½ cup fresh ricotta (see page 44)

Bring a large pot of salted water to a boil for the pasta. Heat 4 tablespoons of the olive oil in a large skillet over medium heat. Add the garlic and rosemary, and cook until the garlic just begins to turn golden, 1 to 2 minutes. Add the tomatoes and sugar, and cook, tossing occasionally, until the tomatoes break down, 7 to 8 minutes, adding the peperoncino once the tomatoes give up their juice.

Meanwhile, cook the pasta until just al dente, remove it with a spider, and add to the tomatoes in the skillet along with about ½ cup pasta water. Toss to coat the pasta in the sauce; then simmer until the sauce comes together, about 2 to 3 minutes, adding a little more pasta water if it seems dry. Remove the skillet from the heat, drizzle with the remaining 2 tablespoons olive oil, and sprinkle with the basil and grated Grana Padano. Season with salt, and toss well. Remove the rosemary sprigs and garlic, and discard. Spoon the pasta into individual shallow bowls, and spoon a fresh dollop of ricotta on top of each one.

SPAGHETTI *with* OIL *and* GARLIC

Spaghetti Aglio Olio

Spaghetti with oil and garlic seems like the quintessential simple Italian dish. However, with this simplicity comes a challenge in preparation: you need the very best ingredients. Traditionally, this recipe is made by sautéing garlic in oil with some peperoncino, but I combine the sauce ingredients in a blender, to yield a creamier sauce with a less intense garlic flavor. It might require a few tries at home, but with practice, this dish will certainly become a family favorite.

—Chef Nicotra

SERVES 6

Kosher salt
⅓ cup extra-virgin olive oil
10 cloves garlic, peeled and sliced
¼ teaspoon peperoncino flakes, or more to taste
1 pound dried spaghetti
1 cup freshly grated Grana Padano
¼ cup chopped fresh Italian parsley

Bring a large pot of salted water to a boil for the pasta. In the meantime, in a small skillet, heat the olive oil over medium-low heat. Scatter in the garlic, and cook, making sure it doesn't burn, until softened and pale golden, about 3 to 4 minutes. Season with salt and the peperoncino.

Begin cooking the pasta. Ladle ½ cup pasta cooking water into a blender, and add the garlic oil and half of the grated Grana Padano. Blend until smooth, then add the parsley. Pour into a large skillet.

When the pasta is al dente, remove with tongs to the skillet. Sprinkle with the remaining grated Grana Padano. Toss to coat the pasta in the sauce, adding a little more of the pasta cooking water if it seems dry. When plating, use the tongs to twirl the pasta into the shape of a bird's nest. This will keep the pasta warmer and make for an attractive presentation. You can also remove the pasta with a large serving fork and twist it into a bird's nest using a ladle, then place it in the pasta bowl. Set the ladle into the pot with the dressed pasta. With a chef's fork start filling the ladle with the spaghetti and start twisting until it is twisted around the fork. Remove the ladle and fork the twisted pasta into the center of a plate and gently guide onto the plate.

BOLOGNESE SAUCE

Ragù alla Bolognese

Bolognese is a versatile sauce that everyone seems to love. I serve it with pasta, with polenta, or as my sauce for baked pasta or lasagna. Making it is a time-consuming process, so many people shy away from doing so at home, but they love to order it at Felidia. Though the sauce gets its name from the city of Bologna, it can be found in some form all around Italy. This recipe makes enough to sauce 2 pounds of dried pasta. After the sauce is cooked, you can divide it and freeze some for later if you're serving less. It's best to grind your own meat, but you can also buy ground beef, pork, and veal if you don't have a grinder.

We like to serve this with dried rigatoni or fusilli, but it is delicious with fresh tagliatelle.

MAKES ABOUT 6 CUPS

1 pound boneless beef chuck, cubed
1 pound boneless pork shoulder, cubed
1 pound boneless veal shoulder, cubed
3 tablespoons extra-virgin olive oil, plus more for drizzling
1 medium onion, finely chopped
1 medium carrot, grated
2 stalks celery, finely chopped
Kosher salt
Peperoncino flakes
3 tablespoons tomato paste
1 cup dry red wine
One 28-ounce can whole San Marzano tomatoes, crushed by hand
1 pound dried rigatoni or fusilli
½ cup freshly grated Grana Padano, plus more for serving

Grind the meats, using a meat grinder set to the coarse plate. Pour 6 cups water into a medium saucepan, and warm to a simmer over low heat. Heat a large Dutch oven over medium heat, then add the olive oil. When the oil is hot, add the onion, carrot, and celery, and cook, stirring often, until tender but not browned, about 8 to 10 minutes.

Crumble in the ground meat and cook, breaking it up with a wooden spoon, over medium heat, stirring frequently, until the meat gives up its juices, 15 to 18 minutes. Increase the heat to medium high to reduce away the juices and concentrate the flavor, about 3 minutes. Season with salt and peperoncino.

Return heat to medium. Clear a space in the pan, and add the tomato paste. Cook and stir the tomato paste in that spot for a minute, then stir into the meat. Pour in the red wine, and adjust heat to reduce the wine by half, 1 to 2 minutes. Add the tomatoes and enough of the simmering water just to cover the meat.

Simmer the sauce over low heat, adding water as

(recipe continues)

needed to keep the meat just covered, until thick and very flavorful, 1½ to 2 hours. The longer you cook it, the better it will be.

When you're ready to serve, put 3 cups of the sauce in a large skillet and bring to a simmer. (Freeze the remaining sauce for another time.) Bring a large pot of salted water to a boil. Add 1 pound of the dried pasta of your choice. When the pasta is al dente, drain, reserving 1 cup pasta cooking water. Add the hot pasta to the sauce, and toss to coat. Drizzle with olive oil, season with salt if needed, and toss again, adding a little pasta water if it seems dry. Remove the skillet from the heat, sprinkle with the grated Grana Padano, and toss. Serve immediately.

If you decide to serve this sauce with a long pasta, when plating, use the tongs to twirl the pasta into the shape of a bird's nest. It will keep the pasta warmer and make for an attractive presentation. Spoon some Bolognese sauce into the center of the pasta mound. Put additional grated Grana Padano in a bowl for the table, in case your guests would like more cheese. This sauce is also wonderful over some piping-hot polenta.

LINGUINE *with* WHITE CLAM SAUCE *and* BROCCOLI

Linguine con Vongole e Broccoli

This great dish has been through many incarnations at Felidia over the years. This is my version. The recipe calls for broccoli, but it works just as well with broccoli rabe in the winter or zucchini in the summer. At Felidia, I typically use different kinds of clams for texture and flavor, such as Manila clams, cooked on the shell directly in the pan, where the pasta is then added and everything is sautéed together. I suggest linguine here, but other suitable pasta shapes include spaghetti and bavette.

—Chef Nicotra

SERVES 6

Kosher salt
4 cups broccoli florets
1 pound dried linguine
¼ cup extra-virgin olive oil, plus more for drizzling
6 cloves garlic, peeled and sliced
36 littleneck clams, or a mix of other medium to small clams, scrubbed
½ teaspoon crushed peperoncino flakes
¼ cup chopped fresh Italian parsley

Bring a large pot of salted water to a boil for the broccoli and pasta. Add the broccoli to the boiling water, and blanch until bright green but still crisp, about 2 minutes. Remove with a spider to a bowl of ice water. Cool, and pat dry. Coarsely chop.

When you're ready to start the sauce, add the linguine to the water. Heat a large skillet over medium-high heat. Add the oil. When the oil is hot, scatter in the garlic, and cook until it just begins to turn golden on the edges, about 1 minute. Add the clams and ½ cup pasta water. Cook until the clams just begin to open, about 2 to 3 minutes. Add the blanched broccoli and crushed red pepper, and cook until the broccoli is sizzling, about 2 minutes. Cover, bring to a simmer, and cook until the clams open fully, 3 to 4 minutes more. Uncover and boil rapidly to reduce the pan juices down by about half, about 2 minutes. Discard any clams that do not open.

When the pasta is al dente, remove with tongs directly to the sauce in the skillet. Season with salt, sprinkle with the parsley, and add a generous drizzle of olive oil. Toss to coat the pasta in the sauce. When plating, use the tongs to twirl the pasta into the shape of a bird's nest. It will keep the pasta warmer and make for an attractive presentation. Arrange clams around each serving. Spoon any leftover sauce over the pasta.

PACCHERI *with* MOZZARELLA *and* TOMATOES

Paccheri alla Caprese

This dish is served in the hot months of July and August, when people are craving pasta but prefer something cooler. Paccheri is the perfect pasta, since it keeps its texture and shape as it cools.

SERVES 6

Kosher salt
1½ pounds heirloom tomatoes, cut into small wedges, or, out of season, cherry tomatoes, halved
½ cup fresh basil leaves, shredded
½ cup extra-virgin olive oil, plus more for drizzling
1 pound dried paccheri
12 ounces buffalo mozzarella, cut into small wedges, or bocconcini, halved
Freshly grated Grana Padano, for finishing (optional)

Bring a large pot of salted water to a boil for the pasta. Combine the tomatoes, basil, and olive oil in a large bowl. Season generously with salt, and toss well. Let the tomatoes sit at room temperature while you cook the pasta.

Add the pasta to the boiling water, and cook until al dente. Drain, and pat very dry on kitchen towels. While it's still slightly warm, add the pasta to the tomatoes, and toss well. Arrange the mozzarella over the top, and finish with a drizzle of olive oil and some grated Grana Padano, if you like.

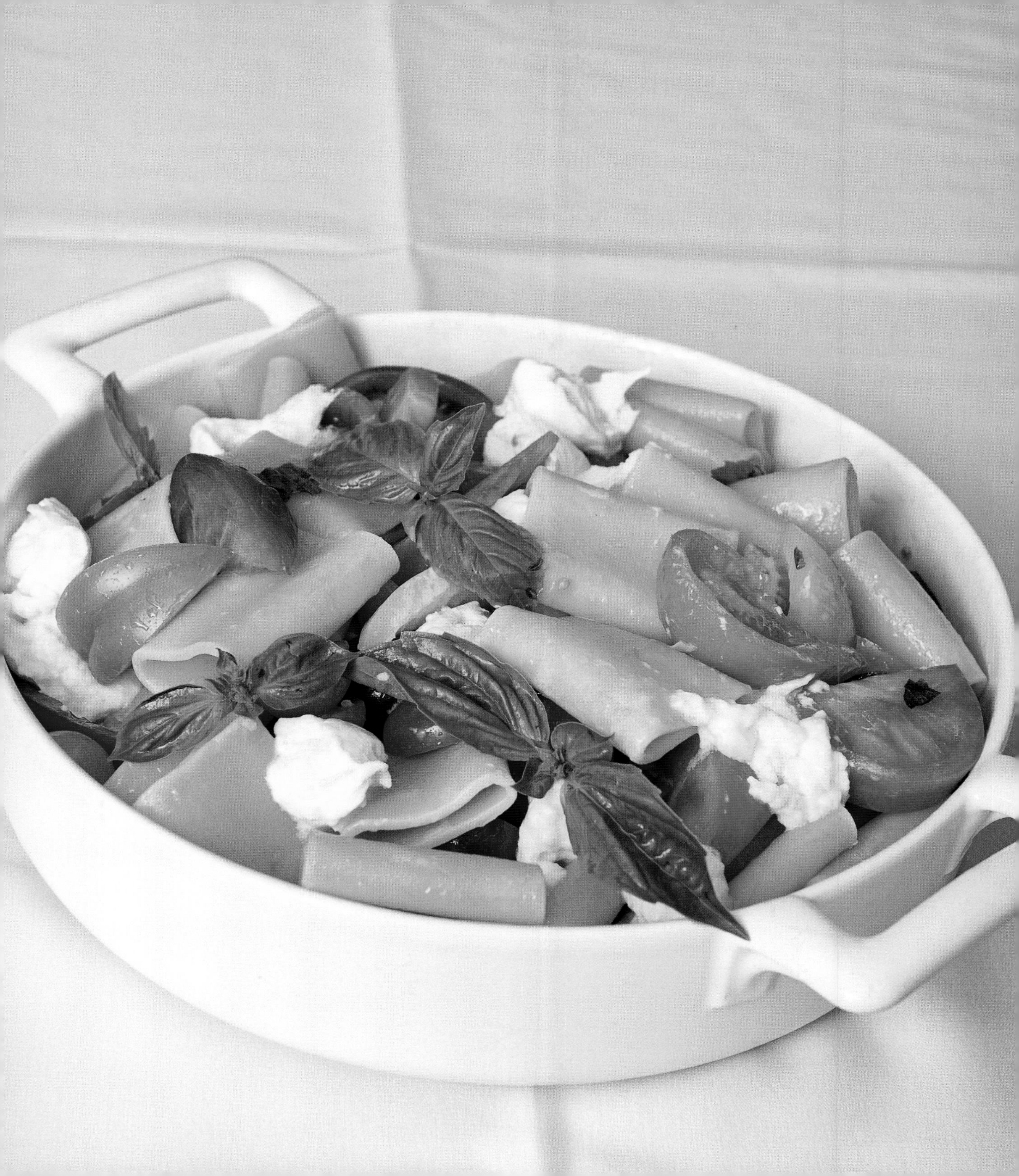

CHEF NICOTRA'S HOME-STYLE LASAGNA

Lasagna dello Chef

We don't always serve lasagna at Felidia, but on certain Sunday family menus, or on other special occasions, you will find it, and people love it. We use fresh pasta at the restaurant, but this version, made with dry ready-to-bake lasagna noodles, is perfect for home cooking, and something I regularly make for my kids. Alex, Julia, and Luca love it.

—Chef Nicotra

SERVES 8

3 tablespoons extra-virgin olive oil
6 cloves garlic, peeled and thinly sliced
Peperoncino flakes, to taste
Two 28-ounce cans whole San Marzano tomatoes, crushed by hand
Kosher salt
2 large sprigs fresh basil
1 cup heavy cream
15 sheets no-boil lasagna noodles (about one 9-ounce box)
4 cups freshly grated low-moisture mozzarella (about 1 pound)
2½ cups freshly grated Grana Padano

For the sauce, heat a large Dutch oven over medium heat, and add the olive oil. When the oil is hot, add the garlic and let sizzle until just golden, about 1 minute. Add a pinch of peperoncino and the crushed tomatoes. Rinse out the cans with 2 cups water, and add that as well. Season with salt, and put the basil sprigs in the sauce. Simmer until flavorful and slightly thickened, about 20 minutes. Discard the basil sprigs, and add the cream. Simmer just until the sauce comes together, 3 to 4 minutes. Season again with salt and peperoncino. You should have 6 to 7 cups of sauce.

To assemble the lasagna, preheat the oven to 400 degrees. Spread about a cup of sauce in the bottom of a 9-by-13-inch baking dish. Cover the sauce with three noodles (there will be extra space around the noodles, and that's okay—they will expand as they absorb the sauce). Spread another cup of sauce over the noodles, then sprinkle with 1 cup mozzarella and ½ cup Grana Padano. Top with another layer of noodles. Continue with sauce, mozzarella, and Grana Padano, layering in the same manner, until you add the fifth layer of noodles. Top that layer just with sauce and grated Grana Padano (not mozzarella).

Tent the lasagna with foil, and place on a baking sheet to catch any drips. Bake until the edges are bubbling, about 30 to 35 minutes. Uncover the lasagna, and bake until the top is browned and crusty, about 20 to 30 minutes more. Let the lasagna rest out of the oven for at least 30 minutes before slicing and serving.

TOMATO ALMOND TRAPANESE PESTO *with* BUSIATI

Pesto Trapanese

This simple pesto is traditionally served with dried busiati pasta from the town of Trapani, in Sicily; some specialty stores might have it, but, if not, gemelli is a great substitute. I serve this dish with our freshly made "black-and-white" pasta, which came about as part of a joke that I played on Lidia's son-in-law, Corrado. Both of us are avid soccer fans but for rival teams, so one day I served Corrado this delicious sauce on fresh black-and-white pasta—the colors of my team, "Juventus," which he did not appreciate. The colors of his team, "Roma," are red and yellow. It's been on the menu since and a point of contention between the two of us. You can also use this pesto with short pasta. In Trapani, it is served with seafood that is added at the last minute. Any small fish that the local fishermen have caught are fried and put on top of the dressed pasta; the larger fish they caught are sold at market.

As a variation, you can also make this with sun-dried tomatoes instead of fresh cherry tomatoes, but choose a good-quality brand that's soft and pliable. Use about 1 cup of sun-dried tomatoes to substitute for the fresh tomatoes here.

—Chef Nicotra

SERVES 4 TO 6

1 pint sweet, ripe cherry tomatoes
½ cup extra-virgin olive oil
Kosher salt
4 cups fresh basil leaves
2 cloves garlic, crushed and peeled
⅓ cup almond slivers, toasted
1 pound dried busiati or gemelli
½ cup freshly grated Grana Padano

Preheat the oven to 500 degrees.

Toss the tomatoes in a large bowl with 2 tablespoons of the olive oil, and season with salt. Spread on a baking sheet, and cook until blistered, about 10 to 15 minutes. Turn off the oven, and let tomatoes dry and cool.

Bring a large pot of salted water to a boil. Add the basil, and cook until it's bright green and just wilted, about 30 seconds. Remove with a spider to an ice bath (leave the water on for the pasta), then wring very dry.

Put the basil in the work bowl of a food processor with the cooled roasted tomatoes, garlic, and almonds, and pulse to make a coarse paste. With the processor running, add the remaining 6 tablespoons of olive oil, and process to make a smooth pesto.

Add the pasta to the boiling water, and cook until al dente. Drain, reserving 1 cup pasta cooking water. Toss the pasta with the pesto and grated Grana Padano in a large serving bowl, adding a little pasta cooking water if it seems dry. Serve immediately.

PASTA PRIMAVERA—OLD *and* NEW SCHOOL VARIATIONS

Fusilli alla Primavera

This classic version of pasta primavera has been served at Felidia from the very beginning. It's a favorite of Tanya and Joe, who grew up at Felidia and spent many hours there doing homework and having meals with family and friends, while I was busy working in the kitchen or greeting clients. Now, when spring is here, Chef Nicotra carries on the tradition.

SERVES 6

Kosher salt
3 tablespoons extra-virgin olive oil, plus more for drizzling
4 cloves garlic, crushed and peeled
4 ounces thin green beans, trimmed and cut into 1-inch lengths
8 ounces asparagus, peeled and cut into 1-inch lengths (about ½ bunch)
1 cup halved grape tomatoes
1 bunch scallions, white and green parts, chopped (about 1 cup)
1 cup frozen peas, thawed
½ cup heavy cream
1 pound dried fusilli
½ cup loosely packed fresh basil leaves, shredded
½ cup freshly grated Grana Padano

Bring a large pot of salted water to a boil for the pasta. Heat a large skillet over medium-high heat, and add the olive oil. When the oil is hot, add the garlic and cook until sizzling, about 1 minute. Once the garlic is sizzling, add the green beans and asparagus. Season with ½ teaspoon salt. Ladle in ½ cup pasta water, cover the skillet, and cook until vegetables are crisp-tender, about 2 to 3 minutes.

Uncover the skillet, add the grape tomatoes, and cook until they begin to wrinkle, about 3 to 4 minutes. Add the scallions, peas, cream, and ½ cup pasta water. Simmer until reduced by half, about 2 minutes.

Meanwhile, add the fusilli to the boiling water and cook until just al dente. Transfer the pasta to the sauce, sprinkle with the basil, and toss to coat the pasta with the sauce, adding a little more pasta water if it seems dry.

Remove the skillet from the heat, and discard the garlic. Sprinkle with the grated Grana Padano, toss, and serve immediately.

VARIATION: Omit the tomatoes. Instead of the shredded basil, make a quick pesto in the food processor with 4 cups fresh basil leaves, 3 tablespoons toasted pine nuts, and ¼ cup extra-virgin olive oil. Add the pesto to the sauce when you add the fusilli, and toss well. (You may need to add a little more pasta water at this point as well, if the pesto thickens the sauce too much.)

RIGATONI WOODSMAN STYLE

Rigatoni alla Boscaiola

I used to make this pasta in our first restaurant, Buonavia, in Forest Hills, Queens, which we opened in 1971. It was so popular there that I brought it with me when we opened Felidia. This was a clear favorite of Tanya's; my husband, Felix, used to make it for her often when they had lunch together at the restaurant. In addition to the mushrooms listed here, you can try other seasonal varieties, such as morels, chanterelles, or porcini, available at your farmers' market. Bosco *means "forest" or "woods" in Italian; the mushrooms in the sauce were originally foraged in the woods.*

SERVES 4 TO 6

Kosher salt
½ cup dried porcini
3 tablespoons extra-virgin olive oil
1 medium onion, chopped
1 pound sweet Italian sausage without fennel seeds, removed from casings
1 pound mixed fresh mushrooms (button, cremini, shiitake, oyster), thickly sliced
6 fresh sage leaves
One 28-ounce can whole San Marzano tomatoes, crushed by hand
Peperoncino flakes, to taste
1 cup frozen peas
1 bunch scallions, white and light-green parts, chopped (about 1 cup)
½ cup heavy cream
1 pound dried rigatoni
1 cup freshly grated Grana Padano

Bring a large pot of salted water to a boil for the pasta. Ladle 1 cup pasta water over the porcini in a small bowl, and let soak until softened, about 10 minutes. Drain, reserving the soaking liquid, and finely chop the porcini.

Heat the olive oil in a large skillet over medium heat. Add the onion, and cook until it begins to soften, about 5 minutes. Add the sausage, and cook and crumble with a wooden spoon until no longer pink, about 4 minutes. Add the mushrooms and sage. Cover, and cook until the mushrooms release their juices, about 5 minutes.

Uncover, increase the heat to bring the mushroom juices to a boil, and reduce them away, about 2 minutes. Add the tomatoes, and season with ½ teaspoon salt and a pinch of peperoncino. Rinse out the tomato can with 1 cup pasta cooking water, and add that as well. Add the porcini, and pour in their soaking liquid, leaving any grit behind in the bowl. Bring to a simmer over medium heat, and cook until sauce is thickened, about 10 to 15 minutes.

Add the peas, scallions, and cream, and simmer until the scallions wilt and the peas are heated through, about 2 to 3 minutes.

When the sauce is almost ready, add the rigatoni to the boiling water and cook until al dente. Transfer the pasta to the sauce with a spider, and toss to coat. Bring to a simmer, and add up to 1 cup pasta water if it seems dry. Off heat, sprinkle with the Grana Padano, toss again, and serve immediately.

FRESH PASTAS AND GNUDI

Our fresh, homemade pasta has been a signature item on the Felidia menu since we first opened our doors. Though it takes quite a bit of effort to make fresh pasta, the rewards and flavors it provides are fantastic. At Felidia, we produce stuffed pastas, flat ribbon pastas, gnocchi, and passatelli for soup. Our fresh pasta comes in many different shapes and sizes, from tagliatelle, orecchiette, fuzi (a pasta that looks like garganelli), and so on down the line. The versatility of pasta is great for a restaurant menu. It is easily partnered with seasonal sauces, such as braised-meat sauces in the winter and spring vegetables in the spring months. Our guests know us for our fresh seasonal pasta and keep coming back for more after all these years.

PAPPARDELLE *with* MIXED FRESH MUSHROOMS

Pappardelle con Funghi Misti

Fresh long pasta like pappardelle or fettucine with mushroom sauce is a classic at Felidia that guests ask for year-round. We serve it with chanterelles and morels in the spring, and it is extraordinary with porcini in the fall. Garganelli, rigatoni, or penne also work with this sauce, as does polenta.

SERVES 4 TO 6

For the Pappardelle

2 cups unbleached all-purpose flour, plus more for working the dough
3 large eggs
1 tablespoon extra-virgin olive oil
½ teaspoon kosher salt, plus more for the pot

For the Sauce

¼ cup extra-virgin olive oil, plus more for drizzling
1½ pounds mixed fresh mushrooms (porcini, chanterelle, morel, shiitake), trimmed and sliced
2 tablespoons unsalted butter
3 cloves garlic, peeled and sliced
2 teaspoons chopped fresh rosemary leaves
Kosher salt
Peperoncino flakes, to taste
1 cup chicken stock
¼ cup chopped fresh Italian parsley
½ cup freshly grated Grana Padano, plus more for serving

For the pappardelle, put the flour in a food processor and pulse several times. Beat the eggs, olive oil, and salt in a spouted measuring cup. With the food processor running, add the liquid; let the machine run until the dough forms a ball on the blade, about 30 seconds. If it's too loose, add a tablespoon or two of flour; if too crumbly, add a tablespoon or so of cold water.

Let the machine knead the dough for about 20 seconds. Turn the dough out onto a very lightly floured surface, and knead by hand for another 30 seconds or so, until it's smooth, soft, and stretchy. Wrap in plastic, and rest the dough for 30 minutes.

Cut the dough into four pieces. Keeping the unused pieces covered as you roll, roll each one through a pasta machine set to the next-to-last setting, to get strips that are about as wide as the machine and about 12 to 14 inches in length.

Cut this pasta in half crosswise to get eight pieces that are about 6 to 7 inches long. Stack a few well-floured pieces, and cut into 1½-inch strips. Dust the pappardelle with flour, and nest them on floured baking sheets. Bring a large pot of salted water to a boil.

For the sauce, heat the olive oil in a large skillet over medium-high heat. When the oil is hot, add about half the mushrooms. Cook and stir until they begin to wilt and leave space in the pan, then add the remaining mushrooms. Cook and stir until they give up their liquid; then increase the heat to boil the liquid away and caramelize the mushrooms, about 8 to 10 minutes in all.

Reduce the heat to medium, add the butter, and

let it melt. Add the garlic and rosemary, and season with salt and peperoncino. Add the chicken stock, and simmer until reduced by half, about 3 minutes.

Meanwhile, add the pappardelle to the boiling water, and cook until al dente, about 3 minutes. Transfer the pasta with tongs to the simmering sauce, drizzle with olive oil, sprinkle with the parsley, and toss to coat, adding a little pasta water if it seems dry. Remove the skillet from the heat, and sprinkle with the grated cheese. Toss and serve, passing more grated Grana Padano at the table.

PEAR *and* PECORINO RAVIOLI

Cacio e Pere

This delicate and quite simple ravioli is a lovely way to enjoy the affinity of pear and cheese. The filling is a lively blend of shredded ripe pear, shredded Pecorino Romano that has been aged for 3 to 6 months, Grana Padano, and mascarpone—just stirred together at the last moment. Tanya and I discovered this recipe in Bologna while we were researching the book Lidia's Italy. *At a small pasta shop, Le Sfogline, near the herb market, a mother and her two daughters were making fresh pasta to sell to locals. The mom rolled out transparent golden-yellow sheets of dough by hand. I observed her making the stuffing for these ravioli and watched her grate some ripe pear into the cheese mixture. The flavors are a match made in heaven . . . or Felidia.*

MAKES 1 POUND PASTA, FOR 24 TO 28 RAVIOLI, SERVING 4 TO 6

For the Dough

2 cups all-purpose flour, plus more for working the dough
4 large eggs
1 large egg yolk
2 tablespoons extra-virgin olive oil

For the Filling

1 large or 2 small firm-ripe Bartlett pears, or other ripe but firm pears
6 ounces Pecorino Romano aged 3 to 6 months, freshly shredded
1 cup freshly grated Grana Padano
2 tablespoons mascarpone, chilled

For the Sauce

1 stick (8 tablespoons) unsalted butter
4 ounces Pecorino Romano aged 3 to 6 months, freshly shredded, plus more for serving
Kosher salt
Freshly ground black pepper

For the dough, put the flour in a food processor, and pulse several times. Beat together three of the eggs, the egg yolk, olive oil, and 2 tablespoons water in a spouted measuring cup. With the food processor running, add the liquid, and let it run until the dough forms a ball on the blade, about 30 seconds. If it's too loose, add a tablespoon or two of flour; if still crumbly, add a teaspoon or two of cold water.

Let the machine knead the dough for about 20 seconds. Turn the dough out on a very lightly floured surface, and knead by hand for another 30 seconds or so, until it's smooth, soft, and stretchy. Wrap, and rest the dough for 30 minutes.

For the filling, peel and core the pear, and shred it against the large holes of a box grater into a medium bowl. Stir in the pecorino, Grana Padano, and mascarpone, and mash to make a paste.

Cut the dough into four pieces. Keeping the pieces you are not immediately working with covered as you roll, roll each piece through a pasta machine set to the next-to-last setting (or the last setting, if you are comfortable with your

(recipe continues)

machine—you want the dough to be quite thin, since you will be folding it over), to get strips that are about as wide as the machine and about 16 to 18 inches in length.

Lay one strip out on a very lightly floured surface, and dollop scant tablespoons of filling at about 3-inch intervals down the center of the strip (you will get about six ravioli per strip). Press the tops of the mounds lightly to flatten. Beat the remaining egg and brush a thin strip of egg along the top, bottom, and side edges of the dough strip and in between each mound of filling. Fold the dough over and seal.

With a pastry-cutting wheel, cut the ravioli into rectangles. Arrange the finished ravioli on a lightly floured towel-lined baking sheet. Make more ravioli from the remaining pieces of dough.

To cook the ravioli, bring a large pot of salted water to a boil. Meanwhile, heat the butter in a large skillet until simmering. Add a cup of boiling pasta water, and simmer until reduced by half, about 3 to 4 minutes. Add the ravioli to the boiling water, and cook about 2 minutes once they return to a boil. Lay the cooked ravioli in the skillet, and toss to coat with the butter. Remove the pan from the heat, and sprinkle over it the shredded aged pecorino, mixing gently so the cheese begins to melt into a sauce. Season with salt and lots of black pepper. If plating individually, gently scoop up the ravioli with a large spoon and place in large shallow bowls, or use a flat plate. Sprinkle with more shredded aged pecorino and freshly ground black pepper.

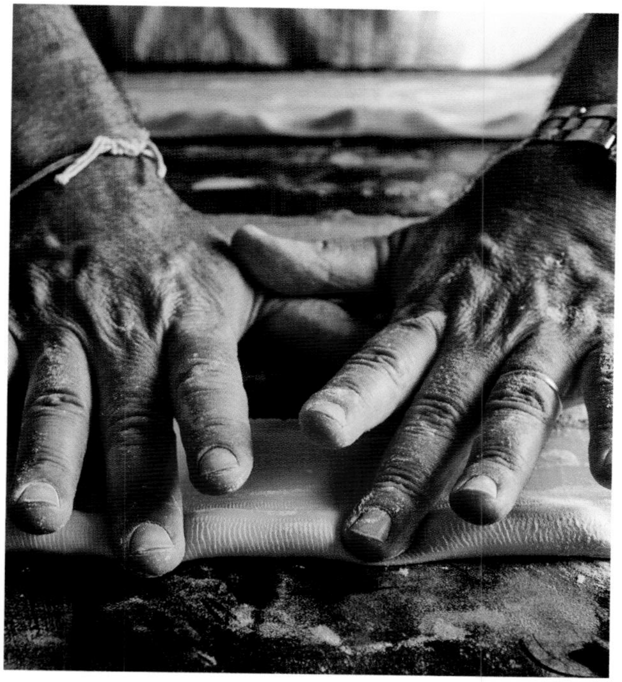

CHOCOLATE RAVIOLI FILLED *with* BURRATA *and* BUTTERNUT SQUASH

Ravioli al Cioccolato, Ripieni di Burrata e Zucca

This was one of my signature dishes at the Michelin-starred restaurants Villa Marchese and Villa Esperanza in Sicily. Bitter cocoa powder is used in a lot of savory preparations there, and when I arrived at Felidia, I wanted to do something similar but using more local ingredients. So I kept the same dough but added butternut squash—a typical sweet ingredient from America that balances the bitterness of the cocoa powder. I make this dish a few different ways. It is sometimes stuffed with ricotta or burrata. Amaretti cookies are often grated on top, as is done with the tortelli di zucca that are served in Mantua, Lombardy.

—Chef Nicotra

MAKES ABOUT 30 TO 34 RAVIOLI, SERVING 6

For the Filling

1 small butternut squash (1½ pounds)
Extra-virgin olive oil, for brushing
Kosher salt
Freshly ground black pepper
2 cups (about 12 ounces) shredded burrata cheese (it's easiest to shred by hand, with your fingers)
1 cup freshly grated Grana Padano
2 large egg yolks, beaten
½ cup toasted breadcrumbs, or as needed

For the Dough

1½ cups all-purpose flour, plus more for working the dough
½ cup Dutch-process cocoa
4 large eggs
1 large egg yolk
2 tablespoons extra-virgin olive oil

For the Sauce

1 stick (8 tablespoons) unsalted butter
12 fresh sage leaves
Kosher salt
Freshly ground black pepper
1 cup freshly grated Grana Padano
6 amaretto cookies, crumbled or grated

Preheat the oven to 375 degrees.

For the filling, cut the squash into quarters lengthwise, and scrape out the seeds. Brush a 13-by-9-inch baking dish with olive oil. Arrange the squash pieces cut side up in the dish, brush lightly with olive oil, and season with salt and pepper. Bake until the squash feels soft and is easily pierced with a knife, about 1 hour. Allow to cool.

Remove the skin from the squash, and place the flesh in a food processor; process until no longer chunky, just a few quick pulses. Transfer the

(recipe continues)

squash to a sieve lined with cheesecloth, and drain into a bowl in the refrigerator overnight.

Transfer the drained squash to a mixing bowl. Stir in the burrata, grated cheese, and egg yolks. Then stir in the breadcrumbs to make a filling that is tight but not dry. Add more breadcrumbs, a tablespoon at a time, if the filling is too loose. Refrigerate the filling while you make the dough.

For the dough, put the flour and cocoa in a food processor, and pulse several times. Beat 3 eggs, the egg yolk, olive oil, and 2 tablespoons water in a spouted measuring cup. With the food processor running, add the liquid, and let it run until the dough forms a ball on the blade, about 30 seconds. If it's too loose, add a tablespoon or two of flour; if still crumbly, add a teaspoon or two of cold water.

Let the machine knead the dough for about 10 seconds. Turn the dough out on a very lightly floured surface, and knead by hand for another 30 seconds or so, until it's smooth, soft, and stretchy. Wrap, and rest the dough for 30 minutes. Line two baking sheets with kitchen towels, and dust with flour.

Cut the dough into four pieces. Keeping the pieces you are not immediately working with covered, roll each piece through a pasta machine set to the next-to-last setting (or the last setting, if you are comfortable with your machine—you want the dough to be quite thin, since you will be folding it over), to get strips that are about as wide as the machine and about 16 inches in length.

Lay one strip out on a very lightly floured surface, and dollop scant tablespoons of filling at about 3-inch intervals down the center of the strip (you will get about six ravioli per strip). Press the tops of the mounds lightly to flatten. Beat the remaining egg and brush a thin strip along the top, bottom, and side edges of the dough strip and in between each mound of filling. Fold the dough over and seal.

Using a round pasta cutter, cut full half-rounds and fold in slightly. Arrange the finished ravioli on a lightly floured towel-lined baking sheet. Make more ravioli from the remaining pieces of dough.

When ready to cook, bring a large pot of salted water to a boil. For the butter-and-sage sauce, heat the butter in a large skillet over medium heat until melted and just foaming. Gently lay the sage leaves in the pan, and heat until they crisp up, about a minute. Ladle in 1 cup boiling pasta water; stir the sauce, and simmer for about 2 minutes, to reduce the liquid by half. Season the sauce with salt and pepper, and keep warm over very low heat while you cook the ravioli.

Add the ravioli to the boiling water, and let return to a simmer, stirring gently. Cook until the edges of the pasta are tender but still firm to the bite, about 3 minutes once the water returns to a simmer.

Transfer the cooked ravioli to the sauce with a spider or slotted spoon. Toss gently to coat. Remove the skillet from the heat, sprinkle with the 1 cup grated Grana Padano, and toss gently. Sprinkle the cookies over the top, and serve. If plating individually, gently scoop up the ravioli with a large spoon and place in large shallow bowls, covering the bottom and layering the ravioli, not piling them up, or use a flat plate.

FUZI *with* BRAISED DUCK

Fuzi all'Anatra

Fuzi—or garganelli, as it is sometimes known—was the pasta of choice at holidays, weddings, and Sunday meals in Istria. Depending on how many people were coming to dinner, we began making the pasta 2 or 3 days in advance, all the young ladies helping to shape it while the older women kneaded the dough, rolled it out, and cut it in a diamond shape. We young ladies then rolled it around our fingers to make the shape of a quill, and pinched it closed. The fuzi was left covered on wooden boards on top of armoires, tables, and beds until it was time to cook and sauce it. Fuzi, a fresh pasta unique to Istria, graced Felidia's menu when it opened. The braised-duck sauce was and still is a favorite even today, typically served with spinach pappardelle.

SERVES 6

3 cups all-purpose flour, plus more as needed
3 large eggs, lightly beaten
2 tablespoons plus ¼ cup extra-virgin olive oil
6 cups chicken stock
½ cup dried porcini
1 whole duck, quartered
4 ounces bacon or pancetta, finely chopped
1 medium onion, finely chopped
2 tablespoons tomato paste
1 cup dry white wine
3 fresh bay leaves
1 sprig fresh rosemary
5 whole cloves
Kosher salt
Freshly ground black pepper
½ cup freshly grated Grana Padano

—

For the fuzi, put the flour in the work bowl of a food processor, and pulse to aerate. Whisk together the eggs, 2 tablespoons oil, and ⅓ cup cold water in a spouted measuring cup. With the food processor running, pour this liquid through the feed tube and process until the dough forms a ball on the blade; add a little more flour if it is too sticky, or more water if it is too crumbly. Process another 20 seconds or so, until the ball of dough becomes smooth.

Dump the dough onto a floured counter, and knead until it comes together in a smooth ball. Wrap in plastic, and let rest for 30 minutes.

Cut the rested dough into six pieces. Keeping the dough lightly floured, roll the pieces through a pasta machine at progressively narrower settings, up to the next-to-the-last. Cut the strips in half crosswise. Lay the strips on floured kitchen towels on top of baking sheets.

Cut the strips into ribbons 1½ inches wide. Cut across the ribbons with parallel diagonal slices, about 1½ inches apart, to make diamonds. Roll each diamond, starting at one of the points, around a lightly floured chopstick to form a thin, hollow tube, resembling a quill. Press on the overlapping pasta to seal, and slide off the chopstick.

For the sauce, warm the chicken broth in a small saucepan. Soak the porcini in 1½ cups of the broth for 15 minutes. Trim the excess skin from the duck. Heat a large Dutch oven over medium heat, and add the ¼ cup olive oil. When the oil is hot, add the duck pieces and cook until crusty, about 3 minutes per side. Remove to a plate.

Add the bacon, and cook until rendered and starting to crisp, about 4 minutes. Add the onion, and cook until wilted, about 5 minutes. Clear a space in the pan, and add the tomato paste. Cook and stir the tomato paste in that spot for a minute, then stir into the onion. Drain the porcini, reserving the soaking water, finely chop them, and add to the pot.

Return the duck to the pan, and add the wine. Bring to a boil, and reduce by half. Tie the bay leaves, rosemary, and cloves into a square of cheesecloth, and add to the pot. Pour in the mushroom soaking liquid and enough of the remaining broth almost to cover the duck pieces. Adjust the heat so the sauce is simmering gently. Cook, adding broth as needed to keep the meat almost covered, until the duck is very tender and falls from the bone, about 2 hours.

Remove the duck pieces and let cool slightly. Skim any excess fat from the top of the sauce. Discard the cheesecloth packet. Remove and discard the skin from the duck, and shred the meat into small pieces. Add the meat back to the sauce, season with salt and pepper, and keep simmering while you cook the fuzi.

Bring a large pot of salted water to a boil for the pasta. If the sauce is very dense, loosen it with more broth (or pasta water). If it is soupy, cook uncovered to evaporate moisture. Add the pasta to the boiling water, and cook until al dente, about 3 minutes. Lift the pasta from the pot with a spider, and add to the simmering sauce. Toss together for a minute or two over medium-low heat, until all the fuzi are coated with sauce. Remove from the heat, add the grated Grana Padano, toss, and serve.

PASTA ALLA CHITARRA *with* AMATRICIANA SAUCE

Pasta alla Chitarra all'Amatriciana

This is a classic dish from Rome that none of my grandkids can resist. The Felidia guests love it as well! Amatriciana usually contains guanciale, or jowl bacon, which is very flavorful and traditional in the Italian rendition of this recipe, and tomato, but here Chef Nicotra adds a pestata *of onion, celery, and carrots with the bacon. Romans will often argue whether this sauce is made with or without the onions. I like it with the onions, but I do use an immersion blender to purée it, so that you don't have the texture of the onions. Instead, I like the texture of the crispy bacon served on top.*

SERVES 4 TO 6

For the Pasta

2 cups all-purpose flour, plus more for rolling the dough
¼ cup extra-virgin olive oil

For the Sauce

Kosher salt
1 small onion, cut into chunks
1 small carrot, cut into chunks
1 small stalk celery, cut into chunks
3 cloves garlic, crushed and peeled
2 tablespoons extra-virgin olive oil, plus more for drizzling
3 thick slices bacon (about 4 ounces), cut into ½-inch pieces
¼ teaspoon crushed peperoncino flakes, or to taste
One 28-ounce can whole Italian plum tomatoes, preferably San Marzano, crushed by hand
¼ cup chopped fresh Italian parsley
½ cup freshly grated Grana Padano, plus more for serving
½ cup freshly grated Pecorino Romano, plus more for serving

For the pasta, put the flour in the work bowl of a food processor, and pulse several times to aerate. In a spouted measuring cup, beat the olive oil and ½ cup cold water together with a fork. With the processor running, add the wet ingredients to the flour, and process until the dough forms a ball around the blade; add a little more water if it is too crumbly, a little more flour if it is too loose. Once the dough forms a ball, knead in the processor until smooth, about 20 to 30 seconds. Flour your work surface, dump the dough out, and knead a few times by hand to bring it together in a smooth ball. Wrap in plastic wrap, and let it rest at room temperature for 30 minutes.

Once the dough has rested, cut it into six pieces, keeping the pieces you are not immediately working with covered as you work. Roll each piece by hand on a floured work surface (or through a pasta machine set to the next-to-last setting) to an ⅛-inch thickness. If using a chitarra, cut the sheets to fit the dimensions of the strings, and press the trimmings together to roll for another sheet.

If using a chitarra, place a floured sheet of pasta on it, and use a rolling pin to roll and press the dough through the strings. Gather the pasta that falls through, and form it into floured nests on a floured baking sheet. Repeat with the remaining sheets of dough. (You can also cut the dough by hand: roll out all of the sheets, then cut into ⅛-inch strands with a sharp knife or pizza wheel.) Let the pasta dry on the baking sheet while you make the sauce.

Bring a large pot of salted water to a boil for the pasta. Combine the onion, carrot, celery, and garlic in a food processor, and pulse to make a coarse vegetable paste or *pestata.* Heat the olive oil in a large skillet over medium heat. Add the bacon, and cook until almost crisp, about 3 minutes. Add the *pestata* and cook, stirring occasionally, until it dries out and begins to stick to the bottom of the pan, about 6 minutes. Season with salt and the peperoncino.

Add the tomatoes. Rinse out the can with 2 cups pasta water, and add that as well. Bring to a simmer, and cook until the sauce is thick and flavorful, about 15 to 20 minutes.

When the sauce is ready, gently shake out any residual flour from the pasta nests, and add the nests to the boiling water. Cook the pasta until al dente, 2 to 3 minutes. Remove with tongs to the simmering sauce. Add the parsley and a drizzle of olive oil, and toss to coat the pasta with the sauce, adding a splash of pasta water if it seems dry. Remove the skillet from the heat, sprinkle with the grated cheeses, toss, and serve. If plating individually, use the tongs to twirl each portion of pasta into the shape of a bird's nest. This will keep the pasta warmer and make for an attractive presentation. Spoon some sauce over the top of the pasta, and serve with grated cheeses.

"NAKED" SPINACH *and* RICOTTA DUMPLINGS *with* BUTTER *and* SAGE SAUCE

Gnudi

Think of this as a pasta dish without pasta; it's all about the filling. The story goes that these delicious little "naked" dumplings were born in Florence when, during a meal, the ravioli that contained the filling broke, so the chef served the filling as it was, or "naked." They were a hit then, and still are, a light and fluffy pasta dish anytime of year. In the spring, the spinach can be replaced by nettles, and often is at Felidia.

MAKES 25 TO 30 GNUDI, SERVING 6 AS A FIRST COURSE OR 4 AS A MAIN DISH

Kosher salt
3 medium bunches spinach (about 2 pounds), stems removed
1 pound fresh ricotta, drained overnight
1 large egg, beaten
Pinch of freshly grated nutmeg
1½ cups freshly grated Grana Padano
¼ cup fine breadcrumbs, plus more if needed
¼ cup all-purpose flour, plus more for rolling
1 stick (8 tablespoons) unsalted butter
12 fresh sage leaves
Freshly ground black pepper

Bring a large pot of salted water to a boil. Add the spinach leaves, and cook until tender, about 3 to 4 minutes. Remove to an ice bath until cold, then drain, and wring very dry in a kitchen towel or press dry in batches through a ricer. When the spinach is dry, chop it. You should have about 1 cup. Crumble the spinach into a large bowl. Discard the water from the pot, fill with clean salted water, and return the pot to a boil for the gnudi.

Add the ricotta, egg, nutmeg, and 1 teaspoon salt to the bowl. Mix to blend. Add ½ cup of the grated cheese, the breadcrumbs, and the flour. Mix until it's blended and the mixture pulls off the sides and holds its shape when rolled into a ball between your lightly floured hands, but don't overmix.

Spread some flour in a shallow bowl. Test the consistency of the dough by scooping up a heaping tablespoon, rolling it between your floured hands, then lightly roll it into the flour, forming it into a ball. Drop it into the boiling water; if it does not hold its shape and rise to the surface of the water within a minute, add a tablespoon or so more breadcrumbs to your dough.

When you have the right consistency, shape the dough into 1-inch balls (a heaping tablespoon), roll them lightly in flour, and lay them out on baking sheets covered in parchment paper. You should get about twenty-five to thirty pieces.

For the butter-and-sage sauce, heat the butter in a large skillet over medium heat until melted and just foaming. Gently lay the sage leaves in the pan, and heat until they crisp up, about a minute.

Ladle in 1 cup boiling pasta water; stir the sauce, and simmer for about 2 minutes, to reduce

(recipe continues)

the liquid by half. Season the sauce with salt and pepper, and keep warm over very low heat while you cook the gnudi.

Drop the gnudi gently, one by one, into the boiling water, and cook for about 2 or 3 minutes, until they rise to the top and the water comes to a rolling boil. To test for doneness, scoop out one of the gnudi and press it with your finger; when cooked, the dumpling dough should bounce back, leaving no indentation.

Transfer the cooked gnudi to the sauce with a spider or slotted spoon. Toss gently to coat with the sauce. Remove the skillet from the heat, sprinkle with the remaining 1 cup of grated Grana Padano, toss gently, and serve.

RISOTTOS

Risotto is an Italian tradition—especially in the north—where rice fields abound. Carnaroli is my preferred rice for making risotto, although Arborio also makes a good risotto; a short-grain rice is essential, because long-grain simply won't result in creamy risotto.

Risottos are known to take a while to stir, so this is not a primo that you find on our menu daily, but it is available when guests ask.

In restaurants, risotto is always a challenge, because you cannot prepare it in advance. So a chef must closely time other parts of an order so everything comes out of the kitchen at the same time. Part of the energy and adrenaline rush in the kitchen during service is the tension of needing to time the food, making it delicious, and serving it beautifully. The chef is like a conductor of the line in the kitchen who needs to give cues, and time and direct all of the orders that come in as the expeditor calls out the dishes for the table. This orchestration needs to happen two to three times per table, depending on how many courses they order. My recurring nightmare—I can say it now that it occurs less often—is that I have a dining room full of guests, the waiters keep on punching in the orders, and I am in a panic and cannot get one dish finished on the line. When I wake up, usually all sweaty, I am so relieved that it is only a dream.

In Italy, risottos are commonly cooked for special occasions and parties. In fact, a nice big pot of risotto is a perfect crowd-pleaser at home. My family say one of the best things I make at home is lobster risotto; they consider it one of my signature dishes. Many people are mystified by risotto and think it is complicated to achieve the creaminess that it is known for. It actually just takes the right rice, patience in stirring, and the right amount of liquid to allow the rice to release the starches that make for a creamy risotto. It is certainly worth trying at home, but if you want to take it easy, there is always a good risotto waiting for you at Felidia.

RISOTTO *with* PEAR, GRANA PADANO, *and* BALSAMIC VINEGAR

Risotto Grana Padano e Pere, Balsamico Tradizionale

First served ten years ago, the cacio-e-pere pasta is one of our signature dishes, and a revolt would ensue if we attempted to take it off the menu. However, for the home cook, a stuffed fresh pasta can be a challenge and a time-consuming prospect. The same great combination of pear and cheese can be made into a simple risotto dish, perfect for an easy family meal or when cooking for a large gathering. Chef Nicotra transferred the flavors of the cacio e pere into a risotto, and we now serve both. If you have a homemade stock to substitute for the water in this recipe, it will enhance the flavor. If not, you can make a quick stock with the cores of the pears and the trimmings of the onion, leeks, and celery. He lastly drizzles each serving with a traditional balsamic vinegar or reduction.

SERVES 6

8 cups light chicken or vegetable stock
¼ cup extra-virgin olive oil
1 cup finely chopped onion
1 cup sliced leeks, white and pale-green parts only, washed
Kosher salt
Freshly ground black pepper
2 cups Carnaroli rice (or Arborio if Carnaroli is not available)
¾ cup dry white wine
2 medium Bartlett pears, peeled and grated
4 tablespoons unsalted butter, cut into bits
1 cup freshly grated Grana Padano
1 cup thinly sliced celery and celery leaves
Aceto Balsamico Tradizionale, or reduction of regular balsamic vinegar (see opposite)

Bring the stock to a simmer in a saucepan. Heat a large skillet over medium heat, and add the olive oil. When the oil is hot, add the onion and leeks. Season lightly with salt and pepper. Cook and stir until the onion and leeks are wilted but not browned, about 7 to 8 minutes.

Add the rice, and stir to coat in the oil. Pour in the wine, and cook, stirring, until it's absorbed, about 1 to 2 minutes. Ladle in enough hot stock just to cover the rice. Adjust the heat so the risotto is simmering, and cook, stirring constantly, until all liquid has been absorbed. Continue to add hot stock in small batches (just enough to moisten the rice completely) and cook until each successive batch has been absorbed, stirring constantly, until the rice mixture is creamy but still al dente, about 18 minutes total; add the grated pears about halfway through the cooking time. It's okay if you have a little stock left over.

Remove the skillet from the heat, and vigorously stir in the butter in teaspoon-size pieces until absorbed. Sprinkle with the Grana Padano, and stir to combine all into a creamy mixture. Season with salt and pepper, if needed. Serve the risotto in shallow bowls, with a sprinkle of celery and celery leaves and a drizzle of balsamic vinegar reduction.

For the balsamic reduction: Pour 1 cup balsamic vinegar into a skillet, and boil until reduced to ⅓ cup. Cool completely before using. It will keep for several weeks refrigerated.

BEET RISOTTO *with* GOAT CHEESE *and* BALSAMIC REDUCTION

Risotto con Barbabietole, Caprino e Riduzione di Aceto Balsamico

The bright color of this dish when it arrives at the table immediately attracts attention. But the real surprise is the flavor, a rich but mellow blend of rice and beets. Beet-and-goat-cheese salads have been around for a while, and turning the concept into a risotto is perfect. If you're using store-bought vegetable stock, make sure to choose one that is light in color and flavor, so as not to muddy the look and taste of the risotto, and that it is not overly salty. Critic Frank Bruni loved this risotto when he reviewed Felidia for The New York Times.

SERVES 6

2 medium beets, trimmed to within 1 inch of the top
8 cups light vegetable stock
3 tablespoons extra-virgin olive oil
1 cup finely chopped onion
2 shallots, finely chopped
Kosher salt
Freshly ground black pepper
2 cups Arborio or Carnaroli rice
¾ cup dry white wine
2 tablespoons unsalted butter, cut into bits
½ cup freshly grated Grana Padano
3 ounces fresh goat cheese, crumbled
Balsamic reduction, for drizzling (see page 124)

Put the beets in a small saucepan, and add water to cover by about 2 inches. Bring to a simmer, and cook until tender, about 30 to 40 minutes, depending on size. Drain, reserving 1 cup of the cooking liquid. Let the beets cool, then peel them and grate them on the coarse holes of a box grater. Strain the reserved cooking liquid through a coffee filter or a sieve lined with cheesecloth. Set the beets and their liquid aside.

Bring the stock to a simmer in a saucepan. Heat a large skillet over medium heat, and add the olive oil. When the oil is hot, add the onion and shallots. Season lightly with salt and pepper. Cook and stir until the onion and shallots are wilted but not browned, about 7 to 8 minutes.

Add the rice, and stir to coat in the oil. Pour in the wine, and cook, stirring, until it's absorbed, about 1 to 2 minutes. Ladle in enough stock just to cover the rice. Adjust the heat so the risotto is simmering, and cook, stirring constantly, until all liquid has been absorbed. Continue to add hot stock in small batches (just enough to moisten the rice completely) and cook until each successive batch has been absorbed, stirring constantly, until the rice mixture is creamy but still al dente, about

(recipe continues)

18 minutes total; add the grated beets about halfway through the cooking time.

Remove the skillet from the heat. Beat in the butter in teaspoon-size pieces until completely melted, then the Grana Padano cheese. Adjust the seasoning with salt and pepper, if necessary. Serve immediately, ladled onto flat plates. Crumble the goat cheese on top, and finish with balsamic reduction.

For the balsamic reduction: Pour 1 cup balsamic vinegar into a skillet, and boil until reduced to ⅓ cup. Cool completely before using. It will keep for several weeks refrigerated.

RISOTTO *with* PORCINI *and* COFFEE

Risotto al Caffè con Porcini

Like most chefs, I love taking a traditional recipe and giving it a contemporary twist. Here I take our basic porcini-risotto recipe and add some espresso powder. It creates a play of flavors between the mustiness and sweetness of the mushrooms and the complexity of the coffee, which reminds me of a cappuccino. I often top off the dish with crispy fried capers for balance. You can also make the risotto with espresso (without porcini) when making it at home. If you have homemade stock on hand, use that instead of water; it will enrich the flavor.

—Chef Nicotra

SERVES 6

8 cups homemade beef or vegetable stock, or water
½ cup dried porcini
¼ cup extra-virgin olive oil
1 cup finely chopped onion
½ cup finely chopped shallot
12 ounces sliced fresh porcini or other mixed mushrooms (such as cremini, shiitake, oyster, or chanterelle)
Kosher salt
Freshly ground black pepper
2 cups Carnaroli rice (or Arborio)
¾ cup dry white wine
1 tablespoon espresso powder
2 tablespoons unsalted butter, cut into bits
½ cup freshly grated Grana Padano

Bring the stock to a simmer in a saucepan. Ladle 1 cup hot stock into a measuring cup, add the dried porcini, and let them soak until softened, about 10 minutes. Drain, reserving the soaking water, and finely chop the porcini. Pour the soaking water into the saucepan of stock, leaving any grit behind in the measuring cup.

Heat a large skillet over medium heat, and add the olive oil. When the oil is hot, add the onion and shallot. Cook until they begin to soften, about 4 minutes. Add the fresh mushrooms, and season with salt and pepper. Cook, stirring occasionally, until the mushrooms are wilted and browned on the edges, about 6 minutes.

Add the rice, and stir to coat in the oil. Pour in the wine, and cook, stirring, until it's absorbed, about 1 to 2 minutes. Ladle in enough hot stock just to cover the rice. Adjust the heat so the risotto is simmering, and cook, stirring constantly, until all liquid has been absorbed. Continue to add hot stock in small batches (just enough to moisten the rice completely) and cook until each successive batch has been absorbed, stirring constantly, until the rice mixture is creamy but still al dente, about 18 minutes total. It's okay if you have a little stock left over.

Stir in the espresso powder until it's dissolved. Remove from heat, and vigorously stir in the butter until absorbed. Sprinkle with the Grana Padano, and stir to combine. Season with salt and pepper, if needed. Serve the risotto in shallow bowls.

RISOTTO MILANESE

Risotto alla Milanese

Risotto Milanese is a sacred risotto in Milan, and, as much as chefs generally like to change and create, with this recipe Italian chefs usually stick to tradition. It can be served by itself or with the ossobuco that was served at Felidia for our first ten years (page 163); still people ask for it. It was originally served with a long, thin marrow knife to remove the succulent marrow from the bone. For those who love Milan or have always wanted to visit that dynamic city, this dish will make you think you are there. It's Italian comfort food.

For the bone marrow, ask your butcher to get you some from veal bones, or to cut the femur bone into 2-inch pieces. Then, with a little knife, you can scoop around the marrow and pull it out. Keep the marrow chilled until you are ready to use it. The remaining bones are good for making stock.

SERVES 6

8 cups homemade beef stock or canned low-sodium beef broth
½ teaspoon saffron threads
3 tablespoons extra-virgin olive oil
1 cup minced onion
½ cup minced shallots
2 cups Arborio or Carnaroli rice
½ cup dry white wine
Kosher salt
2 ounces beef marrow, cut into ¼-inch pieces (optional)
2 tablespoons unsalted butter, cut into pieces
½ cup freshly grated Grana Padano

Warm the stock in a medium saucepan over low heat. Put the saffron in a small bowl, and ladle ½ cup hot stock over it.

Heat a shallow Dutch oven over medium heat. Add the olive oil. When the oil is hot, add the onion and shallots, and cook, stirring, until tender and almost golden, about 8 minutes. Add the rice, and toss to coat in the oil. Cook until the edges of the rice are translucent, about 2 minutes.

Pour in the wine. Cook and stir until absorbed. Ladle in enough stock just to cover the rice. Adjust the heat so the risotto is simmering, and cook, stirring constantly, until all the liquid has been absorbed. Continue to add hot stock in small batches (just enough to moisten the rice completely) and cook until each successive batch has been absorbed, stirring constantly, until the rice mixture is creamy but still al dente, about 18 minutes total. Add the saffron and soaking liquid about 10 minutes after you start simmering the rice. Season with salt.

Stir in the marrow, if using. Off heat, beat in the butter in teaspoon-size pieces, a few at a time until incorporated, add the grated cheese and mix until creamy, and serve immediately in shallow bowls.

RISOTTO *with* HEIRLOOM TOMATOES, MOZZARELLA, *and* BASIL

Risotto alla Caprese

The combination of mozzarella and tomato is Italian heaven. We added those flavors to a steaming risotto to create a winner on our summer menu. Heirloom tomatoes are a real treat at Felidia, and a feature of the menu as soon as they become available. I grow them in my garden, and Chef Nicotra buys them locally in season from Long Island and New Jersey farmers. If you cannot find heirlooms, feel free to use other ripe and flavorful summer tomatoes. Oh, let me count how many ways tomatoes, mozzarella, and basil can be enjoyed.

SERVES 4 TO 6

7 cups chicken or vegetable stock, or water
6 tablespoons extra-virgin olive oil
1 medium onion, finely chopped
2 cups short-grain Italian rice, either Arborio or Carnaroli
Kosher salt
Freshly ground black pepper
1 cup dry white wine
1 cup tomato purée or sauce
1½ cups finely chopped heirloom tomatoes
½ cup freshly grated Grana Padano, plus more for serving
One 8-ounce ball fresh buffalo mozzarella, shredded by hand (or burrata or fresh ricotta)
½ cup fresh basil leaves, shredded

Pour the water or stock into a medium saucepan, and keep hot over low heat.

Heat a large skillet or shallow Dutch oven over medium-low heat. Add 4 tablespoons of the olive oil. When the oil is hot, add the onion, and cook, stirring frequently, until it's tender but not browned, about 8 minutes. Add a splash of water, if needed, to keep it from browning.

Increase the heat to medium to cook away any water in the pan, and add the rice all at once, stirring to coat the rice in the oil. Cook the rice for a minute or so, without letting it brown, and season with salt and pepper. Add the white wine, and adjust the heat so the wine is rapidly simmering. Cook, stirring frequently, until the wine has reduced away, about 2 to 3 minutes.

Once the wine has reduced, add about 1½ to 2 cups of stock or water—or just enough to cover the rice. Simmer, stirring frequently, until the stock has been absorbed. Continue in the same fashion, adding stock as it gets absorbed; add the cup of tomato purée with the second-to-last addition of stock, and the chopped tomatoes along with the last addition. It's okay if you have a little stock left over.

When the risotto is al dente, remove it from the heat, sprinkle with the grated Grana Padano, and drizzle with the remaining 2 tablespoons olive oil. Stir to incorporate. Serve in large, flat bowls, topped with the mozzarella and basil. Pass additional grated Grana Padano at the table.

SPRING FARRO RISOTTO

Farrotto Primavera

Risotto, very popular at Felidia, is traditionally made with short-grain rice. Farro is an ancient grain that is typically used for soups in regions like Umbria and Tuscany. When it is finished as risotto, as we do here, it is sometimes called "farrotto." Farro was often used in ancient Rome, and was milled and used as flour before wheat became common. I love its nutty, complex flavor, its nutritional value, and the resilience it retains when cooked.

SERVES 4 TO 6

Kosher salt
1 cup farro
1½ pounds fresh fava beans, shelled
1 small bunch medium-thick asparagus, stems trimmed and peeled, cut into 1-inch lengths
1 cup fresh peas
3 cups low-sodium chicken or vegetable broth
2 tablespoons extra-virgin olive oil
1 medium onion, chopped
2 ounces pancetta, finely diced, or 2 strips thick bacon, finely chopped
4 tablespoons unsalted butter
½ cup freshly grated Grana Padano

Bring a large pot of salted water to a boil, and add the farro. Cook until al dente and still a bit chewy, 35 to 40 minutes. Drain, and spread on a baking sheet to cool.

Meanwhile, bring a second pot of water to a boil. Add the favas, and boil for 1 minute to shock. Transfer with a spider to an ice bath to cool. Add the asparagus to the boiling water, and blanch until tender but still crisp, about 2 minutes. Add to the ice bath. Repeat with the peas, cooking until just tender, about 5 minutes. Drain, and pat all the vegetables dry. Remove and discard the skins from the favas.

Put the chicken broth in a small saucepan, and warm it over low heat. Heat the olive oil in a medium Dutch oven over medium heat. Add the onion and pancetta. Cook until the onion is tender but not browned and the pancetta has rendered its fat, about 8 minutes.

Stir in the farro, and season with salt. Add a few ladles of the hot stock, and cook, stirring, as you would for risotto, adding stock as each batch gets absorbed. Simmer and stir until the farro is cooked to your liking but still al dente and creamy, about 10 minutes; add the vegetables in the last few minutes of cooking.

When the risotto is done, remove from the heat, and beat in the butter and grated Grana Padano. Serve immediately in flat, shallow bowls.

BASTIANICH
Calabrone
2006
BASTIANICH
Vespa
BIANCO
2010

SEAFOOD

I was born by the sea and often went fishing with my uncle. Chef Nicotra was also born by the sea, in his native Sicily, and has been cooking and serving delicious fish dishes since his early days in the kitchen with his mother. The Italian peninsula has twenty regions, fifteen of which have sea access or are on the sea, so fish dishes can be found from north to south, with different fish and traditions in every port.

The universal law in buying fish is that it be fresh. If a recipe calls for a certain fish but it is not in season, buy and use a similar fish that is fresher. In a restaurant, the relationship between the chef and the fish purveyor is incredibly important. On any given day, there will be several calls between the two. Chef Nicotra knows fishermen up and down the coast. They know what is running and in season and what they are most likely to catch. He puts in his order, and once he has an idea what the fishermen will bring in, he begins to plan the menu for the following day. The fishermen don't always catch what was in their plan, so sometimes we have to substitute what was actually caught, but as long as it is fresh, we can make it into the special of the day. The great team at our restaurant opens every box and bag that is delivered to check for freshness, quantity, and other requirements to meet our expectations. This team is Felidia's first line of defense in getting only the best products.

WHOLE ROASTED BRANZINO

Branzino al Forno

This dish has graced the Felidia menu since the very beginning. It's simple and fresh, and an absolute guest favorite. It is cooked whole, with the bones in, which gives it an intense, delicious flavor, and our captains fillet it table side. Have your fishmonger select fish that are all about the same size, so they cook at the same rate. A fillet of fish is convenient and easy to cook and eat, but there is nothing better than a whole roasted fish for flavor.

Other fish like red snapper, sea bass, or striped bass could be substituted—just be mindful of the size and hence its cooking time.

SERVES 4

¾ cup extra-virgin olive oil
6 cloves garlic, peeled and sliced
1 teaspoon kosher salt, plus more to taste
Freshly ground black pepper
1 pound very small red potatoes, halved
4 whole branzino (about 1¼ pounds each), cleaned
4 sprigs fresh thyme, plus 2 teaspoons chopped leaves
4 fresh bay leaves
4 medium sweet onions, peeled and halved, crosswise
4 small plum tomatoes, cored and halved
¼ cup breadcrumbs
Juice of 1 lemon
¼ cup chopped fresh Italian parsley leaves

Combine the oil, garlic, 1 teaspoon salt, and several grinds of black pepper in a small bowl. Set aside to infuse for 30 minutes. Meanwhile, preheat the oven to 425 degrees.

Put the potatoes in a large saucepan with salted water to cover. Bring to a simmer, and cook until half cooked, still al dente, about 8 minutes. Drain, and rinse to cool. Pat dry.

Wrap the tails of the fish in foil to keep them from burning. Season the fish inside and out with salt and pepper. Stick a sprig of thyme and a bay leaf in the cavity of each fish. Brush all over with the garlic oil, and arrange the fish on a rimmed baking sheet so they don't touch.

Combine the onion halves and tomatoes in a large bowl. Drizzle with 2 tablespoons of the garlic oil, and gently toss to coat the vegetables in the oil. Arrange the vegetables on another baking sheet, setting the tomatoes cut side up.

Roast the fish and vegetables until the fish are cooked through and the vegetables are just tender, about 20 minutes, tossing the vegetables once or twice. Meanwhile, in a small bowl, toss the breadcrumbs with 2 teaspoons of the garlic oil and the chopped thyme. Remove the fish from the oven, and tent with foil to keep warm. Scatter the breadcrumbs over the vegetables, and increase oven temperature to 450 degrees. Roast until crumbs are crisp, about 5 minutes.

Stir the lemon juice and parsley into the remaining garlic oil. Remove the foil from the fish, and serve with the vegetables. Drizzle the remaining oil over all.

PAN-FRIED SOFT-SHELL CRABS *with* LEMON *and* GARLIC SAUCE

Moleche con Salsa all'Aglio e Limone

In Venice, these crabs are called moleche and are about 2 inches in diameter. On the east coast of Italy, they are also available in the spring, although a bit larger than those in Venice. When you buy soft-shell crabs, make sure they are still alive. Usually, soft-shell crabs are lined up in boxes set on wet straw for sale. Have the fishmonger run his finger down the shells, if they're alive, the crabs will move. Soft-shell crabs are soft because they have just shed their shells; since they are only in season for a short time, it is a special experience to eat the entire crab, instead of picking the meat out of the shell. This recipe calls for small-to-medium crabs. During soft-shell crab season, I enjoy as many as I can.

SERVES 4

For the Crabs
8 soft-shell crabs
Whole milk, for dipping
All-purpose flour, for dredging
Vegetable oil, for frying
Kosher salt
Freshly ground black pepper, to taste

For the Sauce
1 stick (8 tablespoons) unsalted butter
3 cloves garlic, crushed and peeled
½ cup dry white wine
2 tablespoons freshly squeezed lemon juice
½ cup fish stock
1 tablespoon fresh thyme leaves
Kosher salt

To clean the crabs, turn them bottom side up and, using scissors, remove the flaps: a narrow, tapered appendage on male crabs; a leaflike tab on females. Turn the crabs over, lift each pointed tip of the top shells, and pull away and discard the exposed featherlike strands. With a sharp knife or scissors positioned just behind the eyes, cut away and discard the articulated section of the head. Rinse crabs under cold running water, and pat dry, or you can ask your fishmonger to clean them for you.

Dip the cleaned crabs in milk, and dredge lightly in flour, shaking off the excess. In a large skillet, heat ½ inch of oil until a pinch of flour sizzles when dropped in. Cook the crabs in batches, stomach side down, until browned and crisp, about 2 minutes. Turn the crabs, and cook about 2 minutes longer, until golden brown. (Take care—the crabs may pop and splatter oil as they cook.) Remove the crabs from the skillet, drain on paper towels, and keep them warm. Season with salt and pepper.

For the sauce, melt the butter in a medium skillet over medium heat. When the butter is melted, add the garlic and cook until sizzling and fragrant, about 1 minute. Add the wine and lemon juice, and bring to a boil. Add the fish stock, and boil until the liquid is reduced and slightly thickened, about 4 minutes; add the thyme leaves in the last minute. Season with salt. Serve the warm crabs with the sauce.

ONE-SIDE-GRILLED TUNA PALERMITANA STYLE

Tonno Quasi Palermitana

This versatile, quick, and healthy dish is something we serve year-round with various seasonal dressings and sides. It can be made on a griddle or in a nonstick pan, but a grill pan is recommended, to impart more flavor. It goes beautifully served with a mixed green salad or asparagus dressed with lemon and extra-virgin olive oil. I first tried this dish while filming near Palermo, and was very happy to see it on the menu at Felidia. Chef Nicotra knew the dish from back home, and it is a guest favorite.

"Palermitana" means that the meat or fish is marinated in a mixture of olive oil and fresh herbs. You then bread it on one side with breadcrumbs and cheese, but without using egg. The tuna palermitana is breaded and cooked on only one side. I don't like my tuna cooked thoroughly on both sides and find that Americans typically do not, either. This is the perfect solution.

SERVES 6

1 cup panko breadcrumbs
2 tablespoons chopped fresh Italian parsley
2 tablespoons chopped fresh chives
Kosher salt
Four 4-to-5-ounce yellowfin tuna steaks, about 1 inch thick
Extra-virgin olive oil, for brushing fish
Caponata (page 183) or lightly dressed mixed greens, for serving

Preheat a grill pan over medium-high heat.

Combine the panko, parsley, and chives in a shallow bowl, and season lightly with salt.

Brush the tuna all over with olive oil. Press one side of each tuna steak into the panko, coating it with crumbs.

Place the tuna, panko side down, on the grill pan, and cook until the crumbs are browned and crisp but the tuna is still raw on top, about 2 minutes. Remove from the grill, season the raw side lightly with sea salt, and serve, raw side up, with the mixed greens or caponata.

PAN-SEARED HALIBUT *with* BALSAMIC REDUCTION

Ippoglosso al Balsamico

Balsamic vinegar is essential in Italian cooking, and chefs love to use it. Authentic Aceto Balsamico Tradizionale comes in a small glass bottle with a 1-inch neck and a pot-belly bottom, and it contains balsamic vinegar certified by the official balsamic-vinegar consortium. It is expensive, and best used by the teaspoonful to drizzle over cheese or roasts, and in risotto. In the grocery store, you will find many bottles of Aceto Balsamico Commerciale, not made and aged in the traditional style, but still good for cooking and dressing salad. You will have some extra balsamic reduction after creating this dish, but it keeps well and can be used for other dishes—grilled meats, in appetizers, and in other seafood preparations, even over ice cream. You can use some of it to decorate in plating the dish as well—just don't overdo it! When I am cooking at home, I love recipes that give me something a little extra to store away. The leftovers become an extra little goody bag in my refrigerator.

SERVES 4

1 cup balsamic vinegar
2 teaspoons honey
1 sprig fresh rosemary
2 fresh bay leaves
Four 6-ounce halibut fillets, with skin, about 1 inch thick
Kosher salt
Freshly ground black pepper
2 tablespoons extra-virgin olive oil

Preheat the oven to 450 degrees.

Combine the vinegar, honey, rosemary, and bay leaves in a small saucepan. Bring to a boil, and boil until it's syrupy and reduced to about a third of its original volume, about 6 to 8 minutes. Let cool slightly. Remove and discard the rosemary and bay leaves.

Season the halibut with salt and pepper. Heat a large, preferably nonstick skillet over high heat. Add the olive oil. When the oil is hot, add the fish, skin side down. Cook, without moving the fish, until the skin is crisp, about 2 to 3 minutes. Flip the fish, and cook an additional 2 minutes to brown the other side.

Put the pan in the oven, and roast until the fish is just cooked through, about another 3 to 5 minutes, depending on thickness. Serve skin side down, drizzling each portion with a little of the balsamic reduction.

SALMON *with* MUSTARD SAUCE

Salmone alla Senape

I used to make this dish in my first restaurant in Queens, Buonavia. It is simple and easy to prepare, and particularly popular during lunch hours. The mustard sauce adds just the right amount of sophistication, complexity, and acidity.

SERVES 4

Four 6-ounce skinless salmon fillets
Kosher salt
Freshly ground black pepper
All-purpose flour, for dredging
2 tablespoons vegetable oil
3 tablespoons unsalted butter
½ cup dry white wine
½ cup fish stock
Juice of ½ lemon
¼ cup heavy cream
2 tablespoons Dijon mustard

Season the salmon with salt and pepper. Heat a large skillet over medium-high heat. Spread some flour on a plate. Lightly dredge the salmon in the flour on all sides, tapping off the excess. When the skillet is hot, add the vegetable oil. Add the salmon, and cook, turning once, until almost cooked through, 2 to 3 minutes per side, depending on the thickness of the fillets. The fish should still be rare in the center, because it will cook more in the sauce. Remove it to a plate.

Carefully discard the oil from the pan. Return the pan to medium heat, and add the butter. Once it has melted, add the wine, and reduce by half, about 2 minutes. Add the fish stock and lemon juice, and bring to a simmer. Simmer until it's reduced by about a quarter and slightly thickened, about 2 minutes. Add the cream, and simmer for 1 minute to blend the flavors. Whisk in the mustard, return the salmon to the pan, and simmer until the fish is just done and heated through and the sauce coats the back of a spoon, about 2 minutes. With a spatula, carefully transfer the fillets to serving plates. Strain the sauce, and spoon a little over each fillet.

GRILLED SWORDFISH TAGLIATA *alle* ERBE

Tagliata di Pesce Spada alle Erbe

Swordfish is abundant in Sicily and Calabria and is therefore a popular choice in restaurants there. I used to make a version of this dish while running two Michelin-starred restaurants in Milazzo, Sicily. New Yorkers dining at Felidia love fresh fish dishes such as this one, particularly in the hotter months, and every time I cook it, it reminds me of home.

—Chef Nicotra

SERVES 4 TO 6

2 skinless swordfish steaks, about 1½ pounds total, 1 inch thick
7 tablespoons extra-virgin olive oil
4 cloves garlic, crushed and peeled
3 tablespoons freshly squeezed lemon juice
Kosher salt
Freshly ground black pepper
2 cups chopped mixed fresh herbs (including some or all of these: chives, basil, parsley, thyme, and fennel fronds)
Flaky sea salt, for sprinkling

Put the swordfish in a snug-fitting baking dish, and toss with 3 tablespoons of the olive oil and the crushed garlic. Marinate in the refrigerator for 2 hours, turning occasionally.

Preheat a grill or grill pan to medium-high heat.

Remove the swordfish from the marinade, and grill, turning once, until cooked to your liking, about 2 to 3 minutes per side for medium to medium rare. Let the swordfish rest while you make the dressing.

In a medium bowl, whisk together the remaining ¼ cup olive oil and the lemon juice. Season with salt and pepper. Stir in the herbs to coat them in the vinaigrette.

Slice the swordfish, and arrange it on plates. Drizzle the herb dressing over, and sprinkle all with flaky sea salt.

GRILLED SEAFOOD *with* SWISS CHARD SALAD

Grigliata di Pesce con Insalata di Erbette

The grigliata di pesce I recall from my childhood was something we made when my uncle Emilio came home from fishing with an assortment of seafood. This dish is a true celebration of the bounty of the sea, and a fun option for an adventurous cook at the grill. At Felidia, we include razor clams, which can be difficult to find in some markets, so here I have added littleneck clams instead. Either way is simply delicious. Serve with a salad and it's a meal that will impress any guest. In the restaurant, the plating of a dish has great importance. Here the salad gives gorgeous color, and the careful placement of the grilled fish can create a visual masterpiece.

SERVES 4

7 tablespoons extra-virgin olive oil, plus more for brushing the grill and drizzling
Kosher salt
1 large bunch rainbow Swiss chard (about 1½ pounds), washed
1 teaspoon grated lemon zest
Freshly ground black pepper
12 littleneck clams, scrubbed
4 lobster tails in the shell (about 4 ounces each), split
12 sea scallops, side muscle or "foot" removed (about 8 to 10 ounces)
8 medium calamari, tubes and tentacles, about 3 inches long (about 12 ounces)
4 jumbo head-on shrimp (about 8 to 10 ounces)
2 tablespoons chopped fresh Italian parsley

Brush the grill with olive oil, and preheat it to high heat.

Bring a large pot of salted water to a boil. Separate the chard stems from the leaves. Trim the tough parts from the stems and discard, then trim the stems into 2-inch pieces. Add the stems to the boiling water, and cook for about 5 minutes. Add the leaves, and cook until both are tender, about 4 to 5 minutes more. Drain, and refresh in an ice bath to stop the cooking. Drain well, and pat very dry. Toss the chard in a medium bowl with 3 tablespoons of the olive oil and the lemon zest, and season with salt and pepper.

Toss the clams and lobster in a large bowl with 2 tablespoons of the olive oil. Season with salt and pepper. Put the clams on the grill. Put the lobster pieces on the grill, flesh side down. Cover, and cook until the clams open, about 5 minutes, and the lobster shell is bright red and the flesh is cooked through, also about 5 minutes. Remove to a platter.

Toss the scallops, calamari, and shrimp in the same large bowl with the remaining 2 tablespoons olive oil, and season with salt and pepper. Put the scallops, calamari, and shrimp on the grill, and cover. Cook, turning everything once, until the pieces are marked from the grill and cooked through, about 3 to 4 minutes for the scallops and calamari and a minute more for the shrimp. Remove to the platter with the clams and lobster. Sprinkle with the parsley, and drizzle with more olive oil. Serve with the chard salad.

LOBSTER *in* ZESTY TOMATO SAUCE

Astice Aragosta in Brodetto

This is one way Chef Nicotra serves lobster at Felidia. I especially like this preparation with al dente spaghetti, but it can also be served as is, with crusty bread, or over polenta. I particularly enjoy shellfish I get to eat with my hands, taking my time to pick through the whole thing. The final piece of enjoyment is mopping up all the tasty sauce with a piece of crusty bread. Though it is difficult to dig in this way in a restaurant, I greatly enjoy myself when eating it at home.

SERVES 4 TO 6

4 live lobsters (about 1¼ pounds each)
¼ cup extra-virgin olive oil, plus more for drizzling
1 medium onion, chopped
2 shallots, chopped
¼ cup tomato paste
⅓ cup red-wine vinegar
One 28-ounce can whole San Marzano tomatoes, crushed by hand
Kosher salt
Peperoncino flakes
¼ cup chopped fresh Italian parsley

To cut the lobsters into serving pieces, place them in the freezer for 15 minutes to stun them. Then pierce the backs of the heads with a knife, about 2 inches down from the eyes, and push straight down and split between the eyes. Twist and remove the claws from the bodies. Twist the knuckles from the claws. Crack the knuckles and claws with the back of a chef's knife to make them easier to open when serving. Remove the small walking legs from the bodies. Split the bodies and tails in half, then cut the tails from the bodies. Clean the body cavities by the eyes, leaving in the green tomalley.

Heat the olive oil in a large, wide Dutch oven over medium heat. Add the lobster tails, meat side down, and cook, shaking the skillet occasionally, until they're golden brown, about 2 minutes. Remove the tails from the oil and set them aside.

Add the onion and shallots, and cook until translucent, 3 to 4 minutes. Add the lobster body pieces, and cook, stirring, until they turn bright red, about 5 minutes. Stir in the tomato paste, and cook until it coats the lobster pieces, about 2 minutes. Blend the vinegar with 2 cups hot water, pour this into the pan, and bring it to a full boil. Add the tomatoes, bring the liquid to a brisk simmer, and cook until the sauce comes together, about 5 minutes. Season with salt and peperoncino. Remove the lobster bodies with tongs to a deep serving platter, allowing all juices to drain back into the sauce, and keep the body pieces warm.

Add the claws to the pot, and cook 7 minutes. Add the reserved tails, lobster legs, and the remaining olive oil. Simmer until the lobster tails are fully cooked, 3 to 5 minutes longer. Remove the tails and claws to the platter, and keep them warm. Bring the sauce to a boil, and boil until slightly thickened, about 3 minutes. Stir the parsley into the sauce with a final drizzle of oil. Fish out and place on the platter any stray lobster pieces, and spoon the sauce over all. Serve with crusty bread.

MEAT AND POULTRY

The secondo of the Italian table is typically a protein, either meat or fish. When eating at home, most Italians have a salad and either a primo or a secondo, not both. But when dining out, they order both. The majority of meat dishes in this chapter are from the more recent years at Felidia. Throughout the evolution of our menu, it has been peppered with items that are not often found in other Italian restaurants, such as rognoni (kidneys) or fegato alla Veneziana (liver Venetian-style), but are common on menus in Italy. These are all parts of the animal I was taught to eat when I was a child, on my grandmother's small farm. Some guests come just for these items. As well, I love long cooking techniques, like roasting and braising. Chef Nicotra is great with big pieces of meat, such as chops, shanks, shoulders, ossobuco, and steak. He also likes his seasonal game meats, as do I. Vegetables, an important part of Italian dining, traditionally make up a large part of the presentation, and at Felidia this is the case, too; you will also find delicious sauces in the final presentation. The side dishes typically associated with the meat dishes are referred to in the headnotes, and corresponding recipes are found in the sides chapter (page 169).

CHICKEN PIZZAIOLA

Petto di Pollo alla Pizzaiola

This dish has quickly become one of our most popular at lunch. The chicken is so tender that you don't need a knife to cut it. And the pizzaiola preparation is a favorite tradition of Italian American cuisine. A lighter and more contemporary way to prepare this recipe would be to use fresh tomatoes.

SERVES 4

4 boneless, skinless chicken breasts (about 2 pounds), trimmed of fat and gristle
Kosher salt
1 cup buttermilk
1½ cups panko breadcrumbs
¾ cup freshly grated Grana Padano
1 teaspoon dried oregano, preferably Sicilian, on the branch
2 tablespoons chopped fresh parsley
2 tablespoons chopped fresh basil, plus ¼ cup leaves, and whole sprigs for garnish
5 tablespoons extra-virgin olive oil
2 cups prepared fresh tomato sauce
4 slices low-moisture mozzarella
4 roasted cherry tomatoes (optional, for garnish)

Season the chicken breasts with salt, and place them in a resealable plastic bag. Pour in the buttermilk, and marinate in the refrigerator for 2 hours.

Drain the chicken, and preheat the oven to 400 degrees.

Line a baking sheet with parchment paper. In a medium bowl, toss together the panko, grated Grana Padano, dried oregano, chopped parsley, chopped basil, 3 tablespoons of the olive oil, and ½ teaspoon salt. Stir to incorporate everything fully into the crumbs.

Put the drained chicken breasts in the bowl with the seasoned breadcrumbs one at a time, and pat well on both sides so the crumbs cover the chicken on all sides. Set the breaded chicken breasts on the parchment paper, arranged so they don't touch each other.

Bake the chicken until the coating is crisp and browned and the chicken is just cooked through, about 15 minutes. While the chicken bakes, combine the tomato sauce, the remaining 2 tablespoons olive oil, and ¼ cup basil leaves in a blender, and purée until smooth. Season with salt. Pour the purée into a small saucepan, and warm it over low heat.

When the chicken is just cooked through, top with the sliced mozzarella and bake until the cheese is just melted, about 2 minutes. Spread the tomato emulsion on plates, top with the chicken and a roasted cherry tomato, if using, and serve.

SHORT RIBS BRAISED *in* BAROLO

Costine di Manzo Brasate al Barolo

This is my spin on a typical dish from Piedmont, where I grew up. Usually in Italy, braised meat is taken from a leg of veal or beef. Since short ribs are not often used there, this recipe involves an American cut of meat with an Italian sauce. The ribs are moist and familiar to U.S. diners, and I often serve them with mashed potatoes or polenta. In Piedmont, we use Barolo wine, but this dish can be made with any hearty red wine of your choice; just remember, a dish is the sum of all its parts.

—Chef Nicotra

SERVES 4

½ ounce dried porcini
Four bone-in beef short ribs (1 pound), cut into 3 pieces each (12 pieces total)
Kosher salt
Freshly ground black pepper
¼ cup extra-virgin olive oil
2 thick slices pancetta or bacon, chopped
1 large onion, chopped
2 medium carrots, chopped
2 tablespoons tomato paste
2 sprigs fresh rosemary
2 fresh bay leaves
Pinch of ground cloves
2 cups Barolo or other good-quality red wine
1 cup canned whole plum tomatoes, preferably San Marzano, crushed by hand
2 cups chicken stock, plus more as needed

Soak the porcini in 1 cup boiling water until softened, about 15 minutes. Drain and chop; reserve the porcini and the soaking liquid.

Heat a large Dutch oven over medium heat. Season the short ribs with salt and pepper. Add 2 tablespoons of the oil to the pot. When the oil is hot, brown the short ribs all over, about 5 minutes total. Remove them to a plate. Pour out any oil left in the pot, and wipe it clean with a paper towel.

Return the pot to medium heat, and add the remaining 2 tablespoons oil and the pancetta. Cook until the pancetta has crisped and rendered its fat, about 2 minutes. Add the onion and carrots, and cook until wilted, about 4 minutes. Clear a space in the pan, and add the tomato paste. Cook and stir the tomato paste in that spot for a minute, then stir into the vegetables. Add the rosemary, bay leaves, and cloves, and stir. Pour in the wine and the reserved porcini and soaking liquid, bring to a boil, and cook until reduced by half, about 2 minutes. Stir in the tomatoes. Add the short ribs back to the pot, and pour in the stock. The level of liquid should just barely come up to the tops of the short ribs. If it doesn't, add more stock. Season lightly with salt, and bring to a simmer. Cover the pot, and cook, turning the short ribs once or twice in the sauce, until they are very tender, about 2 hours.

Remove the short ribs from the sauce. Pass the sauce through a food mill or press through a fine strainer back into the pot. Degrease in a fat-separating cup, if desired. Return the short ribs and sauce to the pot to reheat before serving.

SEARED LAMB CHOPS *with* MINT SALSA VERDE *and* ROASTED POTATO WEDGES

Costolette di Agnello alla Scottadito, Salsa alla Menta, Patate al Forno

Scottadito literally translates as "finger burning," which indicates that the chops should be picked up with your fingers and eaten; this is not done much in restaurants, but it's perfect at home, with family and friends. Just remember to set out a moist napkin for each of your guests. Seared lamb chops are a favorite at Felidia, especially in the early spring, around Easter. For this dish, rib chops cut from a rack of lamb are best, because of the length of the bone. Look for ones with a bright red color a few shades lighter than beef, and a big "eye" of meat—about 2½ inches wide. At Felidia the chops are Frenched, which means scraping all the meat off the rib bone. At home you can certainly leave the meat on the bones of the chops—just make sure it is cooked crisp.

SERVES 4

For the Lamb Chops

8 Frenched rib lamb chops (about 2¼ pounds)
2 tablespoons fresh rosemary leaves
2 tablespoons extra-virgin olive oil
Kosher salt
Freshly ground black pepper

For the Mint Salsa Verde

1½ cups fresh Italian parsley leaves
1½ cups fresh mint leaves
2 tablespoons drained capers in brine
1 clove garlic, crushed and peeled
1 teaspoon Dijon mustard
2 anchovy fillets
¼ to ⅓ cup extra-virgin olive oil
Kosher salt
Freshly ground black pepper

For the Potato Wedges

4 medium Yukon Gold potatoes (about 1¼ pounds), cut into 1-inch wedges
2 tablespoons extra-virgin olive oil
Kosher salt
Freshly ground black pepper

Preheat the oven to 450 degrees with a sheet pan placed on the middle rack.

For the lamb chops, rub them with the rosemary, oil, salt, and pepper, and let them stand at room temperature while you prepare the salsa verde and potatoes.

For the salsa verde, combine the parsley, mint, capers, garlic, mustard, and anchovies in a food processor. Pulse to make a chunky paste, then scrape down the sides of the work bowl. With the processor running, add ¼ cup olive oil to make a smooth

(recipe continues)

sauce. The sauce shouldn't be too thick; if it is, add the remaining olive oil and process again. Transfer to a bowl, season with salt and pepper, and set aside.

For the potatoes, toss in a large bowl with the olive oil, 1 teaspoon salt, and a generous amount of black pepper. Spread on the preheated baking sheet, and roast until tender and golden, flipping once, about 18 minutes.

Meanwhile, heat a large skillet over high heat. Scrape the rosemary from the chops, and put as many chops as will fit in the skillet. Sear on both sides until medium rare, about 2 minutes per side. Repeat with the remaining chops.

Spoon the salsa verde onto serving plates. Place the chops and potatoes gingerly on top of the salsa verde.

POUSSINS *with* BEER, MAPLE SYRUP, *and* BALSAMIC GLAZE

Galletto o Pollo Glassato alla Birra e Balsamico

This is a recipe I created for a James Beard Foundation competition in 1995. My future wife, Shelly Burgess, a friend of Lidia's daughter, Tanya, and the co-producer of Lidia's TV show, was the one who insisted that I enter. Using some of the money from the grand prize, I took Shelly out to dinner; one wedding and three kids later, the rest is history.

A poussin is a young chicken, less than a month old, usually weighing about a pound. It is also called "spring chicken."

—Chef Nicotra

SERVES 4 TO 6

1 cup dark beer
½ cup balsamic vinegar
¼ cup maple syrup
4 poussins (or two 2½-pound small chickens), halved
Kosher salt
Freshly ground black pepper
¼ cup extra-virgin olive oil
2 medium onions, cut into chunks
5 cloves garlic, crushed and peeled
3 fresh bay leaves
4 cups chicken stock
1 pint black figs, halved

Combine the beer, vinegar, and maple syrup in a large measuring cup. Season the poussins with salt and pepper.

Heat 2 tablespoons of the olive oil in a large Dutch oven over medium-high heat. Add the onions and garlic, and cook until browned and wilted, about 5 minutes more. Add the bay leaves, stock, and about a quarter of the beer syrup. Bring to a simmer, and cook until very dark and flavorful and reduced by about half, about 1 hour. Strain and defat.

Preheat the oven to 425 degrees.

Wash and dry the Dutch oven. Heat the remaining 2 tablespoons olive oil in the Dutch oven over medium-high heat. Add the poussins and brown all over, about 5 minutes. Put them on a rimmed baking sheet as they brown. Place them in the oven, and roast until they're crisp and tender and a thermometer inserted into the thigh reads 165 degrees, about 30 to 35 minutes (tent with foil if the skin is getting too brown).

While the poussins finish, brown the figs in the oil left in the pot, 1 to 2 minutes, and remove them to a plate. Add the strained stock and remaining beer syrup to the Dutch oven, and boil over high heat to make a thin glaze, about 8 to 10 minutes. When the poussins are done, add to the Dutch oven with the figs, just to coat everything quickly in the sauce. Serve on a platter, with extra sauce on the side.

QUAIL STUFFED *with* CHESTNUT PANZANELLA

Quaglie Ripiene con Panzanella di Castagne

We have always had fabulous holiday menus at the restaurant, and Chef Nicotra really enjoys making the season special for families who do not want to cook at home. But if you are cooking at home, quail is a great alternative for those who choose not to do a big turkey. The seasonal version of a typical Tuscan bread salad makes a great stuffing, and if there is leftover panzanella stuffing, you can bake this mixture or fry it in a patty and serve with a sunny-side-up egg on top. Keep in mind that you can use frozen or canned chestnuts.

SERVES 4

For the Chestnut Panzanella
1½ cups peeled, cubed butternut squash
2 tablespoons extra-virgin olive oil
Kosher salt
Freshly ground black pepper
1 cup cubed day-old bread
½ cup half-and-half
½ cup chopped red onion
1 cup cooked, peeled chestnuts, coarsely chopped
1 tablespoon red-wine vinegar
2 tablespoons chopped fresh chives

For the Quail
8 semi-boneless quail
Kosher salt
Freshly ground black pepper
16 small fresh sage leaves
8 very thin slices prosciutto or speck
2 tablespoons extra-virgin olive oil
½ cup chopped red onion
½ cup Marsala
2 cups chicken stock

Preheat the oven to 400 degrees.

For the panzanella, toss the squash with 1 tablespoon of the olive oil in a medium bowl, and season with salt and pepper. Spread on a baking sheet, and roast until very tender, about 20 minutes. Let the squash cool, and increase oven temperature to 425 degrees.

Put the bread cubes in a large bowl, and pour the half-and-half over them. Let sit until softened, about 10 minutes.

Meanwhile, heat the remaining tablespoon of olive oil in a medium skillet over medium heat. Add the onion and chestnuts, and cook until the onion is softened, about 8 to 10 minutes. Season with salt and pepper, and let cool.

Put the squash, the bread with the half-and-half, and the onion mixture in a food processor, along with the vinegar and chives. Season with salt and pepper, and process to make a smooth mixture.

Transfer the mixture to a piping bag. Pipe some of the mixture into the cavity of each quail (but don't overfill). Season the filled quail with salt and pepper. Lay a sage leaf on the breast of each quail (so two leaves per bird). Wrap a slice of prosciutto around the breast of each quail, and tie the legs closed with twine, making a tight bundle.

Heat a large skillet over medium-high heat, and add the 2 tablespoons olive oil. Brown the quail on all sides, about 4 minutes per quail, and set them on a rimmed baking sheet. Roast until the quail are cooked through, about 20 minutes.

Meanwhile, reduce the heat under the skillet to medium, and add the red onion. Cook until softened, about 5 minutes. Add the Marsala, and cook until it's syrupy, about 2 minutes. Add the stock, and cook until the sauce is reduced to about ½ cup and just coats the back of a spoon, about 5 minutes.

Remove the quail to a platter, and brush with the sauce. Serve the remaining sauce on the side.

PORK CHOPS MILANESE

Costolette di Maiale alla Milanese

In Milan, a chop usually means veal, but with the rise of good animal husbandry here in the United States, there are all kinds of options available, so I prefer to use Berkshire pork for this recipe. Ask your butcher if he or she has any. There is a world of difference in taste between traditionally and sustainably raised animals. "Frenching" the chops—cleaning the meat off to expose part of the bone—prevents the "eye" of the meat that is pounded out from overcooking before the meat next to the bone is cooked, and it does make the finished chops look extra pretty. You can prepare this recipe without Frenching the chops; just be careful that the meat next to the bones is fully cooked before serving.

The recipe for the Amatriciana sauce makes more than you need for the chops, but it can be used to dress pasta and freezes well.

At Felidia this dish is served topped with a tricolored salad.

SERVES 4

For the Amatriciana Sauce

1 tablespoon extra-virgin olive oil
4 ounces slab bacon or pancetta, finely chopped
1 medium onion, finely chopped
One 28-ounce can whole Italian plum tomatoes, preferably San Marzano, crushed by hand
Kosher salt
Peperoncino

For the Pork Chops

4 pork chops, about 8 to 10 ounces each, ¾ inch thick, Frenched (ask your butcher to do this for you)
Kosher salt
Freshly ground black pepper
All-purpose flour, for dredging
1 cup fine dried breadcrumbs
2 large eggs
Vegetable oil, for pan-frying

Preheat the oven to 400 degrees.

For the Amatriciana sauce, heat the olive oil in a large skillet over medium heat. Add the bacon or pancetta, and let the meat render its fat until it begins to crisp, about 3 to 4 minutes. Add the onion, cover the skillet, and cook until the onion begins to soften, about 3 minutes.

Uncover, and add the tomatoes and 1 cup water. Season with salt and peperoncino. Bring to a simmer, and cook until thick and flavorful, about 15 minutes.

For the pork chops, season with salt and pepper. Spread out the flour and breadcrumbs on two separate plates or sheets of wax paper. Beat the eggs in a wide, shallow bowl until thoroughly blended. Dredge the chops in flour to coat them lightly, and tap off any excess. Dip them in the beaten egg, letting the excess drip back into the bowl. Move the chops to the breadcrumbs, and turn to coat completely, patting them gently to make sure the breadcrumbs adhere.

(recipe continues)

Heat ½ inch of vegetable oil in a large skillet over medium heat until a corner of one of the coated chops gives off a lively sizzle when dipped in the oil. Lay the chops into the oil, and fry, turning once, until golden on both sides, about 8 minutes. Transfer to a baking sheet, and bake until no trace of pink remains near the bone, about 5 to 6 minutes.

Remove the chops from the oven. If they look a little oily, drain them briefly on paper towels. Spoon the Amatriciana sauce on four plates, and serve the chops on top.

VEAL MEDALLIONS *with* CASTELMAGNO FONDUTA

Medaglioni di Vitello con Fonduta di Castelmagno

This is a recipe Chef Nicotra brought with him from Piedmont. It is especially popular from late October through December, when we serve our truffle menu, because it is a perfect main course for truffles. The sauce is a fonduta common to that region, and our guests really enjoy it on veal. It's a deeply satisfying dish, which we often serve with salsify, prepared as the parsnips are below. If you can find salsify in season, feel free to substitute. Castelmagno is a prized cheese from Piemonte—if you cannot find it, Taleggio will be fine.

SERVES 4

1½ pounds parsnips, peeled and cut into large chunks
2 tablespoons truffle butter
¼ cup freshly grated Grana Padano
Kosher salt
Freshly ground black pepper
1 cup heavy cream
2 egg yolks
4 ounces freshly grated Castelmagno cheese (or Taleggio)
1½ pounds veal tenderloin, sliced against the grain into 12 medallions
1 tablespoon unsalted butter
1 tablespoon extra-virgin olive oil
Fresh white truffle (optional)

Put the parsnips in a large saucepan with water to cover. Bring to a simmer, and cook until tender, about 15 minutes. Drain, reserving a little of the cooking water, and return to the pot with the truffle butter. Mash with a potato masher to your desired consistency. Beat in the grated Grana Padano, and season with salt and pepper. If the parsnips seem a little dry, you can stir in a tablespoon or two of the reserved cooking water. Cover and keep warm.

For the fonduta, bring the cream to a bare simmer in a small saucepan. Put the egg yolks in a medium bowl with a pinch of salt. Slowly whisk the hot cream into the yolks, taking care not to scramble them. Pour the mixture back into the saucepan, and cook, stirring constantly, over low heat until slightly thickened, about 6 minutes. Stir in the Castelmagno until the sauce is smooth, and keep it warm while you cook the veal.

Season the veal with salt and pepper. Melt the butter and olive oil in a large skillet over medium heat. When the butter has melted, add the veal, and cook, turning once, until browned and done to your liking, about 5 to 7 minutes total for medium rare.

Serve the veal and parsnips side by side with the fonduta on top, and shave the truffles over all, if desired.

OSSOBUCO MILANESE STYLE

Ossobuco alla Milanese

Ossobuco *is a recipe that goes back to the opening of my first restaurant, in 1971, and it was the favorite dish on the menu at Felidia in the 1980s. Combining good veal shanks with lots of vegetables and herbs, and simmering this for hours, results in fork-tender meat nestled in a complex and savory sauce.* Ossobuco, *literally translated as "a bone with a hole," is a dish that originated in Milan. It still outsells many other meat choices on the menu at Becco, Lidia's Kansas City, and Lidia's Pittsburgh.*

Serve this dish with an espresso spoon—or, even better, a marrow spoon—so that your guests can scoop out the marrow, the ultimate delicacy. Whenever we served this at Felidia in the 1980s, my husband, Felix, was always on the lookout to make sure the marrow spoons returned to the kitchen—they were rather expensive and always seemed to disappear. Once, he saw a guest place one inside his suit jacket after finishing the ossobuco. Felix waited until the guest was leaving, asked him how his meal was, and received a raving review; Felix then proceeded to ask for the marrow spoon.

SERVES 4

4 fresh bay leaves
1 large sprig fresh rosemary
4 cups chicken broth, or as needed
3 tablespoons extra-virgin olive oil
Four 1½-inch-thick *ossobuco,* tied around the circumference
Kosher salt
Freshly ground black pepper
All-purpose flour, for dredging
1 large onion, cut into 1-inch-thick chunks
2 medium carrots, cut into 1-inch chunks
2 stalks celery, cut into 1-inch chunks
3 tablespoons tomato paste
1 cup dry white wine
6 whole cloves
2 small oranges, 1 peeled with vegetable peeler, 1 zested
2 tablespoons chopped fresh Italian parsley

Tie the bay leaves and rosemary together with a string. Pour the chicken broth into a small pot, and keep it hot over low heat.

Heat the olive oil in a large Dutch oven over medium heat. Season the *ossobuco* with the salt and pepper. Spread some flour on a plate. Dredge the *ossobuco* in the flour, tapping off the excess. When the oil is hot, add the *ossobuco* and brown on all sides, about 6 to 7 minutes in all. Remove them to a plate.

Add the onion, carrots, and celery to the Dutch oven. Cook until the onion begins to soften and all of the vegetables are caramelized, about 5 minutes. Clear a space in the pan, and add the tomato paste. Cook and stir the tomato paste in that spot until it is toasted and darkened a bit, about 1 minute, then stir it into the vegetables. Add the wine and the herb package. Bring to a boil, and cook until the wine is reduced by half, about 3 minutes.

(recipe continues)

Drop in the cloves and the orange peel (reserve the zest from the other orange for later). Return the *ossobuco* to the pot in one layer, and pour enough chicken broth over the top that it almost, but not quite, covers the meat. Adjust heat so the liquid is simmering, cover, and cook until the *ossobuco* is tender, about 1½ hours.

Once the meat is tender, uncover it, and remove the vegetable chunks to a platter. Put the *ossobuco* on top of the vegetables. Discard the package of bay leaves and rosemary. Bring the liquid in the Dutch oven to a boil, and cook it down until saucy, about 4 to 5 minutes. Remove the strings from the *ossobuco.* Pour the sauce through a strainer directly over them on the platter, pressing on any remaining vegetable solids with a wooden spoon. Stir together the orange zest and parsley, sprinkle over the shanks, and serve.

TRIPE

Trippa

Tripe has been served at Felidia since 1981, and there are regular guests who eat it only here. Felidia was one of the first restaurants in New York to bring peasant foods to high-end tables. Organ meat and innards were and are so much a part of Italian cuisine and my upbringing, but when we opened, they were almost unheard of in American restaurants. We were doing "nose to tail" cooking before the name even existed. It's a way of eating that makes a huge amount of sense in a world where there is so much waste.

This is one of my mother Erminia's absolute favorites; I bring some home for her from the restaurant at least once a week. You can find veal tripe at your butcher in big pieces. It has usually already been blanched, but you will need to cook it again in water to make it tender, and then braise it with herbs and tomatoes to flavor it. Today, at the restaurant, it is served almost like a risotto—with Grana Padano and butter mixed in before serving. Serve with grilled or toasted country bread, or as we do at Felidia and at home, serve it with polenta.

SERVES 4 TO 6

3 pounds veal tripe
3 tablespoons extra-virgin olive oil
1 medium onion, chopped
Peperoncino flakes
3 tablespoons tomato paste
2 teaspoons chopped fresh thyme
1 cup dry white wine
1½ cups chicken stock
2 fresh bay leaves
1 cup tomato purée
Kosher salt
¼ cup chopped fresh Italian parsley
2 tablespoons unsalted butter, cut into pieces
⅓ cup freshly grated Grana Padano
Toasted bread, for serving

Put the tripe in a medium Dutch oven, and add water to cover by about 2 inches. Bring to a simmer, cover, and cook until the tripe is tender when pierced with a knife, about 1½ hours. Drain and let cool. With the back of a chef's knife, scrape both sides of the tripe clean of excess fat and other residue, and rinse. Pat dry and cut into thin bite-sized strips.

Rinse and dry the Dutch oven, and set it over medium heat. Add the olive oil. When the oil is hot, add the onion and cook until softened, 5 to 6 minutes. Season with peperoncino, then clear a space in the pan and add the tomato paste. Cook and stir the tomato paste in that spot until it is toasted and darkens a bit, about 1 minute, then stir into the onion. Add the thyme and white wine,

(recipe continues)

and boil until reduced by half, about 3 minutes. Add the tripe strips, chicken stock, and bay leaves. Bring to a simmer, and cook 30 minutes. After 30 minutes, add the tomato purée and season with salt. Continue to simmer until the tripe is very tender and the sauce is thick and flavorful, about 20 minutes more. Remove the bay leaves and stir in the parsley and butter. Serve the tripe on a deep plate, finished with some grated Grana Padano, and serve with toasted bread. At Felidia, we sometimes serve it with crispy polenta.

NARDINI
APOVILLA
APPLE BRANDY

SIDES

Italians love their vegetables. Protein is not much in demand on the traditional Italian table, which offers more vegetables, legumes, pasta, rice, or polenta. It is no surprise, when looking at the Mediterranean diet and how healthy it is, that vegetables, legumes, and lean proteins are a large portion of what is eaten in the region. Vegetables play a main role in every Italian meal, and, more and more, our customers are looking for a diversity of vegetables in their meals. Luckily, Chef Nicotra does magic with them.

When my summer garden is in full bloom, my mother and I eat meals composed exclusively of vegetables. I sometimes bring some goodies from my garden to Felidia as well. The versatility of vegetables is endless. The selections given here are served at Felidia with either meat or seafood secondi, according to season and availability. Many are also delicious on their own, or served alongside any simple grilled or sautéed piece of meat or fish.

STRING BEAN *and* PICKLED ONION SALAD

Fagiolini e Cipolle all'Aceto

Although string beans are at their best in early summer, they are available year-round. I particularly like them in a salad, and Chef Nicotra here uses them as a backdrop for an antipasto. String-bean salad is often on the menu at Felidia, enhanced by simply adding mozzarella or burrata and served as an appetizer. Here it makes a nice side, especially with fish or chicken. We often serve this salad with some pickled onions (or ramps, when in season). Extra pickled red onions are great on sandwiches or in other salads.

SERVES 6

For the Pickled Onions

¾ cup white-wine vinegar
1 tablespoon sugar
1½ teaspoons kosher salt
¼ teaspoon peperoncino flakes
2 fresh bay leaves
1 medium red onion, thinly sliced

For the String Beans

Kosher salt
1 pound string beans, trimmed
½ cup loosely packed fresh basil leaves
1 tablespoon red-wine vinegar
3 tablespoons extra-virgin olive oil
Freshly ground black pepper

For the onion, combine the vinegar, ¼ cup water, sugar, salt, peperoncino, and bay leaves in a small saucepan, and bring to a simmer. Put the onion in a nonreactive container with a lid, and pour the vinegar mixture over. Remove the bay leaves, and let cool to room temperature, and then refrigerate until chilled, about 2 hours. (This recipe can also be made a day or two ahead and refrigerated.)

For the string beans, bring a large pot of salted water to a boil. Add the string beans, and blanch until tender, about 6 to 7 minutes. Drain, and rinse to cool slightly.

Shred the basil. Put the string beans in a bowl, and toss with the basil. Drizzle with the vinegar and oil, and season with salt and pepper. Toss to coat, and serve slightly warm or at room temperature, topped with a tangle of pickled onion.

FENNEL *and* ASIAN PEAR SALAD

Insalata di Finocchi, Pere e Pistacchi

Asian pears are not typically used in traditional Italian cuisine, but Chef Nicotra excels at inserting nontraditional but delicious products into his menu. This is a great salad for the fall or winter, when Asian pears are in season. At Felidia, we serve it with puffed wild rice on top, which adds an interesting crunchy texture and gives a bit of bite. The slight licorice flavor of the fennel really complements the sweetness of the crisp Asian pear.

SERVES 4

3 medium fennel bulbs, with fronds
5 tablespoons extra-virgin olive oil
Kosher salt
Freshly ground black pepper
2 to 3 tablespoons freshly squeezed lemon juice
2 large Asian pears
One 2-ounce piece aged pecorino, for grating
⅓ cup chopped pistachios, toasted

Preheat the oven to 400 degrees.

Cut the bulbs from the fennel tops. Reserve 2 packed cups of fronds and chopped tender portions of the tops, and set aside.

Core and very thinly slice two of the fennel bulbs. Keep them in ice water while you prepare the rest of the salad. Core and slice the remaining bulb into pieces about ¼ inch thick. Place on a baking sheet with 1 tablespoon of the olive oil, and season with salt and pepper. Roast, stirring occasionally, until tender and golden, about 20 minutes.

Meanwhile, bring a medium saucepan of salted water to a boil. Add the reserved fennel tops and fronds, and blanch until bright green and tender, about 3 minutes. Shock in an ice bath, and pat dry. Put in a blender with 1 tablespoon of the oil and 2 tablespoons water. Blend to make a smooth purée, adding a little more water if necessary. Season with salt and pepper.

To assemble the salad, whisk 2 tablespoons of lemon juice with the remaining 3 tablespoons of olive oil in a large bowl. Season with salt and pepper. Add up to 1 more tablespoon lemon juice, to taste. Thinly slice the Asian pears, and add them to the bowl. Drain the uncooked fennel, pat very dry, and add to the bowl. Season with salt and pepper, and toss well.

To serve, spread four serving plates with the fennel purée. Top with the roasted fennel, then mound the salad on top of that. Finely grate pecorino over each serving, sprinkle with pistachios, and grind black pepper over all. Serve immediately.

ASPARAGUS *and* LEEKS *in* LEMON VINAIGRETTE

Asparagi e Porri al Limone

When I was a child, I made this salad in the springtime with Nonna Rosa. We foraged for wild asparagus and gathered fresh eggs from the chicken coop to make one of my favorite lunches, made perfect with a few slices of homemade prosciutto and crusty bread. The recipe has been modified throughout the years, but it's still on the menu at Felidia in the spring. This dish can be served with or without the hard-boiled eggs. With the eggs, it's a complete dish for a light lunch. Without the eggs, it is a perfect side to simply prepared white fish dishes. The dish also does very well served as an appetizer, with or without eggs. Leeks are underused, in my opinion, and this easy-to-make dish gives them a starring role.

SERVES 4 TO 6

Kosher salt
2 bunches medium-thick asparagus, trimmed, lower third of stalks peeled (about 2 pounds)
1 bunch medium leeks, white and pale-green parts, halved lengthwise and washed
Juice of 1 large lemon
¼ cup extra-virgin olive oil
Freshly ground black pepper
3 hard-boiled eggs, coarsely chopped

Bring a large pot of salted water to a boil. Cut the peeled asparagus into thirds crosswise. Cut the leeks into thirds crosswise as well. Add the leeks to the boiling water, and cook for 2 minutes. Add the asparagus, and cook until leeks and asparagus are just tender, about 3 minutes more. Drain, and plunge into an ice bath to stop the cooking and set the color. Drain and pat very dry.

Put the asparagus and leeks in a serving bowl. Drizzle with the lemon juice and olive oil, and season with salt and pepper. Toss well. Mound the asparagus and leeks on a serving platter, and scatter the hard-boiled eggs over the top.

ROASTED POTATO WEDGES *with* MUSHROOMS

Patate al Forno con Funghi

This side dish works well alongside any fall-inspired meat dish. Any form of roasted potato is gobbled up in my house, but this recipe is particularly beloved. An extremely satisfying pairing of the starch of the potatoes and the earthiness of the mushrooms, it will be equally popular at your house, I'm sure. Once you master the roasting technique, you can try it with other seasonal vegetables as well.

SERVES 4 TO 6

8 tablespoons extra-virgin olive oil
2 tablespoons fresh rosemary leaves
4 cloves garlic, peeled and sliced
¼ cup chopped fresh Italian parsley
2 pounds medium russet potatoes, halved crosswise, then cut into 1-inch wedges
Kosher salt
Freshly ground black pepper
1 pound mixed fresh mushrooms (cremini, shiitake, chanterelle, oyster, etc.), trimmed and thickly sliced

---

Preheat the oven to 425 degrees.

In a small bowl, combine ¼ cup of the olive oil, the rosemary, garlic, and parsley, and leave this to steep while you roast the potatoes.

On a rimmed baking sheet, toss the potatoes with 2 tablespoons of the olive oil. Season with salt and several grinds of black pepper. Roast on the lower rack until golden on one side, about 15 to 20 minutes. Flip, and roast until potatoes are golden on the other side, just cooked through, and very crispy, about 10 to 15 minutes more.

While the potatoes roast, heat the remaining 2 tablespoons olive oil in a large skillet over medium-high heat. Add the mushrooms, and season with salt and several grinds of black pepper. Cook and toss the mushrooms until tender and well browned, about 10 minutes.

Add the mushrooms to the roasted potatoes, toss, and roast until both are very tender, about 5 minutes more.

Immediately dump the hot potatoes and mushrooms into a large serving bowl, and strain the garlic-rosemary oil over. Toss to coat, and season with black pepper. Use tongs to crush the potatoes lightly, then toss again to coat the exposed parts of the potatoes with oil. Serve immediately.

ROASTED ROOT VEGETABLES

Radici Invernali al Forno

Roasting is one of my favorite cooking techniques, and I particularly love the earthiness of these roasted root vegetables.

SERVES 4 TO 6

3 small leeks
2 large carrots (about 12 ounces), cut into 2-by-½-inch sticks
2 large parsnips (about 12 ounces), cut into 2-by-½-inch sticks
1 small celery root (about 16 ounces), cut into 1-inch cubes
6 tablespoons extra-virgin olive oil
2 sprigs fresh rosemary, needles removed
Kosher salt
Freshly ground black pepper
6 small red or white new potatoes (about 8 ounces), cut into chunks
2 small red onions, peeled and quartered through the root
1 head garlic, crushed and peeled
¼ cup chopped fresh Italian parsley

Preheat the oven to 400 degrees.

Trim the dark green leaves from the leeks and cut the whites in half lengthwise. Trim the root ends of the leeks, leaving enough of the root core intact to hold the leek halves together. Rinse the leek halves under cold water, separating the layers to rinse out any grit from between them.

Toss the carrots, parsnips, and celery root in a large bowl with 3 tablespoons of the oil and half of the rosemary. Season with salt and pepper. Spread on a baking sheet. Toss the leeks, potatoes, red onions, and garlic cloves in the same bowl with the remaining 3 tablespoons olive oil and the remaining rosemary. Season with salt and pepper. Spread on a second baking sheet. Roast until everything is tender, about 40 minutes for the carrots and parsnips and about 30 minutes for the potatoes and onions. Remove the pans from the oven and stir the vegetables gently several times and rotate pans from top to bottom while they roast so they cook and brown evenly. Sprinkle with the parsley, toss, and serve.

MUSHROOM GRATIN

Gratinati di Funghi

Mushroom gratin is typically prepared and finished together with a battutina, a thin slice of veal or beef quickly grilled or sautéed, topped with seasonal vegetables, and occasionally finished with cheese—a classic at Felidia for years. This gratin is also delicious as a side dish with meat or plain polenta.

SERVES 4 TO 6

2 cups small grape tomatoes
¼ cup extra-virgin olive oil
Kosher salt
Freshly ground black pepper
2 tablespoons unsalted butter
1½ pounds fresh porcini or shiitake mushrooms, stems removed, thickly sliced
½ cup freshly grated Grana Padano
¼ cup fine dried breadcrumbs
8 ounces fresh mozzarella, diced
¼ cup fresh basil leaves, coarsely chopped

Arrange a rack in the top half of the oven, and preheat to 425 degrees.

Toss the tomatoes with 2 tablespoons of the olive oil in a 9-by-13-inch baking dish. Season with salt and pepper. Roast until the tomatoes begin to burst and give up their juices, about 15 minutes.

Meanwhile, heat a large skillet over medium-high heat. Add the remaining 2 tablespoons olive oil and the butter. When the butter is melted, add the mushrooms, and season with salt and pepper. Cook, without stirring, until the mushrooms begin to brown on the underside, then stir. Continue to cook, stirring occasionally, until the mushrooms are wilted and browned, about 6 to 7 minutes.

Toss the grated Grana Padano and breadcrumbs together in a small bowl.

Once the tomatoes have roasted, about 15 minutes, remove the baking dish from the oven and add the sautéed mushrooms. Sprinkle with about half of the breadcrumb mixture, add the diced mozzarella and the basil, stir, and then sprinkle the remaining breadcrumb mixture over the top.

Bake until the top is browned and crusty, about 20 minutes more. Serve hot.

BRUSSELS SPROUTS BRAISED *with* VINEGAR

Cavolini di Bruxelles all'Aceto

This is one of my favorite ways to cook Brussels sprouts, and the way I cooked them for many years at Felidia. Brussels sprouts have become wildly popular on menus over the past few years, but that was not the case when we opened. Cooking them with vinegar removes the sulfurous taste, and when they are browned just right, they are delicious. Today Chef Nicotra typically serves these Brussels sprouts with lamb, duck, or quail.

SERVES 6

1½ pounds Brussels sprouts
3 tablespoons extra-virgin olive oil, plus more for drizzling
6 cloves garlic, crushed and peeled
Kosher salt
2 tablespoons red-wine vinegar or white balsamic vinegar
Freshly ground black pepper

Trim the bases of the sprouts. Remove the discolored outer leaves, and cut each sprout vertically in half. Wash them thoroughly, and drain well.

Heat the olive oil in a large skillet over medium heat. Add the garlic cloves, shaking the pan until they turn golden, about 2 minutes.

Stir the sprouts into the oil, season them lightly with salt, and stir until they turn bright green, about 3 minutes. Pour in 1 cup water, and bring to a boil. Lower the heat so the liquid is simmering.

Cook, uncovered, until the sprouts are tender and almost falling apart and the liquid is almost completely evaporated, about 10 to 15 minutes depending on the size of the sprouts. If the liquid is evaporated before the sprouts are tender, add more water, about ¼ cup at a time, as necessary. Increase the heat to high, sprinkle with the vinegar, and toss to coat. Season with salt and pepper to taste. Spoon the sprouts into a warm serving bowl, drizzle with a little olive oil, and serve.

SAUTÉED SPINACH

Spinaci Saltati al Pane

At Felidia, breadcrumb spinach is served with our chicken pizzaiola, a popular current lunch-menu item. We serve the chicken placed on top of the bed of spinach. The addition of a tablespoon or two of breadcrumbs to sautéed vegetables like spinach or escarole—vegetables that release water when cooked—helps absorb the released water and adds a little bit of extra flavor.

SERVES 4 TO 6

2 bunches spinach, stemmed (about 2 pounds)
3 tablespoons extra-virgin olive oil
5 cloves garlic, crushed and peeled
Kosher salt
Freshly ground black pepper

Wash the spinach, but don't dry it completely. The water that clings to the leaves will steam the spinach as it cooks.

Heat the olive oil in a wide, heavy skillet over medium heat. When the oil is hot, add the garlic, and cook, shaking the pan, until golden, about 2 minutes. Scatter the spinach into the pan, a large handful at a time, waiting until each batch wilts before adding another. Season lightly with salt and pepper, and cover the pan. Cook until the spinach begins to release its liquid, 3 to 5 minutes. Uncover the pan, and cook, stirring, until the spinach is wilted and the water has evaporated, 1 to 3 minutes. Taste, and season with additional salt and pepper if you like. Serve hot.

VARIATION: Spinach Sautéed with Breadcrumbs: Prepare the sautéed spinach as described above, but sprinkle 2 to 3 tablespoons of fine dried toasted breadcrumbs over it just before removing it from the heat. (Adding some breadcrumbs to the pan near the end of cooking is a traditional Istrian way of preparing spinach. Breadcrumbs not only add flavor but also absorb some of the liquid that the spinach gives off, making the spinach neater when you're plating.)

FENNEL *with* OLIVES *and* ONION

Finocchi con Cipolle e Olive

I enjoy fennel raw and sliced to munch on, but when it's prepared as it is here, the subtle licorice flavor really comes out. What makes this dish especially delicious is the balance between the sweetness of the fennel and the onions, the intensity of the olives, and the acidity of the vinegar. It is a side dish that can be made in advance and reheated when you are ready to serve it, and is great with grilled or broiled fish.

SERVES 4 TO 6

Kosher salt
3 medium fennel bulbs
4 tablespoons unsalted butter
1 medium red onion, thickly sliced
Freshly ground black pepper
½ cup quartered pitted Italian green olives, such as Cerignola
¼ cup cider vinegar

Bring a large pot of salted water to a boil. Trim the tops from the fennel bulbs, reserving some of the tender fronds. Cut out the cores from the fennel bulbs, and slice the bulbs into pieces about ¼ inch thick. Add the fennel to the boiling water, and cook until just tender but still with a little bite, about 4 minutes. Drain well, reserving about ½ cup cooking liquid, and pat dry.

Heat a large skillet over medium heat. Add the butter. Once the butter is melted, add the onion, and cook until it begins to wilt, about 4 minutes. Add the fennel, and season with salt and pepper. Cook until the fennel and onion are just golden, about 4 minutes. Add the olives, and toss. Add the vinegar, and bring to a boil. Add the reserved ½ cup cooking water, bring to a rapid simmer, and cook until the liquid has reduced and lightly glazes the fennel and onion, about 2 to 4 minutes. Season with salt and pepper, garnish with some of the reserved fronds, and serve.

BRAISED SPRING VEGETABLES

Scafata

Many of the recipes at Felidia are based on my childhood memories. This one is inspired by my recollection of how, every spring, particularly if Nonna Rosa was preparing a big Sunday meal, I would be sent into the garden with my basket to collect the mature peas and fava pods. I would have to shell them, and then Grandma would do the cooking. This is a good recipe for the tougher, outer leaves of romaine lettuce that aren't tender enough for salad. It's a natural side for spring lamb dishes or any other simple preparation of meat or fish. This side is always on the menu at Felidia for Easter. It is a particular favorite of my Roman son-in-law, Corrado, who is a huge fan of fava beans.

SERVES 4 TO 6

Kosher salt
2½ pounds washed fava beans, shelled (or 1 cup frozen peeled favas)
1 pound peas in the pod, shelled (or 1¼ cups frozen peas)
3 tablespoons extra-virgin olive oil, plus more for drizzling
1 small onion, finely chopped
2 small zucchini, diced
1 bunch scallions, white and green parts, chopped (about 1 cup)
Peperoncino flakes, to taste
4 cups shredded romaine lettuce, preferably the tough outer leaves
2 tablespoons chopped fresh mint leaves

Bring a large pot of salted water to a boil. Add the fava beans, and blanch for 1 minute. Transfer with a spider to an ice bath. Add the peas to the boiling water, and cook until bright green, about 2 to 3 minutes. Drain, and add to the ice bath. Peel the outer skins from the favas, and pat the peas and favas dry.

Heat the olive oil in a large skillet over medium heat. Add the onion, and cook until tender but not browned, about 7 to 8 minutes. (Add a splash of water to the pan if the onion starts to brown.) Add the zucchini and scallions, and cook until wilted, about 4 minutes. Add the favas and peas, and season with salt and peperoncino. Cover, and cook until the vegetables are just tender, about 6 minutes. (If the vegetables are browning, add a splash of water to the pan.)

Add the romaine, cover, and cook until it's wilted, about 4 minutes. Sprinkle with the mint, drizzle with olive oil, adjust the seasoning, stir, and serve.

WINTER CAPONATA

Caponata d'Inverno

Summertime caponata, made with eggplant, is something one finds in almost any Sicilian household. I was born in Sicily, though I grew up in Torino, and my parents returned to Sicily when they retired. My father cultivated a large garden there for decades, and my mother continued to cook.

This winter version of caponata reminds me of my parents. It's a terrific dish that uses butternut squash in place of the eggplant and goes beautifully with the Palermitana-style tuna (page 138) when eggplant is not in season.

—Chef Nicotra

SERVES 6 TO 8

¼ cup white-wine vinegar
2 tablespoons sugar
¼ cup fresh mint leaves
Vegetable oil, for frying
1 small celery root, peeled and cut into ½-inch cubes (about 1½ cups)
Kosher salt
½ small butternut squash, peeled and cut into ½-inch cubes (about 2 cups)
¼ cup extra-virgin olive oil
1 medium onion, chopped
2 stalks celery, sliced
1 medium red bell pepper, chopped
½ cup golden raisins
¼ cup coarsely chopped pitted green olives
1 tablespoon pine nuts, toasted
1 tablespoon drained capers in brine
Peperoncino
2 medium-sized ripe tomatoes, seeded and diced

Bring the vinegar to a boil in a small saucepan. Add the sugar and the mint, reduce the heat to low, and simmer until lightly syrupy, about 5 minutes. Set aside.

Heat a film of vegetable oil in a large skillet over medium heat. Add the celery-root cubes, and fry, stirring and turning them so they cook evenly, until the celery root is golden brown on all sides, about 4 to 5 minutes. Remove the celery root with a slotted spoon, drain on a paper-towel-lined plate, and season lightly with salt. Add the butternut squash to the skillet, and cook, stirring occasionally, until golden, about 5 minutes. Remove with a slotted spoon, and add to the celery root, seasoning the squash lightly with salt. Pour out the vegetable oil and wipe the skillet clean with a paper towel.

Heat the olive oil in the skillet over medium heat. Add the onion and celery, and cook until the vegetables are wilted, about 5 minutes. Add the bell pepper, and cook until crisp-tender, about 3 minutes more. Season lightly with salt. Return

(recipe continues)

the celery root and squash to the skillet. Stir in the raisins, green olives, pine nuts, and capers. Season with peperoncino, and continue cooking, stirring, until the vegetables are just soft but not mushy, about 5 minutes. Add the diced tomatoes, and cook until they just soften, 3 to 4 minutes.

Strain the vinegar syrup (without the mint leaves) into the skillet, and bring to a simmer. Cook until the syrup coats the vegetables and everything is very tender but not falling apart, 2 to 3 minutes more. Serve warm or at room temperature.

MASHED POTATOES *and* SAVOY CABBAGE

Patate e Verza

I love cabbage in the winter, especially Savoy cabbage. Grandma Rosa taught me this recipe, and I have been cooking it ever since, at home and in the restaurant, and now Chef Nicotra also includes it on the menu in the winter. It is a side dish that can be made in abundance and reheated the next day. Adding vegetables to mashed potatoes is common in the Italian tradition, and certainly at Felidia. It really lightens the potatoes up. The vegetable can vary—green beans in the spring, Swiss chard as it becomes available. At Felidia, we also like to use parsnips, which takes the recipe to a new level, but this version with cabbage is especially good.

SERVES 4

1 pound Savoy cabbage, cleaned, cored, and coarsely chopped
1 pound Idaho potatoes, peeled and sliced 1½ inches thick
Kosher salt
1 bunch scallions, white and tender green parts, trimmed, cleaned, and sliced thin (about 1 cup)
½ cup whole milk
4 tablespoons unsalted butter
1 apple
1 teaspoon grated lemon zest
Freshly ground black pepper

Pour enough cold water over the cabbage and potatoes in a 3-to-4-quart saucepan to cover them by three fingers. Season generously with salt, and bring to a boil over high heat. Cook until tender, about 15 minutes. Add the scallions, and cook for 3 minutes.

Meanwhile, heat the milk and butter in a saucepan over low heat until the butter is melted. Drain the vegetables thoroughly, and return them to the empty pot. Mash the vegetables with a potato masher, gradually adding the milk and butter, to get a smooth texture. Finely dice the apple. Stir in the lemon zest, and season to taste with salt and pepper. Add the apple, and serve immediately.

ROASTED WINTER SQUASH *with* CRANBERRY SAUCE

Zucca Arrostita con Cranberry

In Modena, they use squash a lot and combine it with fruit, such as mostarda di Cremona, to serve with a holiday roast. Cranberries are an American tradition; one does not find them in Italian food. Winter squash is popular at the restaurant during the colder months, and the cranberry sauce creates a little holiday flavor during that special time of year. Even though they are not native to Italian cuisine, I always have cranberries on my holiday table. This dish will work next to your holiday turkey slices or any roasted meat.

SERVES 4 TO 6

For the Squash
1 small butternut squash
1 acorn squash
2 tablespoons extra-virgin olive oil
2 tablespoons unsalted butter, melted
Kosher salt
Freshly ground black pepper

For the Cranberry Sauce
2 cups fresh or frozen cranberries
½ cup orange juice
2 to 3 tablespoons honey
Kosher salt

Preheat the oven to 425 degrees.

For the butternut squash, remove the peel with a sharp vegetable peeler or paring knife. For the acorn squash, strip off the peel from the top of the ridges only (this will help the pieces cook faster and create a decorative striped look). Halve and seed both squash, and cut them into 1-inch-thick wedges or chunks.

Toss the squash in a large bowl with the olive oil and melted butter, and season with salt and a generous amount of black pepper. Spread the squash on two rimmed baking sheets. Bake about 15 to 20 minutes, then flip the pieces over and bake for another 20 to 25 minutes, until they are tender all the way through (poke with a fork to check) and nicely caramelized on the edges.

Meanwhile, for the cranberry sauce, combine the cranberries, orange juice, and 2 tablespoons honey in a medium saucepan. Season with a pinch of salt. Bring to a simmer, and cook until the berries pop and the juices are thick but saucy, about 6 to 7 minutes. Add the remaining tablespoon of honey if the sauce is too tart.

Remove the squash from the baking pan and place on the 4–6 plates evenly and next to each other. Spoon the cranberry sauce on top of each of the pieces of squash and use any extra to drizzle on top of the plate.

BROCCOLI RABE BRAISED *with* GARLIC *and* OIL

Cime di Rape all'Aglio e Olio

Home cooks can always rely on this dish in the fall and winter months. It's slightly bitter, really healthy, and a great go-to side dish for almost any main course. Broccoli rabe is a favorite in the Italian culinary tradition, as well as in the Italian American one. It is extremely versatile, as a side, with pasta, or in a filling for stuffed pasta. At Felidia, it is sometimes served with the main course, but also often as the base of an appetizer salad, sometimes with roasted squash and burrata or fresh house-made ricotta. In my many years in the restaurant business, I have seen a lot of Italian products slowly permeate the U.S. market, but nothing so much as broccoli rabe, which is now grown on acres upon acres of land in California. It can be found in every major food market, and in homes all over America.

SERVES 4

2 bunches broccoli rabe
3 tablespoons extra-virgin olive oil
6 cloves garlic, peeled and thinly sliced
Kosher salt
¼ teaspoon crushed peperoncino flakes, or to taste

Cut off the tough ends of the stems of the broccoli rabe. Then, holding a stem with the florets in hand, nick a little piece at the end of the stem with a paring knife, and pull the little piece of the stem toward you, peeling the stem partially. Continue working your way around the stem until it is peeled. As you peel, some of the large, tough outer leaves will also be removed; discard those as well. Repeat with the remaining stems. Wash and drain them in a colander.

Heat the olive oil in a large skillet over medium heat. Scatter the garlic over the oil, and cook, shaking the pan, until golden brown, about 1 minute. Add the broccoli rabe, and season lightly with salt and the crushed red pepper flakes. Stir and toss to distribute the seasonings.

Pour ¼ cup water into the skillet, and bring to a boil. Cover the skillet tightly, and cook, lifting the lid to turn the stalks occasionally, until the broccoli rabe is tender, about 10 minutes. Taste, and season with additional salt and crushed red pepper if necessary. Serve hot.

JEWISH-STYLE ARTICHOKES

Carciofi alla Giudia

Roman-style carciofi alla giudia *originated in the Jewish community in Rome, and I first tried them in the Jewish Quarter there in the early 1970s. They are great served by themselves, or as a side with lamb chops. People love to eat artichokes but do not like to clean and prepare them, so our guests are thrilled when they find them on the menu. But once you get the hang of it, artichokes are actually pretty easy to clean and prepare. Of course, making them when they are in peak season will give the most flavor.*

SERVES 4

Vegetable oil, for frying
2 lemons, halved, plus wedges for serving
4 young spring artichokes, with stems
Kosher salt
Freshly ground black pepper

Fill a large pot with oil deep enough to submerge the artichokes, and heat to 320 degrees.

Squeeze the lemons into a large bowl of water. Pull off the tough outer leaves of the artichokes, proceeding from the bottom to the top. With a serrated knife, cut off roughly the top third of each artichoke. Peel the stems, and place the artichokes in the lemon water until you have finished cleaning all the artichokes and are ready to cook them. Remove the artichokes from the water, drain well, and pat them dry with a towel. Take each artichoke by the stem, and press against a flat surface so that the leaves open up, using your fingers to help them if needed. There should not be much choke in a young artichoke; if there is, remove it with a spoon. Season the artichokes with salt and pepper.

Add as many artichokes to the pot with the oil as will fit (don't crowd them; you may have to do two batches). The artichokes will take about 10 to 12 minutes to cook, depending on size. Turn the artichokes in the oil as they fry, slowly increasing the heat during the first 7 to 8 minutes to 365 degrees. Continue to fry at 365 degrees until the artichokes are deep golden brown, and crisp and tender when pierced. Drain on paper towels and season with salt and pepper. Repeat with the remaining artichokes as needed. They can be served family-style, in the middle of the table on a long platter, or plated individually. Serve with lemon wedges.

WHOLE-WHEAT SPAETZLE

Spätzle di Farina Integrale

Spaetzle are dumplings that look like miniature gnocchi, made by pressing a sticky dough through a perforated tool right into boiling water. It is one of the simplest of all the techniques by which pasta is made. These whole-wheat spaetzle are especially delicious, dressed simply with butter and grated Grana Padano cheese, and make a good alternative to potatoes as a contorno accompanying roasts or braised meats. The key to making spaetzle is having the right tool or utensil, with holes large enough to let the dough pass through easily and quickly. You might have a colander that works, but there are spaeztle makers designed for the job. Often spaetzle are thought of as a German or Austrian food, but I ate them as a young girl, and they are still often found in the northeastern regions of Italy.

SERVES 6

2 large eggs
¾ to 1 cup whole milk
Kosher salt
¼ teaspoon freshly grated nutmeg
1¼ cups whole-wheat flour
½ cup all-purpose flour
3 tablespoons unsalted butter
¼ cup chopped fresh Italian parsley
Freshly ground black pepper
½ cup freshly grated Grana Padano

Whisk the eggs, ¾ cup milk, 1 teaspoon salt, and nutmeg together in a large bowl. Whisk in the flours to make a smooth dough. The dough should be thick, but still drip like a batter. If it is too thick, whisk in the remaining milk a tablespoon at a time to achieve the right consistency. Let the dough rest at room temperature for 30 minutes.

Meanwhile, bring a large pot of salted water to a boil. Fill the spaetzle maker, if using, with the batter, hold it over the pot, and force the dough through the holes into the water in small blobs. If you don't have a spaetzle maker, scoop or pour the batter into a colander and press it through the holes with a spatula.

Press all the batter into spaetzle, stirring occasionally so they don't stick together or sink to the bottom. Return the water to a steady, gentle boil, and cook for 4 or 5 minutes, until the spaetzle are all floating and cooked through; slice and taste one to check for doneness.

As the spaetzle cook, melt the butter in a large skillet over low heat. Scoop the cooked spaetzle out of the pot with a spider or large strainer, let drain for a moment, and add to the skillet. Still over low heat, toss the spaetzle to coat them all with butter and evaporate excess water. Add the parsley, and toss. Turn off the heat, season with salt and pepper, sprinkle the grated Grana Padano on top, and toss again. Serve. Spaetzle reheats well with the addition of some stock.

BUTTERNUT SQUASH PARMIGIANA

Parmigiana di Zucca

This side dish is typically served with Felidia's popular chicken pizzaiola in the fall and winter. Many adore eggplant Parmigiana, but this dish, which doesn't include eggs or flour, results in a much lighter version with a popular fall-and-winter ingredient, butternut squash. It's delicious by itself or next to any grilled or roasted piece of meat, such as chicken or pork. This dish looks best if you only use the neck of the squash, so look for squash with longer necks and smaller bulbs. You can save the bulbs to use for a soup or the filling for a stuffed pasta.

SERVES 4 TO 6

2½ cups prepared tomato sauce
2 butternut squash, peeled, cut lengthwise into ¼-inch-thick planks (about 8 slices from each squash)
Vegetable oil, for frying
Extra-virgin olive oil, for frying
Kosher salt
1 pound fresh mozzarella, thinly sliced into 16 slices
1 cup freshly grated Grana Padano
16 fresh basil leaves (or 1 for each slice of squash)

Preheat the oven to 425 degrees.

Warm the tomato sauce in a small saucepan. Pat the butternut-squash slices very dry with paper towels. Over medium heat, fill a large nonstick skillet with ½ inch of oil (equal parts vegetable and olive oil).

When a tip of a piece of squash sizzles when dipped in the oil, add half of the squash, and cook, turning once, until golden, about 2 minutes per side. Drain on paper towels, and season with salt. Repeat with the remaining squash.

Ladle enough tomato sauce into a 9-by-13-inch baking dish to cover the bottom, about 1 cup. Arrange the butternut squash in one layer (it is okay if they overlap), and top with the remaining 1½ cups sauce. Add a slice of mozzarella to each piece of squash, and sprinkle the grated Grana Padano over all. Top each slice of mozzarella with a basil leaf. Bake until the squash is tender and the cheese is browned and bubbly, about 20 minutes.

ESCAROLE *and* WHITE BEANS

Scarola e Fagioli Bianchi

This was one of the first dishes on the menu when we opened, and it is still a family favorite at home. These vegetables were typically served in a loose broth under stuffed calamari, but they are great on their own or with simply grilled calamari or octopus, and delicious with sautéed or grilled shrimp.

SERVES 6

1½ cups dried cannellini or other white beans, soaked overnight and drained
2 fresh bay leaves
½ cup extra-virgin olive oil, plus more for drizzling
Kosher salt
2 cloves garlic, crushed and peeled
2 whole dried peperoncini
8 cups packed coarsely shredded escarole leaves, preferably the tough outer leaves, washed and drained
1 cup prepared tomato sauce
3 tablespoons chopped fresh chives

Transfer the drained beans to a large Dutch oven. Pour in water to cover by 2 inches, add the bay leaves, and bring to a boil. Adjust the heat so the water is simmering, pour in ¼ cup of the olive oil, and cook until the beans are tender, about 1 hour. Drain the beans, reserving 1 cup cooking liquid. Season the beans to taste with salt and discard the bay leaves.

Wipe the Dutch oven dry, and add the remaining ¼ cup olive oil. Add the garlic and peperoncini, and cook until they are sizzling and golden, about 2 minutes. Add the escarole, and cook and stir until it begins to wilt, about 2 to 3 minutes. Add beans, tomato sauce, and reserved cooking liquid. Simmer until thick but still saucy, about 7 to 8 minutes. Season with salt, and sprinkle with the chives.

SAUTÉED ARTICHOKES *and* SUNCHOKES *with* PISTACHIOS

Carciofi e Topinambour al Burro con Pistacchi

If you have not tried sunchokes, this is a great way to introduce them to your repertoire. In Italy, I find they are most often used in the Piedmont region. At Felidia, we use these delicious tubers quite often while they're in season. By combining them with artichokes in a simple sauté, you create a great new vegetable side to share with your family and friends. If you want a richer version, grate a little Pecorino Toscano over them at the very end.

SERVES 6

1 lemon
6 small, firm artichokes (no more than 3 inches wide)
Kosher salt
Freshly ground black pepper
12 medium Jerusalem artichokes
2 tablespoons unsalted butter
2 tablespoons chopped fresh Italian parsley
3 tablespoons chopped pistachios, toasted

Squeeze the lemon into a large bowl of water. Pull off the tough outer leaves of the artichokes, proceeding from the bottom to the top. With a serrated knife, cut off roughly the top third of each artichoke. Peel the stems, and place the artichokes in the lemon water. Remove one of the artichokes from the water, drain it well, and pat it dry with a towel. Take it by the stem, and press against a flat surface so that the leaves open up, using your fingers to help them if needed. There should not be much choke in a young artichoke; if there is, remove it with a spoon. Repeat with the remaining artichokes. Season the artichokes with salt and pepper.

For the Jerusalem artichokes, don't peel them, but use a brush to wash them very well under water. Thinly slice both the artichokes (lengthwise) and the Jerusalem artichokes (crosswise).

Melt the butter in a large skillet over medium heat. Add the artichokes and Jerusalem artichokes, cover, and let sweat until they begin to wilt, about 5 minutes. Uncover, and cook until tender, about 10 minutes more. Add the chopped parsley, and season with salt.

Transfer to a serving dish, and top with the pistachios and several grinds of black pepper.

GRILLED ROMAINE CAESAR SALAD

Insalata Cesare alla Griglia

This variation on the ubiquitous salad is typically served with the pork chops Milanese (page 158) but also works well with any grilled piece of meat. The grill adds a smoky flavor to the romaine, and softens it so it is easy to cut through and wonderful to eat.

SERVES 6

2 cups ½-inch cubes day-old country bread
4 tablespoons red-wine vinegar
2 large hard-boiled egg yolks
1 large clove garlic, peeled
4 anchovy fillets
1 tablespoon Dijon mustard
⅓ cup extra-virgin olive oil, plus more for brushing the romaine
Kosher salt
Freshly ground black pepper
3 heads romaine hearts, trimmed, halved lengthwise
½ cup freshly shredded Grana Padano

Preheat a grill to medium-high heat (you can also use a grill pan) and the oven to 350 degrees.

Scatter bread cubes on a baking sheet, and toast until crisp throughout, about 8 to 10 minutes. Set croutons aside to cool.

In a mini–food processor, combine the vinegar, egg yolks, garlic, anchovies, and mustard. Process until smooth, scraping down the sides of the work bowl as needed. With the processor still running, pour the ⅓ cup oil through the feed tube to make a smooth dressing. Season with salt and pepper. If the dressing is too thick (you should be able to drizzle it from a spoon), add a tablespoon or so of water and process again.

Brush the romaine lightly with olive oil, and season with salt and pepper. Grill until the leaves are charred but not wilted, about 2 minutes per side, turning once. Put the romaine on a platter, and drizzle with the dressing. Sprinkle with the shredded Grana Padano and croutons, and serve immediately.

DESSERTS

As a young girl, I was always called to help knead the bread and work the dough, and ultimately to cut and shape the desserts we ate at home: sweet breads, cookies, fruit tarts, strudels, and fried dough. My first experience in a real bakery was in 1962, when I began to work in Walken's Bakery in Astoria, Queens, for Paul Walken, a German immigrant. Here I began learning about all kinds of desserts, such as cheesecake, napoleons, stollens, and éclairs. It was a weekend job, but I got my hands into the cream.

The desserts at Felidia have evolved over the years. Initially, most were in cake form and displayed on a large table by the bar, along with the antipasti. If you ordered the chocolate rigójancsi cake, you received a fairly oversized slice with zabaglione sauce. There was a large fruit crostata with pastry cream, which was Tanya's favorite, and of course tiramisù. Diners can still find the tiramisù, although it has gone through quite a few iterations since the early 1980s. Today the desserts are individually plated with a more elaborate presentation, more flavor elements in each dessert, and usually some contrast, whether it be sweet and sour or crunchy and creamy. Dessert has come a long way in all restaurants in the past four decades. Often at Felidia, desserts are Italian classics with American twists or ingredients, such as a peach tiramisù when stone fruit is in season, or meringue served with local strawberries and passion-fruit sorbet—something classic and something modern.

WARM CHOCOLATE-HAZELNUT FLAN

Sformato di Nutella

Nutella is to Italians what peanut butter is to Americans. It is incorporated into a lot of desserts such as crêpes, cakes, and much more. Many Italian children eat Nutella on toast in the morning before heading off to school. The chocolate-hazelnut combination is undeniably good and works really well in many desserts. Since the flavor is so pervasive in Italian sweets, it only made sense to use it in a dessert that would have typically been made with just chocolate. Lidia is not an avid fan of chocolate desserts, but I won her over with this take on flan.

—Chef Nicotra

SERVES 6

4 tablespoons unsalted butter, plus melted butter for the ramekins
Turbinado sugar, for lining the ramekins
4 ounces bittersweet chocolate, chopped
⅓ cup chocolate-hazelnut spread
2 large eggs, separated
½ cup confectioners' sugar
2 teaspoons cornstarch

Brush six 5-ounce ramekins with melted butter. Line the bottoms and sides with turbinado sugar. Preheat the oven to 350 degrees.

Melt the chocolate and 4 tablespoons butter in a double boiler. When it's melted, add the chocolate-hazelnut spread, and stir until smooth. Let cool slightly.

In an electric mixer fitted with the paddle attachment, beat the egg yolks and ¼ cup of the confectioners' sugar until pale and fluffy. With the mixer at low speed, pour in the melted chocolate mixture and mix until smooth.

In a separate mixer bowl, combine the egg whites, remaining ¼ cup confectioners' sugar, and cornstarch. Whisk at high speed until the whites form stiff peaks. Fold about a third of the whites into the chocolate mixture to lighten it. Gently fold in the remaining whites until just combined. Divide the mixture among the ramekins. Place them on a baking sheet, and bake until the flans are puffed and set, about 17 to 20 minutes. Serve right away.

You can serve these in the individual ramekins, like a soufflé, or you can unmold them onto small serving plates. Vanilla, hazelnut, fudge-swirl, or white-chocolate ice cream works well with this dessert. You can also serve it with unsweetened whipped cream.

PECAN TART

Crostata di Pecan

Both the gluten-free and the regular crust options of this "grande finale" dish are listed here. Pecans are not often found in Italy, but are much loved by Americans, and this hybrid dessert at Felidia is a favorite. It is another example of how we take American ingredients and make something Italian with them.

SERVES 8

For the Gluten-Free Crust
(for a non-gluten-free version, see opposite)
1¼ cups gluten-free flour blend, plus more for rolling
2 tablespoons granulated sugar
½ teaspoon xanthan gum
¼ teaspoon kosher salt
6 tablespoons unsalted butter, cold, cut into pieces
1 large egg, beaten

For the Filling
2 large eggs
½ cup light corn syrup
½ cup dark corn syrup (or pure maple syrup)
¼ cup light brown sugar
3 tablespoons unsalted butter, melted and cooled
1 teaspoon pure vanilla extract
¼ teaspoon kosher salt
1½ cups coarsely chopped pecans

For the crust, combine the flour blend, sugar, xanthan gum, and salt in a food processor, and pulse several times to combine. Add the butter, and pulse until the bits of butter are the size of oatmeal. Drizzle in the egg, and pulse until incorporated. See if the dough will clump together when pressed with your fingers. If it doesn't, add up to 3 tablespoons water, a tablespoon at a time, pulsing in between additions. Once you can clump the dough together in a ball, dump it onto the counter, press it into a disk, and wrap it in plastic wrap. Chill in the refrigerator for 30 minutes.

Preheat the oven to 375 degrees.

Lightly flour the disk of dough, and roll between two pieces of parchment paper to get about a 12-inch circle. Lay it in a 9-inch fluted tart pan, and trim to fit. Chill for 30 minutes.

Line the chilled crust with a sheet of parchment paper. Fill with pie weights or dried beans. Bake until the crust is set but still blond, about 18 to 20 minutes. Carefully remove weights or beans and parchment paper and bake until pale gold, 5 to 7 minutes more.

Once the crust has been blind-baked, make the filling. Reduce oven temperature to 350 degrees. Whisk the eggs in a large bowl. Add both corn syrups, the brown sugar, melted butter, vanilla, and salt, and whisk until smooth. Stir in the pecans. Pour the filling into the crust, and set on a foil-lined baking sheet (for easier cleanup, in case there are drips). Bake on the bottom rack of the oven until the edges of the crust are golden and the filling is set, 20 to 25 minutes. Cool on a rack before serving.

To serve, cut the tart from the center to the border into eight individual pieces. Serve on individual plates with vanilla ice cream, or even walnut or banana ice cream. You can also add toasted pecans for crunch. At Felidia, this is served with bourbon-and-artisanal-maple-syrup ice cream.

Traditional Crust

1 cup plus 4 tablespoons all-purpose flour, plus more for rolling
2 tablespoons granulated sugar
½ teaspoon baking powder
¼ teaspoon kosher salt
1 stick (8 tablespoons) unsalted butter, cold, cut into pieces
2 large egg yolks

Combine the flour, sugar, baking powder, and salt in a food processor, and pulse several times to combine. Add the butter, and pulse until it's in pieces the size of oatmeal. Drizzle in the egg yolks, and pulse until incorporated. See if the dough will clump together when pressed with your fingers. If it doesn't, add up to 3 tablespoons water, a tablespoon at a time, pulsing in between additions. Once you can clump the dough together in a ball, dump it onto the counter, press it into a disk, and wrap it in plastic wrap. Chill, roll, and blind-bake as for the gluten-free crust.

ALMOND *and* CHOCOLATE TART CAPRESE

Torta Caprese

One of Chef Nicotra's creations, this is a deliciously moist chocolate dessert that is easy to make and keeps well for several days. The crackly, flourless top gives way to a rich, fudgy interior when you slice into it.

SERVES 8 TO 10

1¼ cups sliced blanched almonds, toasted
1 stick unsalted butter, plus more for greasing the baking dish
2 tablespoons dried breadcrumbs
8 ounces bittersweet chocolate, chopped
4 large eggs, at room temperature, separated
1 cup granulated sugar
Zest of 1 orange, grated
2 tablespoons rum or amaro
1 teaspoon pure vanilla extract
¼ teaspoon kosher salt
Confectioners' sugar, for garnish

Preheat the oven to 350 degrees.

In a food processor, grind the almonds until fine but not clumpy. Grease a 9-inch springform pan with butter, and sprinkle with the breadcrumbs. Coat the bottom and sides of the pan with the breadcrumbs, and tap out any excess. Combine the chocolate and 1 stick butter in a double boiler set over simmering water, and melt over low heat. Stir to combine, and let cool slightly.

In an electric mixer fitted with the paddle attachment, whisk the egg yolks and ¾ cup of the granulated sugar at medium-high speed until thick and pale gold in color, about 2 minutes. Beat in the orange zest, the rum or amaro, the vanilla, and the salt. At low speed, beat in the cooled chocolate mixture just until smooth. Fold in the ground almonds.

In the mixer, in a clean bowl fitted with the whisk attachment, whisk the egg whites and remaining ¼ cup sugar to stiff peaks. Stir a third of the whites into the chocolate mixture to lighten it, then gently fold in the rest. Spread into the prepared pan, and bake until the top is firm and crackly (a toothpick will come out with some thick batter still on it), about 35 to 40 minutes.

Let the cake cool on a rack for 5 minutes, run a knife around the edge to loosen it, and unmold. Serve sprinkled with confectioners' sugar.

BLUEBERRY APRICOT FRANGIPANE TART

Crostata di Mirtilli ed Albicocche al Frangipane

This tart can be made with many different seasonal fruits, such as berries, other stone fruit, or apples or pears. Italians are big fans of fruit desserts and love crostate. During the early days at Felidia, we always had a fruit crostata on the menu, but it usually involved pastry cream with fresh sliced fruit fanned out on top of the cream. This was one of Tanya's favorites, but I prefer a much simpler tart. The fruit tarts today at Felidia are not as sweet and do not have cream; rather, the fruit is baked into the crust, imparting all of the natural juices and giving the dessert just enough sugar. The fruit crostate today reflect evolving tastes toward less sugary desserts.

SERVES 8

For the Crust

1½ cups all-purpose flour, plus more for rolling the dough
¼ cup sugar
½ teaspoon baking powder
Pinch of kosher salt
1 stick (8 tablespoons) unsalted butter, cold, cut into bits
Zest of 1 lemon, grated
1 large egg yolk

For the Filling

½ cup apricot jam
1 stick (8 tablespoons) unsalted butter, softened
½ cup sugar
2 large eggs
1 teaspoon pure vanilla extract
1¼ cups almond meal (ground almonds)
2 tablespoons all-purpose flour
6 apricots, pitted, and quartered or sliced
½ cup blueberries

For the crust, combine the flour, sugar, baking powder, and salt in the work bowl of a food processor. Pulse to combine. Add in the butter pieces and lemon zest, and pulse until they are about the size of peas. Add the egg yolk and a tablespoon of ice water, and pulse until the dough just comes together (it should clump when pressed with your fingers, but shouldn't be wet). If the dough doesn't come together, continue to add water, a tablespoon at a time, and pulse quickly until it does (you may need up to 3 to 4 tablespoons of water all together). Dump the dough onto the counter, press it into a disk, and wrap it in plastic. Let it rest in the refrigerator for 1 hour. (The dough can also be made a day ahead, but let it sit out of the fridge for 10 minutes or so to soften a bit before trying to roll it.)

Dust the dough with flour, and roll out into about a 12-inch round. Transfer to a 9-inch tart pan and press into the pan. Roll the rolling pin over the edges of the pan to trim any excess dough. Chill the tart shell for 30 minutes. Meanwhile, preheat the oven to 375 degrees.

Line the chilled shell with parchment paper, and fill with pie weights or dried beans. Bake on the middle rack until set but not colored, about 20 minutes. Remove the parchment paper and weights or beans, and bake until the edges are just beginning to turn golden, about 5 minutes. Cool on a rack. Reduce the oven temperature to 350 degrees.

For the filling, warm the jam in a small saucepan until melted, then strain to make a smooth glaze for brushing. Combine the butter and sugar in a food processor, and process until light and smooth, about 30 seconds, scraping down the sides a few times. Add the eggs and vanilla, and process until smooth. Add the almond meal and flour, and pulse again until smooth.

Brush the cooled crust with about half of the jam glaze. Spread the filling into the crust, and arrange the apricots and blueberries as you like. Bake until the crust is golden on the edges and the filling is lightly browned and set, about 35 minutes. Let cool on a rack for 15 minutes, then rewarm the remaining strained jam, and brush it all over the tart.

Serve slightly warm or at room temperature. Cut the tart into eight equal slices, and serve on individual small plates with any sort of berry sorbet. At Felidia, this dessert is sometimes served with poached apricots and with blueberry coulis.

ALMOST *a* TIRAMISÙ

Quasi un Tiramisù

Tiramisù is typically made from simple leftovers. Coffee, cake or cookies, and cream or mascarpone come together to create one of Italy's most famous and delicious desserts. Though it all sounds simple, a good tiramisù has to be just moist enough without being soggy, and just cakey enough without being dry. We serve all different types of tiramisù, depending on the season. There's a classic tiramisù, of course, as well as peach, squash, limoncello, and chocolate-hazelnut versions. When we change an ingredient, such as adding shavings of chocolate or playing slightly with the technique, like whipping the mascarpone to make it lighter, we call it "quasi un tiramisù," or "almost a tiramisù," no matter what the flavor, since it does not exactly follow the traditional recipe.

SERVES 10 OR MORE

2 cups heavy cream
2 cups mascarpone, at room temperature
1 cup confectioners' sugar
½ cup chocolate-hazelnut spread
2 cups freshly brewed espresso
½ cup granulated sugar
½ cup coffee liqueur
24 Savoiardi cookies (ladyfingers), broken in half
½ cup chopped toasted hazelnuts
2 ounces bittersweet chocolate

Whisk the heavy cream to soft peaks in an electric mixer fitted with the whisk attachment, about 1 minute. Be careful to not overwhip: you will be whisking again, with the mascarpone.

In a separate mixer bowl, whisk the mascarpone with the paddle attachment at medium speed until smooth, about 1 minute. Sift in the confectioners' sugar, and beat until smooth. Switch to the whisk attachment, add the whipped cream, and whisk until the mixture is just combined and smooth.

Pour half of the mixture into a separate bowl. Add the chocolate-hazelnut spread to the half still in the mixer, and whisk until smooth. You now have one bowl of traditional tiramisù mixture, and another bowl of a mixture of chocolate-hazelnut spread and tiramisù.

In a medium saucepan, combine the espresso and granulated sugar over low heat. Cook until the sugar has dissolved, stir, then remove from the heat and stir in the coffee liqueur. Pour the espresso mixture into a shallow pan.

To serve, add a tablespoonful or so of the traditional tiramisù mixture to serving glasses or bowls. Soak some of the Savoiardi in the espresso mixture, four or five at a time so they don't get too soggy, and add one Savoiardi on top of each, followed by a tablespoonful or so of the chocolate-hazelnut tiramisù mixture. Sprinkle a teaspoon of hazelnuts on top, followed by another soaked Savoiardi. Repeat this soaking and layering process another three or four times, depending on the size of your glass. Using a fine cheese-grater, finish with a shaving of bittersweet chocolate on the top of each tiramisù and serve.

VARIATION: If you would like to serve the tiramisù family-style, it can be layered as follows in an 8-by-8-inch glass or ceramic baking dish. Pack the bottom with twelve soaked Savoiardi. Spread over this all of the chocolate-hazelnut tiramisù mixture. Sprinkle with all of the hazelnuts. Add another layer of twelve soaked Savoiardi, then spread with the traditional tiramisù mixture. Grate the chocolate over this, and chill at least 2 hours before serving.

LIMONCELLO TIRAMISÙ

Tiramisù al Limoncello

At Felidia, we serve several different versions of tiramisù. This version, with limoncello, is a bit higher in alcohol content and is inspired by the traditional delizia al limone *that is so popular along the Amalfi Coast.*

SERVES 12 OR MORE

5 or 6 lemons
1⅓ cups limoncello liqueur
1 cup sugar
5 large eggs, separated
1 pound (2 cups) mascarpone, at room temperature
40 Savoiardi cookies (ladyfingers), or more as needed
Candied lemon peel, for serving (optional)

Remove the zest of two or more of the lemons, using a fine grater, to get 2 tablespoons of zest. Squeeze out and strain all five or six lemons to get ¾ cup fresh lemon juice.

For the soaking syrup, combine the lemon juice, 1 cup of the limoncello, 1 cup water, and ½ cup sugar in a small saucepan. Bring to a simmer, just to dissolve the sugar. Transfer to a shallow pan, and let cool completely.

For the zabaglione, bring a medium saucepan of water to a simmer. Put the egg yolks in a metal bowl that is large enough so it will fit on top of the saucepan, to make a double boiler. Off the heat, combine the yolks and ¼ cup of the sugar. Whip with a handheld electric mixer at high speed until the mixture is thick, pale, and fluffy, about 3 minutes. At low speed, slowly add the remaining limoncello. Once all of the limoncello is added, whip at high speed again, to aerate and incorporate it, about 30 seconds.

Set the bowl over the simmering water and whisk the egg yolks constantly with a balloon whisk, being sure to whisk the entire contents of the bowl to avoid getting pockets of scrambled eggs, until the mixture is very thick and forms ribbons that slowly melt back into itself when you lift the whisk from the zabaglione, about 7 to 8 minutes. Remove from heat, and whisk until cooled, about 2 minutes.

In another large bowl, stir the mascarpone with a wooden spoon to soften it, drop in the grated lemon zest, and beat it until light and creamy. In another bowl (or in an electric mixer), whip the egg whites with the remaining ¼ cup sugar until the mixture holds moderately firm peaks. When the zabaglione is cooled, scrape about a third of it over the mascarpone, and fold it in with a large rubber spatula.

Fold in the rest of the zabaglione in two or three additions. Now fold in the whipped egg whites in several additions, until the limoncello-mascarpone cream is light and evenly blended. One at a time, roll a ladyfinger in the cooled syrup, and quickly place it in a 9-by-13-inch Pyrex pan. Wet each cookie briefly—if it soaks up too much syrup, it will fall apart. Arrange the moistened Savoiardi in neat, tight rows in the pan, filling the bottom of the pan completely. You should be able to fit about twenty Savoiardi in a single layer.

Cover the Savoiardi with half of the limoncello-mascarpone cream in a smooth layer. Dip and arrange a second layer of Savoiardi in the pan, and cover it completely with the remainder of the cream. Smooth the cream with a spatula, and seal the tiramisù airtight in plastic wrap. Refrigerate for 6 hours or up to 2 days, or put it in the freezer for 2 hours, before serving.

To serve, cut portions of tiramisù in any size you like, and lift them out of the pan onto dessert plates. It looks great served with a bit of candied lemon peel on top.

PEANUT BUTTER *and* JELLY PALACINKE (CRÊPES)

Palacinke con Marmellata e Burro di Arachidi

Palacinke (or crêpes) have been on the Felidia dessert menu from the first day. I originally served them with rosehip jam, which is how I ate them as a child. Felix, my husband, often made a tableside show in the dining room of flaming the palacinke with Grand Marnier or grappa. They were served with chocolate sauce and hazelnuts, and sometimes with strawberries and cream. The versatility of palacinke is never-ending. Chef Nicotra was introduced to peanut-butter-and-jelly sandwiches when he and his wife, who grew up in West Virginia, attended her family reunion. This only child from Sicily was all of a sudden surrounded by ten new nephews and nieces between the ages of three and eighteen, and these sandwiches were part of lunchtime. He took the combination and brought it back to Felidia, serving my palacinke during the early-fall months with Concord-grape jam and peanut butter.

MAKES 12 PALACINKE, SERVING 6

For the Crêpes
1 large egg
2 tablespoons sugar
Pinch of kosher salt
1¼ cups whole milk
¾ cup all-purpose flour
1 teaspoon freshly grated lemon zest
1 teaspoon freshly grated orange zest
Melted butter, for cooking the crêpes

For Filling and Finishing
3 ounces chopped bittersweet chocolate
1½ cups heavy cream
¾ cup chunky peanut butter
¾ cup Concord-grape jam
4 tablespoons unsalted butter
Sugar, for sprinkling

For the crêpes, whisk the egg, sugar, and salt in a medium bowl. Whisk in the milk until combined. Mix in the flour, to make a smooth batter, then stir in the zests. The batter should have the consistency of melted ice cream. Cover, and let it rest in the refrigerator for 30 minutes.

To cook the crêpes, brush an 8-inch nonstick skillet with melted butter. Pour in a scant 3 tablespoons of batter, and, off heat, turn the pan to coat the bottom evenly. Return to the heat, reduce the flame to moderate, and cook the crêpe until lightly browned, about 30 seconds to 1 minute. Flip it carefully with a spatula, and cook the second side until brown spots appear, about 30 seconds. Remove from the pan, and repeat the process with the remaining batter, to make 12 crêpes in all.

To finish, combine the chocolate and ½ cup cream in a bowl, and microwave at 50 percent power in 30-second intervals, stirring in between, until the mixture is melted, about 1½ minutes. Stir until smooth. In a medium bowl, whip the remaining 1 cup cream to soft peaks.

Lay the crêpes out on your work surface. Fill the center of each with peanut butter and jelly (about 1 tablespoon). Fold in half, then in half again, to form a triangular shape. Heat a large nonstick skillet over medium heat. Melt half of the butter, and add six of the folded crêpes. Turn the pan to coat the bottom of the crêpes in the butter. Sprinkle the tops with sugar and flip to caramelize, about 30 seconds to 1 minute. Repeat with the remaining butter and crêpes. Serve 2 crêpes, sugared side up, per plate, drizzled with the chocolate sauce and topped with the whipped cream.

OPEN CANNOLO

Cannolo Aperto

Chef Nicotra created this dish when he was working at the helm of the Michelin-starred restaurants Villa Marchese and Villa Speranza in Sicily. It is the most-ordered dessert whenever it appears on the Felidia menu.

SERVES 6

2 cups homemade ricotta (about 1 pound) (see page 44)
1½ cups all-purpose flour
2 tablespoons granulated sugar
¼ teaspoon kosher salt
2 tablespoons extra-virgin olive oil
1 teaspoon white vinegar
⅓ cup dry red wine, or more as needed
¾ cup confectioners' sugar, plus more for garnish
3 tablespoons chopped bittersweet chocolate
3 tablespoons finely chopped candied orange peel, plus more for garnish
3 tablespoons chopped pistachios, toasted, plus more for garnish
Vegetable oil, for frying
Honey, for drizzling

Spoon the ricotta into a large fine-mesh sieve, or a colander lined with a double-folded cheesecloth or a basket-type coffee filter. Place the sieve or colander over a bowl, and cover with plastic wrap. Allow the ricotta to drain in the refrigerator at least overnight, or up to 24 hours. Discard the liquid in the bottom of the bowl.

For the dough, combine the flour, granulated sugar, and salt in the work bowl of a food processor fitted with the metal blade. Add the oil, vinegar, and ⅓ cup wine. Process the dough, adding more red wine a few drops at a time if necessary, until the dough is smooth and supple and comes together on the blade. Wrap the dough in plastic wrap, and refrigerate for at least 2 hours or up to overnight.

For the filling, combine the drained ricotta and ¾ cup confectioners' sugar in a mixing bowl. Beat with a handheld electric mixer until the mixture is light and fluffy, about 2 minutes. Fold in the chocolate, orange peel, and pistachios. Store in the refrigerator until needed.

On a lightly floured surface, roll out half the dough to 1/16 inch thick, about the thickness of a dime. Cut the dough into 2-inch rounds, and transfer them to a lightly floured kitchen towel. Repeat with the other half of the dough. Gather the scraps together, reroll them, and cut as many rounds as possible. You should have about twenty-four. Poke each circle with a fork a few times so it doesn't puff when fried. Let the dough rest at least 15 minutes before continuing. (You can also cut the dough into quarters and run it through a pasta machine at the next-to-last setting.)

Pour enough of the oil into a large, heavy skillet to fill to about 1 inch, and heat to 350 degrees, measuring with a deep-fry thermometer. Add as many rounds of the dough to the oil as will fit

(recipe continues)

without touching one another. Fry, turning the cannoli once, until both sides are golden brown, about 2 minutes total.

Transfer the cooked cannoli to paper towels to drain, and fry the remaining rounds, waiting for the oil to reheat as necessary. Cool the cannoli completely before continuing.

To assemble the cannoli, place a circle of the fried dough in the center of a serving plate, and top with a scant 2 tablespoons of the ricotta filling. Place another circle of dough on top, followed by another 2 tablespoons of the ricotta filling, and then another dough circle. Make 5 more stacks of cannoli in the same way. Drizzle honey over each, and sprinkle with confectioners' sugar. Sprinkle some of the chopped toasted pistachios and orange peel around the cannoli.

HONEY ALMOND ICE CREAM

Gelato alle Mandorle e Miele

This is one of Chef Nicotra's favorite flavors of ice cream, and it pairs well with many of the desserts at Felidia. Honey and almond are a natural combination, often found together in desserts in Sicily. I enjoy both flavors immensely, and, put together like this, they make for a wonderful creamy treat.

SERVES 4 TO 6

2 cups heavy cream
1 cup whole milk
½ cup sugar
1 vanilla bean, split lengthwise
¼ teaspoon kosher salt
5 large egg yolks
⅓ cup honey, plus more for drizzling
¼ teaspoon almond extract
½ cup roughly chopped toasted almonds

Combine the cream, milk, and ¼ cup of the sugar in a medium saucepan. Scrape in the seeds of the vanilla bean, and add the salt. Bring to a simmer over medium heat to dissolve the sugar.

Whisk the egg yolks and remaining ¼ cup sugar in a medium bowl. Slowly pour in the cream-milk mixture, whisking constantly. Once it's all combined, pour it back into the saucepan and set over medium-low heat. Cook, stirring constantly, until the mixture has thickened and coats the back of a wooden spoon, about 8 to 10 minutes.

Strain the mixture through a fine sieve into a clean bowl or container, and stir in the honey and almond extract. Refrigerate until cold, at least 3 hours, stirring occasionally.

Transfer the mixture to an ice-cream machine, and churn according to the manufacturer's instructions, adding the almonds in the last minute. Transfer to a quart container, cover, and freeze until scoopable, 2 hours or more. Serve with a drizzle of honey and some toasted almond slices.

STRAWBERRY YOGURT ICE CREAM

Gelato allo Yogurt e Fragole

The homemade ice creams that complement our seasonal and ever-changing dessert menu are well known at Felidia. In the early years, we served the more common flavors of Italian ice cream: chocolate, vanilla, and hazelnut. Now there are often many more options, such as seasonal fruit sorbets and light yogurt creams. This is a versatile one that can be made easily at home (it is, of course, best when strawberries are in season).

SERVES 4 TO 6

8 ounces very ripe strawberries, hulled and halved
¾ cup sugar
2 teaspoons freshly squeezed lemon juice
1 cup whole-milk Greek yogurt
1 cup heavy cream
1 cup whole milk
Pinch of kosher salt
4 large egg yolks
1 teaspoon pure vanilla extract
Sliced strawberries
Honey, for drizzling

Combine the halved strawberries, ¼ cup of the sugar, and the lemon juice in a medium bowl. Let sit at room temperature for 30 minutes, then mash with a potato masher. Combine the mashed strawberries and yogurt in a blender, and blend until smooth. Refrigerate while you make the ice-cream base.

Combine the cream, milk, ¼ cup of the sugar, and the salt in a medium saucepan. Bring to a simmer over medium heat to dissolve the sugar.

Whisk the egg yolks and remaining ¼ cup sugar in a medium bowl. Slowly pour in the cream-milk mixture, whisking constantly. Once it's all combined, pour it back into the saucepan and set over medium-low heat. Cook, stirring constantly, until the mixture is thickened and coats the back of a wooden spoon, about 8 to 10 minutes.

Strain the mixture through a fine sieve into a clean bowl or container, and stir in the vanilla and the yogurt mixture. Refrigerate until cold, at least 3 hours, stirring occasionally.

Transfer the mixture to an ice-cream machine, and churn according to the manufacturer's instructions. Transfer to a quart container, cover, and freeze until scoopable, 2 hours or more. Serve with some fresh sliced strawberries and a drizzle of honey.

PISTACHIO BRITTLE

Croccantino al Pistacchio

This crunchy delight is simplicity at its best: just two ingredients. If you want to splurge and give it an extra kick, buy the fabulously flavorful pistachios from Bronte, a small town in Sicily. Bronte pistachios can be found in Italian specialty-food stores and on the Internet. They are deemed the best pistachio in Italy.

SERVES 12

2 cups sugar
1½ cups shelled salted pistachios

Line a rimmed baking sheet with a silicone baking mat.

Spread the sugar in the bottom of a medium saucepan, and drizzle over it ½ cup water, to make the sugar look like wet sand. Set the saucepan over medium heat and cook, without stirring, until the sugar is melted and turns a deep-caramel color, about 7 to 8 minutes. (Resist the urge to stir, but you can swirl the pan if the sugar is coloring unevenly, and wash down the sides with a pastry brush dipped in water if the sugar crystallizes on the edges.)

Once the caramel is ready, remove it from the heat and quickly stir in the pistachios. Pour the mixture onto the prepared baking sheet, and spread flat. Let harden, about 30 minutes, then break into pieces.

CHOCOLATE ESPRESSO COOKIES

Biscotti al Cioccolato e Caffè

Guests at Felidia have come to love the small cookie treats served with coffee at the end of a meal, a tradition that started when Chef Nicotra became chef. The selection varies, but these crispy chocolate-espresso cookies can always be found on the table. They complement an Italian espresso. Dutch cocoa imparts a rich dark-chocolate color, but any dark cocoa will do.

MAKES ABOUT 48 COOKIES

1 cup all-purpose flour
½ cup Dutch-process cocoa powder
1 tablespoon espresso powder
½ teaspoon baking powder
¼ teaspoon baking soda
¼ teaspoon kosher salt
1 stick (8 tablespoons) unsalted butter, at room temperature
1 cup sugar
1 large egg
1 teaspoon pure vanilla extract

Stir the flour, cocoa, espresso powder, baking powder, baking soda, and salt together in a medium bowl.

Cream the butter and sugar in an electric mixer fitted with the paddle attachment at medium-high speed until light, about 2 minutes. Add the egg and vanilla, and beat until well combined, about 1 minute. Add the flour mixture, and beat at low speed until the mixture just comes together to form a dough.

Divide the dough into two equal pieces. Roll one piece into a squarish log, 1 inch in diameter and 8 to 9 inches long. Set it on a double-folded piece of plastic wrap, and roll up. Roll the plastic wrap around the log, and secure the ends. Roll on the counter to reshape it into a log, if needed. Repeat with the remaining dough. Freeze until the logs are firm, about 1 to 2 hours.

Preheat the oven to 350 degrees. Line two baking sheets with parchment paper.

Unwrap one log, and cut it into scant ¼-inch-thick slices. Place these on the baking sheets, about an inch apart. Repeat with the remaining log (or save that one for another time, if you don't want to make the whole batch; it will keep in the freezer for several weeks). Bake, rotating the trays from top to bottom once, halfway through the baking time, until the cookies are crisp throughout, about 10 to 11 minutes. Allow them to cool on racks.

CRANBERRY NUT BISCOTTI

Biscotti di Cranberries, Pistacchio e Mandorle

Cranberries are not something one finds in Italy very easily, but this fall fruit was welcomed onto the Felidia menu by Chef Nicotra. Their tart quality goes well with the nuts to make an Italian favorite, biscotti, with an American twist. You can also use dried cherries or dried currants. I love a simple crunchy biscotto or two to dunk in my espresso after I finish lunch at Felidia. It is a perfect small sweet bite to end the meal.

MAKES 30 BISCOTTI

2¼ cups all-purpose flour
1 teaspoon baking powder
½ teaspoon ground cinnamon
½ teaspoon kosher salt
6 tablespoons unsalted butter, at room temperature
1 cup sugar
2 large eggs
1 teaspoon pure vanilla extract
Zest of 1 small orange, grated
½ cup dried cranberries
⅓ cup salted pistachios
⅓ cup slivered almonds

Preheat the oven to 350 degrees. Line a baking sheet with parchment paper.

Sift the flour, baking powder, cinnamon, and salt together in a medium bowl.

Combine the butter and sugar in the bowl of an electric mixer fitted with the paddle attachment. Beat at medium-high speed until light and fluffy, about 2 minutes. Add the eggs one at a time, making sure each one is incorporated before adding the next. Beat in the vanilla and orange zest. Add the flour mixture, beat at low speed until just incorporated, then stir in the cranberries and nuts.

Divide the dough in half, and form into two logs, 2 inches in diameter and 10 inches long; set them about 3 inches apart on the prepared baking sheet. Bake until the logs are puffed, pale gold, and just cooked through, about 25 minutes. Let them cool slightly on the baking sheet, and reduce the oven temperature to 300 degrees.

Once the logs are cool enough to handle, cut them with a serrated knife into ½-inch-thick biscotti. Spread the biscotti in one layer on the baking sheet, and bake, flipping them once, until crisp throughout, about 15 to 20 minutes. Let cool on the baking sheet.

POLENTA CURRANT COOKIES

Zaletti

These rustic cornmeal cookies from the Veneto region of Italy are a perfect accompaniment to ice cream or an espresso. The contrast of the crispy cookie and chewy currants is delightful. Preparing a wide selection of cookies daily creates an extra challenge for the pastry kitchen, but guests enjoy the cookie plate so much that it has become a Felidia tradition.

MAKES ABOUT 48

¾ cup dried currants
¼ cup dark rum
1 cup all-purpose flour
¾ cup fine polenta
1 teaspoon baking powder
¼ teaspoon kosher salt
1 stick (8 tablespoons) unsalted butter, at room temperature
¾ cup sugar
1 large egg
2 teaspoons pure vanilla extract

Combine the currants and rum in a small bowl, set aside to let the currants plump, about 15 minutes, then drain off the excess rum. Stir the flour, polenta, baking powder, and salt together in a medium bowl.

Cream the butter and sugar in an electric mixer fitted with the paddle attachment at medium-high speed until light and fluffy, about 1 to 2 minutes. Add the egg and vanilla, and beat until well combined, about 1 minute. Add the flour mixture, and beat at low speed until the mixture just comes together to form a dough. Add the currants, and mix just to distribute them evenly.

Divide the dough into two equal pieces. Roll one piece into a log 1 inch in diameter and 8 to 9 inches long. Set it on a double-folded piece of plastic wrap, and roll up. Roll the plastic wrap around the log, and secure the ends. Roll on the counter to reshape it into a log, if needed. Repeat with the remaining dough. Freeze until the log is firm, about 1 to 2 hours.

Preheat the oven to 350 degrees. Line two baking sheets with parchment paper.

Unwrap one log, and cut it into scant ¼-inch-thick slices. Place on the baking sheets, about an inch apart. Repeat with the remaining log (or save that one for another time, if you don't want to make the whole batch; it will keep in the freezer for several weeks). Bake, rotating the trays from top to bottom once, halfway through the baking time, until the cookies are crisp throughout, about 10 to 11 minutes. Allow them to cool on racks.

PISTACHIO COOKIES

Paste di Mandorle al Pistacchio

These cookies are full of Sicilian flavors. Bronte pistachios are famous in Sicily, and pasta di mandorle is a typical base for many cookies there. It's been a favorite ever since Chef Nicotra added it to the cookie platter. You can also omit filling the cookies with jam and serve them as is.

MAKES ABOUT 30

8 ounces almond paste
¾ cup sugar
3 tablespoons pistachio paste
2 large egg whites, beaten
Pinch of kosher salt
⅓ cup all-purpose flour
¼ cup almond meal
Red currant jelly, for filling

Break the almond paste into a food processor. Add the sugar and pistachio paste, and pulse until combined. Add the egg whites and salt, and process to make a smooth paste. Add the flour and almond meal, and process until very thick and smooth. Scrape into a bowl, and chill until firm, about 1 hour.

Preheat the oven to 350 degrees, and line two baking sheets with parchment paper.

With wet hands, roll the dough into balls or squares slightly less than 1 inch in diameter. Arrange them on the baking sheets with 2 inches between them. Bake, rotating the trays from top to bottom once, halfway through the baking time, until the balls or squares are puffed and golden on the edges, 17 to 20 minutes.

Immediately press a small indentation in the top of each cookie with the back of a teaspoon-sized measuring spoon. Let the cookies cool on racks, and fill the indentations with the jelly.

VARIATION: Omit the jam, and simply dust the cookies with confectioners' sugar.

ITALIAN MERINGUES

Meringa all'Italiana

These meringues are light, airy, and not too sweet, and can add a touch of sophistication to many different desserts. But they are just as delicious by themselves, too.

MAKES ABOUT 100 TO 120 VERY SMALL MERINGUES

1 cup sugar
4 large egg whites, at room temperature
Pinch of kosher salt
2 teaspoons freshly grated lemon zest
2 teaspoons freshly squeezed lemon juice
½ teaspoon pure vanilla extract

Preheat the oven to 225 degrees. Line two baking sheets with parchment paper. Fit a large pastry bag with a large star tip.

Combine the sugar and ¼ cup water in a small saucepan, and bring to a boil. Boil, without stirring, until the mixture reaches 240 degrees (soft-ball stage) on a candy thermometer.

Meanwhile, in an electric mixer fitted with the paddle attachment, beat the egg whites and a pinch of salt at high speed to form soft peaks. (If the whites reach soft peaks before the sugar is at 240 degrees, turn the speed to low but keep mixing, so they don't deflate.)

As soon as the sugar reaches 240 degrees, remove it from the heat and, with the mixer at medium low, add the sugar syrup to the whites in a slow stream. (Take care here not to add the syrup too quickly, which might cook the whites; also, let the syrup slide in along the side of the bowl, not directly onto the whisk or whites.)

Once all of the syrup is incorporated, increase the speed to high, and beat until the whites are very thick and glossy and the bottom of the bowl is no longer warm, about 3 to 4 minutes. Beat in the lemon zest and juice and the vanilla, just to combine.

Transfer the mixture to the pastry bag, and pipe small rosettes (1 inch in diameter or a bit smaller) close to one another, but not touching, on the prepared baking sheets. Bake in the oven until set but still white, about 1½ hours. Turn the oven off and, without opening the door, let the meringues cool and harden, about 2 more hours or overnight.

Index

(Page references in *italics* refer to illustrations.)

B

G

H

S

T

V

DISTILLATO A BAGNOMARIA
CAPOVILLA
CONTENTS 375 ML
ALC. 46% BY VOL.
litri 0,700
Grappa
NARDINI
Moscato Cru
NONINO

A Note About the Authors

LIDIA BASTIANICH, Emmy Award–winning public-television host, best-selling cookbook author, restaurateur, and owner of a flourishing food-and-entertainment business, has married her two passions in life—her family and food—to create multiple culinary endeavors.

Lidia's cookbooks, co-authored with her daughter, Tanya, include *Lidia's Celebrate Like an Italian, Lidia's Commonsense Italian Cooking, Lidia's Favorite Recipes, Lidia's Italy in America, Lidia Cooks from the Heart of Italy,* and *Lidia's Italy*—all companion books to the Emmy-winning and three-time-nominated television series *Lidia's Kitchen, Lidia's Italy in America,* and *Lidia's Italy,* which have aired internationally, in Mexico, Canada, the Middle East, Croatia, and the U.K. Lidia has also published *Lidia's Mastering the Art of Italian Cuisine, Lidia's Family Table, Lidia's Italian-American Kitchen, Lidia's Italian Table,* and *La Cucina di Lidia,* and three children's books: *Nonna Tell Me a Story: Lidia's Christmas Kitchen, Lidia's Family Kitchen: Nonna's Birthday Surprise,* and *Lidia's Egg-citing Farm Adventure*, as well as a memoir, *My American Dream*. Lidia is the chef-owner with her son, Joseph, and daughter, Tanya Manuali, of three acclaimed New York City restaurants—Felidia, Becco, and Del Posto—as well as Lidia's Kansas City with Tanya. She is also the founder of Tavola Productions, an entertainment company that produces high-quality broadcast productions. Lidia also has a line of pastas and all-natural sauces, called LIDIA'S. Along with her son, Joe Bastianich, and Oscar Farinetti, she opened Eataly, the largest artisanal Italian food-and-wine marketplaces in New York City, Chicago, Boston, Los Angeles, Las Vegas, and São Paulo, Brazil.

FORTUNATO NICOTRA After earning Michelin stars at two restaurants in Sicily before his thirtieth birthday, Fortunato Nicotra arrived in New York City to work for celebrity chef Lidia Bastianich in 1996. Hired as Executive Chef of her famous flagship restaurant, Felidia, he earned the restaurant three stars just months after his arrival and again a decade later. *Wine Spectator* named Felidia one of the Top Ten Italian Restaurants in the United States, and *USA Today* named it number two in its yearly roundup of restaurants around the world. Nicotra has appeared on several television shows including *Lidia's Kitchen,*

Lidia's Italy, and Food Network's *Iron Chef.* He prepared meals for Pope Benedict XVI and Pope Francis I during their visits to New York.

TANYA BASTIANICH MANUALI'S visits to Italy as a child sparked her passion for the country's art and culture. She dedicated herself to the study of Italian Renaissance art during her college years at Georgetown; she then earned a master's degree from Syracuse University and a doctorate from Oxford University. Living and studying in many regions of Italy for several years, she taught art history to American students in Florence, although she met her husband, Corrado Manuali from Rome, in New York.

Tanya is integrally involved in the production of Lidia's public television series as an owner and executive producer of Tavola Productions, and is active in the family restaurant business. With her mother, she is co-owner of two restaurants: Felidia and Lidia's Kansas City. In 2019, Tanya joined her brother in operating several other restaurants, including Del Posto, Babbo, Lupa, Otto, Pizzeria Mozza, Osteria Mozza, and Chi Spacca. She has also led the development of the website lidiasitaly.com, and the related publications and merchandise lines of tableware and cookware. Tanya is a member of Les Dames d'Escoffier (New York chapter), a philanthropic organization of women leaders in the fields of food, fine beverage, and hospitality.

Together with her husband, Corrado, Tanya oversees the production and expansion of the LIDIA'S food line of all-natural pastas and sauces. Tanya has co-authored several books with her mother, including *Lidia's Celebrate Like an Italian, Lidia's Mastering the Art of Italian Cuisine, Lidia's Commonsense Italian Cooking, Lidia's Favorite Recipes, Lidia's Italy, Lidia Cooks from the Heart of Italy,* and *Lidia's Italy in America.* In 2010, Tanya co-authored *Reflections of the Breast: Breast Cancer in Art Through the Ages*, a social-art-historical look at breast cancer in art from ancient Egypt to today. In 2014, Tanya co-authored *Healthy Pasta* with her brother, Joe. Tanya and Corrado live in New York City with their children, Lorenzo and Julia.

Felidia

A Note on the Type

This book was set in Adobe Garamond. Designed for the Adobe Corporation by Robert Slimbach, the fonts are based on types first cut by Claude Garamond (ca. 1480–1561). Garamond was a pupil of Geoffroy Tory and is believed to have followed the Venetian models, although he introduced a number of important differences, and it is to him that we owe the letter we now know as "old style." He gave to his letters a certain elegance and feeling of movement that won their creator an immediate reputation and the patronage of Francis I of France.

Composed by North Market Street Graphics,
Lancaster, Pennsylvania

Printed and bound by LSC Communications,
Crawfordsville, Indiana

Designed by Anna B. Knighton

ALEJO Y SU PANDILLA

Misterio en Cartagena de Indias

Edi numen

ISBN Lectura: 978-84-9848-176-1
ISBN Lectura con CD: 978-84-9848-173-0
Depósito Legal: M-8673-2010
Impreso en España
Printed in Spain

Coordinación pedagógica:
María José Gelabert

Coordinación editorial:
Mar Menéndez

Diseño de portada:
Carlos Casado
Diseño y maquetación:
Carlos Casado
Ilustraciones:
Olga Carmona y Carlos Casado
Fotografías:
Archivo Edinumen
Impresión:
Gráficas Glodami. Coslada (Madrid)

Editorial Edinumen
José Celestino Mutis, 4. 28028 - Madrid
Teléfono: 91 308 51 42
Fax: 91 319 93 09
e-mail: edinumen@edinumen.es
www.edinumen.es

En la grabación de la lectura se han eliminado algunas acotaciones de los diálogos para conservar la naturalidad de los mismos.

Índice

Contenido **Página**

Antes de empezar a leer

1. **Identifica la silueta de Colombia entre todos estos países.**

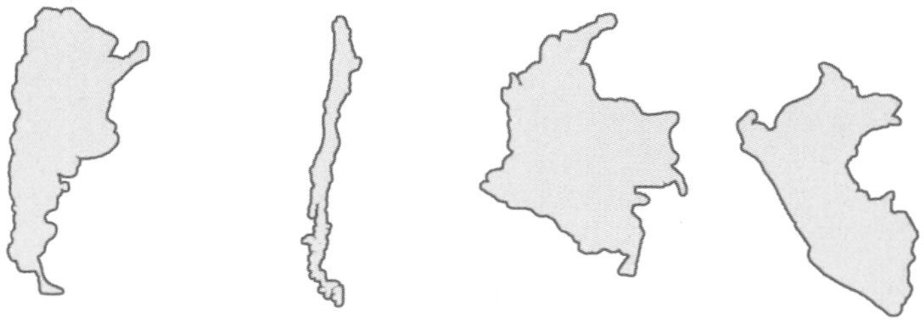

1. .... 2. .... 3. .... 4. ....

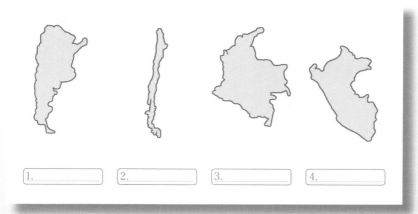

2. **Asocia las siguientes ciudades y países.**

1. Medellín •
2. Quito •
3. Valparaíso •
4. Bogotá •
5. Córdoba •
6. Cartagena de Indias •
7. Guayaquil •
8. Montevideo •
9. Mendoza •
10. Cali •

• **a.** Ecuador
• **b.** Chile
• **c.** Colombia
• **d.** Argentina
• **e.** Uruguay

3. **¿Cuáles de estos personajes son colombianos?**

	Sí	No
a. Diego Maradona.	☐	☐
b. Ingrid Betancourt.	☐	☐
c. Hugo Chávez.	☐	☐
d. Rafael Nadal.	☐	☐
e. Fernando Botero.	☐	☐
f. Jorge Luis Borges.	☐	☐
g. Gabriel García Márquez.	☐	☐
h. Gabriel Batistuta.	☐	☐

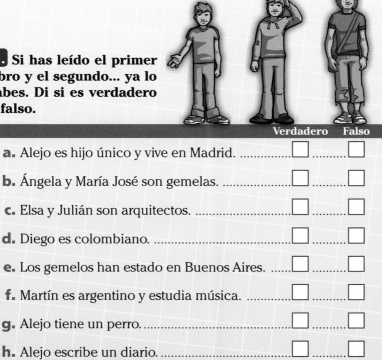

4. **Si has leído el primer libro y el segundo... ya lo sabes. Di si es verdadero o falso.**

	Verdadero	Falso
a. Alejo es hijo único y vive en Madrid.	☐	☐
b. Ángela y María José son gemelas.	☐	☐
c. Elsa y Julián son arquitectos.	☐	☐
d. Diego es colombiano.	☐	☐
e. Los gemelos han estado en Buenos Aires.	☐	☐
f. Martín es argentino y estudia música.	☐	☐
g. Alejo tiene un perro.	☐	☐
h. Alejo escribe un diario.	☐	☐

5. Sopa de letras. Identifica 7 cosas por las que es famosa Colombia.

B	I	M	E	T	O	C	V	I	A	D	U
I	R	E	S	M	E	R	A	L	D	A	S
O	Q	U	E	S	A	D	I	L	L	A	S
D	I	C	A	F	E	P	U	N	T	O	S
I	L	V	A	L	L	E	N	A	T	O	C
V	Z	A	R	O	N	U	N	C	A	T	O
E	B	R	U	R	O	X	A	C	E	R	G
R	S	U	R	E	C	A	M	A	S	T	A
S	A	M	B	S	Y	A	S	R	I	L	E
I	E	S	T	C	U	M	B	I	A	O	L
D	I	A	M	A	N	T	E	B	E	S	L
A	B	S	O	L	U	T	A	E	S	S	O
D	I	N	O	S	A	U	R	I	O	U	S

6. Di si es verdadero (V) o falso (F).

	Verdadero	Falso
a. Colombia limita con Venezuela.	☐	☐
b. Colombia es el país más pequeño de América del Sur.	☐	☐
c. La capital de Colombia es Caracas.	☐	☐
d. En Colombia no hay montañas.	☐	☐
e. Cartagena de Indias está en la costa.	☐	☐

Capítulo 1

Alejo levantó la vista de su diario, dispuesto a ir al trastero de la terraza y a hacer callar de una vez a las gemelas y a Lorenzo. Desde que volvieron de Argentina, hace ya unos cuantos meses, Lorenzo se tomó muy en serio la idea del grupo de rock. No le fue difícil convencer a las gemelas, ya que ellas también saben música. Elsa, la madre de Alejo, y Julián, su marido y padre de las gemelas, aceptaron prestarles el trastero para ensayar. Lo limpiaron, lo ordenaron y pegaron unas cuantas cajas de huevos en las paredes para insonorizarlo. Pero el truco no resultó, y hasta Félix, el gato, se ponía tan nervioso con el ruido que no le quedaba más remedio que entrar y sentarse a dormir en un sillón. A su vez, esto enfurecía a Elsa, que no soporta la casa llena de pelos.

Alejo se levantó a cerrar la puerta de su habitación y leyó lo que tenía escrito:

Querido diario:

Ayer llamó Jorge desde Buenos Aires. Es el marido de Etelvina, la madre de las gemelas. Era para contarnos que nació Nina, su hija. Las gemelas se pusieron locas de contentas y le pidieron una foto. Jorge les prometió algo mejor: una hora más tarde nos conectamos a skype y pudimos ver a Etelvina en la maternidad con el bebé en brazos. Roberta y Ángela decían que su hermanita era preciosa, pero a mí me pareció bastante fea, la verdad. Etelvina dijo que se parecía a ellas, pero Nina tiene el pelo oscuro y las gemelas son muy rubias.

En la cena las chicas le dijeron a su padre que querían ir a Buenos Aires a conocer a Nina.

–Podrían viajar para Semana Santa –sugirió Julián.

–Eso es dentro de diez días. ¿Encontraremos billetes?

–Todo es cuestión de intentarlo. Mañana llamo a la agencia –dijo Elsa.

–Yo también quiero ir –anunció Alejo.

–Cariño, no podemos pagar tantos billetes. Ten un poco de paciencia que en pocos meses nos vamos a Colombia –le explicó su madre.

Alejo estuvo en Argentina el verano anterior, con su madre, Julián, las gemelas y los gemelos, que son los hijos de Oriana, la mujer de Ramón, su padre. Fue un viaje fantástico. Allí conoció a Etelvina, a Jorge y a la abuela Susy. Además coincidieron con Martín, un amigo del colegio de Madrid que es argentino, y Silvia, su hermana. Pasaron con ellos unos días en el campo y vivieron una aventura muy emocionante.

Además, durante ese viaje, Ángela, una de las gemelas y Pablo, uno de los gemelos, se hicieron novios. Martín y Roberta, la otra gemela, estuvieron a punto, pero al volver a Madrid a ella empezó a gustarle Lorenzo, el compañero colombiano con el que formaron el grupo de rock.

Lorenzo llegó a España cuando tenía diez años, con sus padres y sus hermanos. Antes vivían en Bogotá, pero como la familia de su madre es de Cartagena de Indias, solían pasar todos los veranos y las vacaciones allí. Sus abuelos tienen una casa grande en el casco antiguo y su abuelo, que ahora está jubilado, fue alcalde de la ciudad.

Hace un par de meses, a Elsa y Julián, que son arquitectos, les propusieron un trabajo en Colombia, concretamente en un pueblo cerca de Cartagena, por el que pasó el coletazo de un huracán y lo destruyó todo. La Agencia Española de Cooperación Internacional va a subvencionar la reconstrucción de uno de los pueblos arrasados, y Elsa y Julián tienen que viajar para poder luego armar el proyecto.

Capítulo 2

Querido diario:

Siento mucho no haberte escrito antes, pero el caso es que desde abril he estado liadísimo.

Las gemelas consiguieron viajar a Buenos Aires en Semana Santa. Se fueron cargadas de regalos para toda la familia, pero sobre todo para Nina. Volvieron supercontentas porque su nueva hermana es muy guapa y muy buena. Aprendieron a cambiarle los pañales, a cantarle canciones de cuna antes de dormir y sacaron un montón de fotos.

Además, contaron que su madre y Jorge hicieron obras en la casa y unieron los dos departamentos, así que, la próxima vez, tendremos donde quedarnos.

Los gemelos lograron pasar otro año de escuela y se clasificaron para participar en un torneo de tenis juvenil.

Lorenzo y las gemelas dieron su primer concierto y tuvieron mucho éxito. Ahora dicen que quieren grabar un CD.

Mientras tanto, mi madre y Julián empezaron a planear el viaje a Colombia y se pusieron de acuerdo con los padres de Lorenzo para dejarnos solos, a las gemelas y a mí, unos días en Cartagena, en la casa de los abuelos de Lorenzo. Mi madre estaba bastante preocupada porque dice que Colombia es un país peligroso, pero parece que Cartagena es un lugar seguro.

Y aquí estamos, todos en el avión, esperando aterrizar en Bogotá.

El avión llegó a la capital de Colombia a las dos de la tarde. En la salida internacional había un montón de gente.

–Ahí está –exclamó Julián cuando vio a un hombre de unos cuarenta años, alto y con bigote, que llevaba un cartel de la Agencia de Cooperación.

Julián se acercó a él y le dio la mano.
–Encantado.
–El gusto es mío. Bienvenidos a Colombia.
–Gracias. Le presento a la arquitecta Sánchez –dijo señalando a Elsa.
Ismael Pizarro era el encargado de acompañarlos al hotel, de mostrarles la ciudad y llevarlos de nuevo al aeropuerto al día siguiente.
Cuando llegaron a la ciudad era casi de noche.
–Les reservamos dos habitaciones en el hotel Cundinamarca, en el barrio de La Candelaria. Es el corazón histórico y cultural de la ciudad.
–Ahí está la iglesia del Carmen, ¿verdad? –preguntó Alejo, que consultó mucho Internet.
–Sí, Nuestra Señora del Carmen. Miren, miren, ¡ese es el cerro de Monserrate!
Todos miraron hacia arriba para ver un edificio en medio de inmensas nubes negras.
–¿Qué es? –preguntó Roberta.
–Es un santuario. Si quieren, mañana los acompaño. Hay una vista hermosísima de la ciudad.

–Papi, me siento mareada –se quejó Ángela.

–Claro... Estamos a 2600 metros sobre el nivel del mar. Te tomas un aguapanela y ya está –le explicó Ismael.

Cenaron en un restaurante cerca del hotel con Ismael, su mujer y sus dos hijos: Andrea y Gerardo. Julián, Elsa e Ismael hablaron de trabajo, Alejo descubrió que Gerardo era un experto en la Liga española. Andrea y su madre tenían mucha curiosidad por saber cómo se vivía en Madrid: las gemelas estaban en su salsa, aunque ahora las dos se sentían mareadas.

–¡Tienen que probar el ajiaco!

–¿Lleva carne? –preguntó Alejo.

–Lleva pollo y una hierba especial que se llama "guasca" –dijo Andrea orgullosa.

Al día siguiente se levantaron muy temprano para aprovechar el día.

–El vuelo para Cartagena sale a las 6 y media de la tarde. Daos prisa, por favor –dijo Elsa.

Visitaron el centro histórico de la ciudad, el museo del Oro y el famoso cerro Monserrate.

–La próxima vez los llevamos al museo Botero –anunció Ismael.

"¡Qué suerte!", pensó Alejo que también se sentía algo mareado.

Todos se quedaron dormidos durante el vuelo. Cuando el avión aterrizó era completamente de noche.

Capítulo 3

Lorenzo y sus abuelos ya estaban allí y los esperaban en el aeropuerto. La abuela tenía un ramo de flores en la mano y una caja de dulces.

—¡Qué calorcito! —dijo Ángela.

—¡Ya me siento bien! —dijo Roberta.

—¡Bienvenidos al Caribe, chicos!

Lorenzo abrazó a Alejo y a las gemelas. Sobre todo a Roberta. Estaba moreno y llevaba pantalones cortos y una camiseta.

El aeropuerto está junto al mar y soplaba una brisa fresca.

—Tenemos una reserva en el hotel Santa Clara.

—¡Huy! ¡Qué lujo! Los acompañamos —dijo el abuelo de Lorenzo.

El hotel ocupaba el edificio del antiguo convento de Santa Clara. Se construyó en el siglo XVII y durante un tiempo fue hospital. Hoy en día es un hotel de cinco estrellas, ubicado en la plaza de San Diego, en pleno casco antiguo de la ciudad.

Se despidieron en la puerta del hotel y el abuelo de Lorenzo prometió acompañarlos a dar un paseo por la ciudad al día siguiente.

Elsa y Julián se levantaron muy temprano.

—¡Qué raro es el día en el trópico! —comentó Julián.

—Sí, todo empieza y termina muy pronto.

A las siete de la mañana Cartagena estaba ya en plena actividad: repartidores de hielo, puestos ambulantes de jugos de fruta, de arepas, de plátano frito. A esa hora hacía ya muchísimo calor y el sol quemaba tanto como al mediodía.

Cuando bajaron al salón comedor, Alejo y las mellizas estaban desayunando, rodeados de un grupo de camareros. Al ver a Elsa y a Julián les explicaron sus recientes descubrimientos.

–El maracuyá es una fruta de América, ¿quieren probar?

–Probad el jugo de tomate de árbol. No es salado –sugirió Alejo.

–El de mango es más rico –añadió Roberta.

–Bueno, por lo visto se han adaptado muy rápido –dijo Julián.

–En un rato pasará a buscarnos el abuelo de Lorenzo. Daos prisa –comentó Elsa.

–Pero si son las ocho de la mañana...

A las nueve de la mañana Don Efraín pasó a buscarlos por el hotel. Llevaba una guayabera y un sombrero vueltiao.

–Pónganse un sombrero porque el sol está muy fuerte –ordenó.

–¿Y Lorenzo? –quiso saber Roberta.

–Fue a acompañar a su abuela al hospital. Nada grave –concluyó el abuelo.

Salieron a la plaza de San Diego y giraron a la derecha. Se pararon frente a una esquina rodeada de un inmenso muro y muchos árboles.

–Miren, esta es la casa de Gabo.

–¿Quién es Gabo? –preguntó Alejo con curiosidad.

–Gabriel García Márquez, el escritor. Nuestro Premio Nobel de Literatura.

A Alejo le dio mucha vergüenza no saber quién era Gabo, porque le encanta leer. Además, antes de viajar leyó un montón de páginas de Colombia, pero ese dato se le escapó.

—No se preocupe —le dijo Efraín pasándole una mano por la cabeza—, en mi casa tengo todos los libros, se los presto.

—Miren, el mar... —exclamó Ángela.

—Y la muralla —continuó Roberta.

—Vamos a empezar por el principio, vengan conmigo —dijo Efraín.

Anduvieron por una calle llena de gente y de tiendas y llegaron al otro lado de la muralla.

—Esta es la Puerta del Reloj —dijo Efraín orgulloso—. La Torre del Reloj está en la puerta que era la entrada principal a la ciudad amurallada. Lo primero que se ve dentro es el Patio de los Coches y el Portal de los Dulces. ¿Quieren probar? Son muy sabrosos...

Todos se acercaron al puesto de una mujer negra, vestida de blanco.

—¿Qué es esto? —preguntó Roberta.

—Son cocadas —respondió el abuelo.

—¿Y esto?

—Se llaman suspiros.

Los chicos, entusiasmados con los dulces, no paraban de hacer preguntas. Un grupo de turistas con un guía, rodeaba una estatua.

—Es Pedro de Heredia, fundador de Cartagena en 1533.

—¿Y por qué hay tanta gente de color? —preguntó Alejo con timidez.

—Porque Cartagena era un puerto de esclavos. Los traían de África.

—¡Qué horror! —comentó Ángela.

—Sí, pero hubo muchos rebeldes que se escaparon y se refugiaron en los llamados "palenques".

—Como Palenque de San Basilio —intervino Julián.

—Sí, voy a llevar a los niños un día de estos —anunció el abuelo.

—Mañana, Elsa y yo vamos a trabajar a un pueblo que está muy cerca de ahí —dijo Julián.

Capítulo 4

Querido Diario:

Fue un día estupendo. Todos se quejaban del calor, pero la verdad es que no me pareció para tanto. Cartagena es una ciudad guapísima y voy a tratar de describirla lo mejor posible.

Es antigua y está rodeada de una muralla. Aquí hubo de todo: piratas, corsarios y esclavos rebeldes a los que llamaron cimarrones.

Hay muchísimas iglesias y el abuelo de Lorenzo nos hizo entrar en todas: la de Santo Domingo, la catedral, la de San Pedro y otras más que ya no recuerdo. Las calles son muy alegres y suena música por todos lados. A veces se mezclan las canciones y ya no se sabe qué escuchar.

Las casas son muy antiguas y bonitas, con balcones de madera llenos de flores, rejas de madera en las ventanas y unos portones muy originales que tienen unas cerraduras con figuras. Mi madre dice que se llaman aldabas, pero esa palabra no la había oído nunca.

En algunas calles no hay carros, que es la palabra que aquí se usa para decir "coche".

Esta mañana mi madre y Julián se han marchado y nosotros nos hemos quedado en la casa de Efraín. Marta, la abuela, es muy cariñosa y la casa es preciosa. Como hace mucho calor, yo he decidido dormir en una hamaca, en el patio. ¡Es muy cómoda!

Roberta está como atontada con Lorenzo, así que esta tarde, después de la playa, me iré a dar un paseo con Ángela. Ella también está como tonta y se pasa el día en los locutorios con Internet a ver si hay algún correo de Juan Carlos. En fin... sin comentarios.

Marta y los chicos se subieron a la buseta a las nueve y media de la mañana. Llegaron a Bocagrande, y a las diez y cuarto estaban en la playa. A lo largo de la costa se veían rascacielos, tiendas de moda y restaurantes. Era

casi como estar en Benidorm.

–Parece otra ciudad –comentó Alejo.

–A mí me gusta más la ciudad antigua –exclamó Ángela decidida.

–¡Qué olas más bacanas! –gritó Lorenzo.

La temperatura fuera del agua era casi insoportable. Marta compró el periódico, se sentó debajo de una carpa y se puso a leer. Mientras tanto, los chicos se bañaron infinidad de veces y Lorenzo les enseñó a coger las olas en el momento justo. Le compraron agua de coco a un vendedor ambulante y también unas bolas de tamarindo. Son unos dulces de fruta y azúcar. A las doce volvieron a la casa, almorzaron y... a dormir la siesta. Alejo se acercó a Don Efraín:

–¿Puedo ver sus libros?

–Claro, venga.

Subieron las escaleras y entraron en una inmensa habitación llena de librerías, de fotos antiguas y de trofeos.

–Te dejo solo. Puedes mirarlos todos...

–¿Están en orden alfabético?

–¿Buscas los de Gabo? Ahí están, cerca de la ventana. Yo me voy a descansar un ratico.

Alejo descubrió un auténtico tesoro en aquella habitación. Se acercó a las fotos que se encontraban en una de las paredes: Don Efraín joven, rodeado de gente; en otra está recibiendo una medalla; en otra, junto a Marta. De repente, Alejo se detuvo frente a una serie de fotos pequeñas, enmarcadas y colocadas en fila. "Las aldabas de las puertas", dijo en voz alta. Las fotografías eran antiguas y en blanco y negro. En algunas, casi no se distinguían las figuras.

Distraídamente Alejo se acercó al estante donde estaban los libros de García Márquez. Había por lo menos diez ediciones de *Cien años de soledad*. Alejo decidió coger la menos lujosa. Abrió la primera página y leyó:

Dentro había también una fotografía. Era de una de las aldabas de las puertas, pero completamente dorada. Volvió a ponerla dentro del libro y cerró la puerta tras de sí.

Capítulo 5

Alejo levantó la vista del libro cuando empezó a oír ruido a su alrededor.

—¿Vamos a dar una vuelta? —le preguntó Ángela.

—¿Y los chicos?

—No se les puede ni hablar. Solo quieren estar juntos todo el día —contestó fastidiada.

—Igual que como te pones tú con Juan Carlos...

—Antipático —le respondió y le sacó la lengua.

—Dame un minuto, que quiero llevar la cámara de fotos. Se me ha ocurrido una idea...

—Si no te importa...

—Sí, ya sé, quieres pasar por el locutorio. Vale, yo también iré a ver cuál de mis admiradoras me ha escrito —respondió riéndose.

En la calle reinaba una extraña calma. A lo lejos se oía un vallenato mezclado con una cumbia. Los vendedores de collares, aretes y anillos empezaban a ocupar la plaza de San Diego.

—Me los compraría todos —exclamó Ángela con un collar de semillas en la mano.

—Pero si tú no llevas nunca nada —le respondió Alejo claramente aburrido de mirar cosas de chicas.

—Pero este lugar me inspira —le respondió Ángela.

El locutorio estaba bastante lleno y solo quedaban dos ordenadores libres. Alejo entró en la página de su correo y se encontró con varios mensajes nuevos. De Fernando, de los mellizos, de Ramón, su padre, y uno de María José. Sintió que se ponía colorado y echó un vistazo a su derecha para saber si Ángela lo estaba mirando. Nada, ella estaba absorta en la lectura y hasta le pareció que se le caía una lágrima.

El correo de María José no ponía nada en "asunto". Lo abrió y se quedó de piedra:

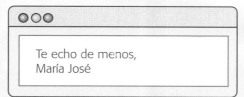

> Te echo de menos,
> María José

"¿Y ahora qué le contesto?", pensó.

–Estoy afuera –le dijo a Ángela mientras cerraba su correo.

–Esperame, que ya voy.

Cuando salieron del local con aire acondicionado, volvieron a sentir el calor de la tarde.

–Quiero sacar unas fotos. ¿Me acompañas?

–Sí, ¿qué vamos a fotografiar?

–Puertas.

–¿Puertas? ¿Puertas normales?

–Las puertas de aquí no son normales. ¿No te has fijado en las aldabas? –preguntó con aire intelectual.

–¿Las qué?

–Esas piezas metálicas que sirven para llamar a la puerta.

–No, la verdad es que no.

–Ven, que te muestro algo.

Alejo tomó muchísimas fotos y logró entusiasmar a Ángela en el proyecto. Las aldabas eran todas diferentes, pero muchas de las figuras estaban repetidas, sobre todo las de leones, caballitos de mar e iguanas.

–Acá tenés otro león. Es rarísimo –gritó Ángela.

Alejo documentó todas las puertas hasta que cayó la noche. Y en todo momento tuvo la impresión de que alguien lo estaba mirando.

–Mañana seguimos. No quiero usar *flash* –anunció, dándose la vuelta para ver si veía a alguien.

–Yo quiero comprarme un collar. ¿Me acompañás?

–Vale, pero solo si me prestas tu ordenador para una cosa que tengo que hacer.

–Trato hecho –respondió Ángela dándole la mano.

Cuando regresaron a la plaza de San Diego no se podía ni caminar. Artesanos con tejidos colocados en el suelo y cubiertos de bisutería intentaban convencer a los turistas de la originalidad de cada pieza. Los restaurantes habían instalado sus terrazas fuera, y había además grupos de cartageneros fumando, charlando y tomando ron. Ángela volvió decidida al puesto que había visto antes.

–A mí este es el que más me gusta.

–Esa semilla la protege contra la mala suerte, mami. Se llama "ojo de venado".

–A mí me gusta más el collar rojo –comentó Alejo.

–No, es muy común. Lo usan todas.

–Yo voy a llevar el rojo –concluyó Alejo sacando la cartera del bolsillo.

–¿Y vos para qué querés un collar?

–Para regalar –respondió. Y agradeció que hubiera poca luz. Tenía las mejillas ardiendo.

Párate un momento

1. Señala cuál de estas afirmaciones resume mejor lo dicho en el texto.

1. Capítulo 1
a. Elsa y Julián van a viajar a Colombia para hacer turismo.
b. Alejo, las gemelas y los gemelos van a viajar a Colombia.
c. Elsa y Julián van a viajar a Colombia por trabajo.

2. Capítulo 2
a. Todos se aburrieron mucho en Bogotá.
b. En Bogotá conocieron a gente interesante.
c. No tuvieron tiempo de visitar la ciudad.

3. Capítulo 3
a. Cartagena de Indias es una ciudad antigua.
b. Cartagena de Indias no es una ciudad turística.
c. Cartagena de Indias está a orillas de un río.

4. Capítulo 4
a. Las aldabas sirven para cerrar las ventanas.
b. En Cartagena hay mucho tráfico.
c. El abuelo Efraín conoció a Gabriel García Márquez.

5. Capítulo 5
a. Alejo y Ángeles tomaron fotos de los principales monumentos.
b. Alejo y Ángela tomaron fotos de las puertas.
c. Roberta se compró un collar.

2. Elige la opción correcta.

1. Nuestra Señora del Carmen es un a. museo/b. santuario que está en el cerro de Monserrate.

2. Gabo es el nombre por el que se conoce al a. escritor/b. pintor Gabriel García Márquez.

3. La guayabera es una prenda para a. mujeres/b. hombres.

4. Una aldaba es una pieza de hierro que se pone en las puertas para a. llamar/b. atar los caballos.

Capítulo 6

Ángela estrenó de inmediato su collar nuevo. Alejo y ella regresaron a la casa antes de la hora de cenar.

—La comida está servida —dijo Marta recibiéndolos en la puerta.

—Gracias, aunque me cuesta pensar que la comida es la cena —concluyó Alejo.

Alejo y Ángela se lavaron las manos y se sentaron a la mesa. Lorenzo y Roberta ya estaban allí, al igual que los abuelos.

—¿Dónde se metieron? —preguntó Roberta un poco enfadada.

—Nos fuimos a dar una vuelta —¿Y ustedes?

—Nosotros estuvimos ensayando un rato. Te recuerdo que en el grupo somos tres...

—Pero...

—Nada de peleas, niñas —dijo Efraín levantando un poco la voz.

El abuelo tenía una voz tan dulce y tan decidida al mismo tiempo, que las gemelas se callaron.

—¿Qué pescado es este? —preguntó Alejo.

—Es pargo rojo, y ahí tienes patacones. Sé que te gustan —le respondió Marta guiñándole un ojo.

Cuando terminaron de cenar eran apenas las ocho de la noche. Alejo le pidió a Ángela el ordenador y le pidió permiso a Don Efraín para subir a la biblioteca. Se llevó también el ejemplar de *Cien años de soledad*.

–Eligió la mejor edición. Cuídemela mucho.

Las gemelas tenían un ordenador portátil que les regalaron los Reyes Magos. Alejo lo encendió y conectó su cámara de fotos. Apretó la tecla derecha del ratón y creó una carpeta que llamó "Aldabas de Cartagena". Descargó las fotos, borró la tarjeta de memoria de la cámara y se preparó a mirar las imágenes. Creó varias subcarpetas: *león, caballito de mar, iguana, otros*. Pero antes de colocar las fotos en su carpeta correspondiente, les echó una mirada a todas. Abrió el libro y sacó la foto del abuelo Efraín. Era un maravilloso hipocampo dorado. Encontró uno igual entre sus fotos, pero el de su foto era de hierro. "¡Qué raro!", pensó, "Son idénticos". Amplió un poco la foto y comprobó cómo era la puerta. Parecía tratarse del mismo portón de madera. Si de algo estaba seguro era de que en Cartagena no había dos puertas iguales. Miró alternativamente la foto del abuelo y la suya varias veces. Jugó a acercar la imagen que él mismo había tomado, y a alejarla. Analizó cada detalle. El hipocampo parecía antiguo, salvo por un detalle: los tornillos eran nuevos, brillaban mucho. Recordó un comentario de Julián mientras montaba una estantería en el piso de Madrid:

–¡Estos tornillos con cabeza de estrella son maravillosos! Antes no había.

Miró la foto del abuelo y trató de identificar los tornillos.

–Nada, esta foto es muy vieja –comentó en voz alta.

En ese momento oyó una voz y la puerta se abrió. Era Ángela.

–¿Estás hablando solo? –le dijo riéndose.

–Ven, siéntate y mira esto conmigo –le propuso.

Alejo le contó a Ángela lo que acababa de descubrir.

–Pero, ¿cómo se te ocurrió? –quiso saber Ángela.

–Nada, en realidad quería regalarle unas fotos al abuelo Efraín. Mira todas las que tiene... –Alejo se puso de pie y le mostró a Ángela la colección del abuelo.

–Como estas son muy viejas, pensé en regalarle una nueva colección.

–Comparemos las otras fotos –propuso Ángela.

–Excelente idea. Por ahora, esto es un secreto entre tú y yo...

–Pero si somos más, podemos descubrir más cosas.

Alejo reflexionó un momento.

–¿Llamamos a Roberta y a Lorenzo? –dijo.

Capítulo 7

Al día siguiente los chicos decidieron no ir a la playa. Querían aprovechar las horas de luz para sacar todas las fotos posibles.

–¿Y por qué hay que tomar fotos? –preguntó Lorenzo.

–Para no llamar la atención. Es mejor fingir que estamos tomando fotos de la ciudad, de las iglesias, de las calles. Le damos al *zoom* y...

–Y nadie se da cuenta de lo que estamos haciendo –concluyó Roberta.

–Sí, además ayer tuve la sensación de que alguien nos miraba –continuó Alejo.

–No nos asustes, che –dijo Ángela.

–¿No es mejor si hablamos con mi abuelo?

–No, todavía no. Vamos a ver si descubrimos algo más.

Alejo distribuyó las tareas del día. Por la mañana tenían que terminar de tomar las fotos y él intentaría escanear la imagen que encontró dentro del libro del abuelo Efraín.

A las diez de la mañana ya estaban todos en la calle. Ángela y Alejo recorrieron varios locutorios hasta encontrar uno con escáner. Además, Alejo quería aprovechar para responderle a María José.

Ángela también chequeó su correo y casi saltó en la silla al ver que tenía un mensaje de Juan Carlos. Alejo abrió su casilla, luego, el mensaje de María José y le respondió:

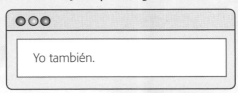

> Yo también.

Encontró un mensaje de Gerardo, el chico colombiano que conocieron en Bogotá:

> Hola, amigos:
> Me da mucho pesar, pero creo que no podremos ir a Cartagena. Mi madre no puede llevarnos.
> Les deseo a todos unas felices vacaciones. ¿No vuelven por Bogotá?
> Un abrazo,
> Gerardo

Ese mensaje podía esperar, pensó Alejo. Sacó la foto de su mochila y escaneó la imagen con la máxima resolución. Detrás de él estaba parado uno de los empleados del locutorio, así que se apresuró a sacar la llave, pasar la imagen, eliminarla del ordenador y vaciar la papelera.

–Vamos a casa inmediatamente. Necesitamos tu ordenador.

Cuando regresaron eran más de las once y media. Subieron el portátil a la biblioteca, Alejo conectó su llave y sí, tenía razón, los tornillos eran diferentes.

Diez minutos más tarde llegaron Roberta y Lorenzo.

–A nosotros también nos pareció que alguien nos miraba –dijo Lorenzo jadeando, después de haber subido las escaleras corriendo.

–¿Sacaron las fotos? –preguntó Ángela.

–Sí, aquí están.

Alejo conectó la máquina de fotos y descargó las nuevas imágenes. Las colocó en las carpetas correspondientes y luego los cuatro miraron atentamente todas las imágenes. Al concluir, Roberta exclamó:

–¿Se dieron cuenta de que solo los caballitos de mar y las iguanas tienen tornillos nuevos?

Todos se quedaron atónitos ante el descubrimiento.

–Eso quiere decir que no es casual... –sugirió Alejo.

–¿Significará algo? –preguntó Lorenzo.

–Chicos, esta tarde, todos al locutorio. Tenemos que saber qué significado tienen esos animales.

–¿Por qué no le pedimos ayuda a Martín? ¡Es un genio para esto de la informática! –propuso Roberta. Lorenzo le echó un vistazo de reproche y Roberta le dio un beso en la mejilla.

–Buena idea. Yo le escribo. ¿Está en Argentina? ¿Cuántas horas habrá de diferencia? –dijo Alejo.

–Creo que dos. Vayamos tempranito, y así le va a dar tiempo a contestarnos –concluyó Ángela.

–Todos con el Messenger abierto, por favor. Tenemos que disimular –dijo Lorenzo.

Por la tarde los chicos se dedicaron a buscar en Google toda la información que necesitaban.

A las cuatro de la tarde se reunieron en la biblioteca del abuelo y pusieron en común sus conclusiones.

–El caballito de mar, o hipocampo, es un pez... –empezó Roberta.

–¿Un pez? –preguntaron todos a coro.

–Un pez. Es símbolo de la fidelidad, porque eligen una pareja para toda la vida.

–¡Ajá! –dijo Alejo.

–Y además, se lo consideraba doble, mitad caballo, mitad marino.

–La iguana –continuó Ángela– también es doble, porque es un reptil. Y es el símbolo de la fertilidad y de la abundancia.

–Tenemos que seguir buscando, chicos. Vamos a ver qué nos dice Martín.

Los cuatro se tomaron la tarde libre y dieron un paseo por la ciudad.

Capítulo 8

Cuando volvieron a la casa, todos tenían la sensación de que los habían estado observando.

–¿Viste al que nos sacó la foto? –preguntó Roberta.

–Yo vi a alguien escondido mirándonos –dijo Lorenzo.

–¿Qué están tramando? –dijo una voz grave a sus espaldas.

Era el abuelo Efraín, que había oído parte de la conversación. Entre todos le contaron los descubrimientos. Y le mostraron las fotos. El abuelo se acarició el mentón y dijo:

–Bueno, en primer lugar, hay una leyenda que dice que algunas aldabas de Cartagena son de oro...

–La de su foto –dijo Alejo tímidamente. Abrió su mochila y se la mostró al abuelo.

–Veo que no pierdes el tiempo. Y que además eres un niño muy observador.

–La aldaba de la foto existe, y es de oro. Pero es la única y está expuesta en el museo.

–Pero a lo mejor no es la única –continuó Alejo.

–Y por eso las están cambiando –dijo Roberta.

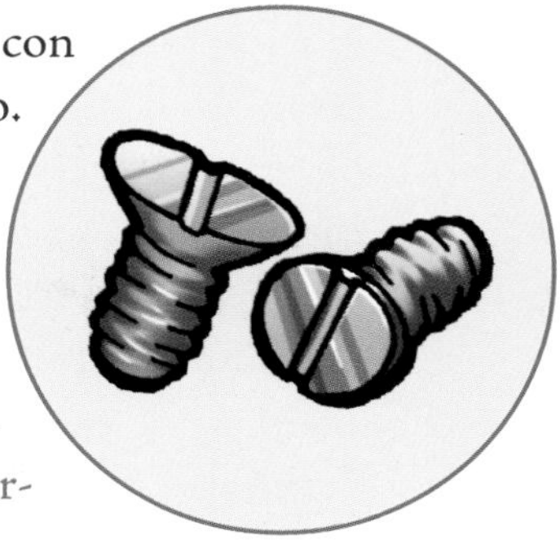

–Los tornillos son una evidencia. Acá, con el aire del mar, todo se oxida muy rápido. Estos tornillos están nuevecitos –murmuró el abuelo.

–¡Tengo una idea! ¿Hay muchas ferreterías en Cartagena? –preguntó Alejo.

–No, solo dos o tres, pero pueden haberlos comprado en el mercado de Bazurto –siguió el abuelo.

–O en cualquier otro lado –concluyó Lorenzo, desanimado.

–Esta noche vamos a quitar un tornillo de alguna aldaba y mañana vamos a recorrer las ferreterías –propuso el abuelo.

Por seguridad sacaron tres tornillos, de diferentes aldabas. Nadie se asombró al comprobar que eran idénticos. Esa noche los chicos durmieron muy mal, un poco por el calor, y otro poco porque estaban muy emocionados con todo lo que estaba pasando. Marta no podía creer que a las seis estuvieran todos de pie. Efraín propuso ir temprano, para evitar las colas de gente. Y a los curiosos. Como todo el mundo lo conocía en la ciudad, estaba seguro de que no iba a tener problemas para obtener la información.

En la primera ferretería le dijeron que ellos no vendían ese tipo de tornillos.

–Una menos –dijo el abuelo al salir.

Entró en la de al lado e hizo la misma pregunta. Si tenían tornillos como esos. Nada. Le recomendaron ir al mercado de Bazurto.

–Por suerte ahí hay solo dos ferreterías –dijo el abuelo durante el viaje en taxi.

Se bajaron en una calle ancha, llena de gente, de camiones que entraban, descargaban y salían. Un verdadero caos.

El abuelo preguntó dónde estaban las ferreterías y caminaron por unos pasillos oscuros y sucios a los que daban puestos y tiendas. Había una zona dedicada a la fruta y la verdura, otra a la carne, otra al pescado. Aquello era inmenso. El olor a especias se mezclaba con el olor a carne cruda.

En la primera ferretería había ya bastante gente. El abuelo volvió a mostrar el tornillo.

–Sí, tenemos. Pero nos quedan pocos porque se los han llevado todos –le dijo el empleado.

–¿Quién es el que está haciendo un barco con ellos? A lo mejor quiere revenderlos... –le respondió el abuelo tratando de sacarle información.

–Bueno, no pierde nada con probar. Un momentico, que voy a ver la factura y le digo quién los compró.

Regresaron a la casa para el almuerzo, con calor y satisfechos.

–Y ahora, ¿qué hacemos? –preguntó Lorenzo.

–Ahora almorzamos, dormimos la siesta y esta noche damos un paseo con un destornillador, quitamos una aldaba y analizamos si es original o no –concluyó Efraín.

Capítulo 9

Por la tarde Alejo fue al locutorio a ver si había algún correo de Martín. Encontró tres mensajes nuevos.

Primer mensaje:

¡Hola, Alejo!

Te mando la información que logré encontrar.

1. "Aldaba" es una palabra de origen árabe, que originalmente significa "lagarta" por su parecido con dicho animal.
2. La figura del león representa al Sol, pero en las puertas y entradas de las casas simboliza la protección divina.
3. Encontré también un estudio sobre las aldabas en La Habana. Por lo que dice el estudio, hay muchos puntos en común con Cartagena. Las dos ciudades eran puertos de esclavos. Es bastante largo, así que te resumo la idea principal: la técnica empleada es hispánica, pero la presencia de elementos con forma de animales es africana. Salvo el caso del león, que se encuentra también en Europa.

Bueno, espero haber sido útil. Por lo que veo, me estoy perdiendo una superaventura.

Un abrazo muy fuerte a todos. Saludos de mis padres, de Silvia y de Irma.
Martín

Segundo mensaje:

Te mando un beso,
María José

Tercer mensaje:

¡Hola, Alejo!
Los invitamos a pasar los últimos días en Bogotá, en nuestra casa.
Escríbeme cuando puedas.
Un abrazo a todos,
Gerardo

Alejo gastó unos pesos más e imprimió el mensaje de Martín para mostrárselo a todos. Y les contó que Gerardo los había invitado a Bogotá. Pero para eso tenían que esperar a Elsa y a Julián.

–A mí me parece que es auténtica –comentó Efraín, con una lupa en la mano.

–Entonces, nada tiene sentido –dijo Alejo.

–Alguna explicación tendrá. Pelados, mañana, a primera hora, vamos a la policía y ponemos una denuncia.

–Sí, como además nos siguen... –dijo Roberta casi pensando en voz alta.

–¿Los siguen? ¿Quién? ¡No me dijeron nada!

–Era para no preocuparte, abuelo –se disculpó Lorenzo.

–¡Eso no se hace! ¡No se puede jugar con estas cosas! Y ahora... todos a la cama.

–¿Y la aldaba? ¿No vamos a ponerla en su sitio? –preguntó tímidamente Alejo.

–¡A la cama, he dicho!

Capítulo 10

Los chicos durmieron muchas horas. Cuando se levantaron el abuelo los esperaba con bollos frescos para el desayuno. Todos se sorprendieron al verlo tan contento. La noche anterior parecía enfadado.

–Fui a la policía y hablé directamente con el Coronel. Para algo fui alcalde...

–¿Y? ¿Qué pasó? –preguntó Lorenzo.

–Los que los seguían eran policías vestidos de civil. Estaban siguiendo una pista y como vieron que ustedes sacaban muchas fotos, pensaron que...

–¿Que los ladrones éramos nosotros? –dijo Ángela riéndose.

–O sea, ¿que sabían que alguien estaba quitando las aldabas de las casas? –preguntó Alejo.

–En realidad todo empezó cuando detuvieron a un turista extranjero, en el aeropuerto, con una maleta cargada de aldabas. Declaró que se las había comprado a alguien en la calle, cosa muy probable.

–Y por eso mandaron a los agentes de civil a ver si descubrían algo –dijo Roberta.

–Les di el nombre y la dirección que nos dio el ferretero. Con un poco de suerte esta tarde sabremos algo –concluyó el abuelo.

Los chicos estaban terminando el café con leche y los bollos cuando de repente llamaron a la puerta. Eran Elsa y Julián.

–¡Qué alegría! –gritaron todos y corrieron a abrazarlos.

–¿Se portaron bien? –preguntó Julián mirando a Efraín y a Marta.

–Son unos niños muy buenos –dijo Marta.

–Y excelentes detectives –añadió Efraín.

—¿Otra vez? —exclamó Elsa.

Los chicos se interrumpían unos a otros para contarles las novedades a sus padres.

—Esto se merece un premio —dijo Julián entusiasmado.

—Tenemos un día libre. Así que mañana nos vamos de excursión a las islas del Rosario —anunció Elsa.

—¿Podemos ir a Bogotá a casa de Gerardo? —preguntó Alejo.

—Efraín dice que él nos puede llevar al aeropuerto y allí nos recoge Ismael —insistió Ángela.

—Y Lorenzo también quiere venir —continuó Roberta.

En ese momento sonó el teléfono. El abuelo fue a responder, y mientras tanto los chicos intentaban convencer a Elsa y a Julián para ir a Bogotá. A los quince minutos regresó Efraín.

—Buenas noticias, mi gente.

Se hizo silencio de inmediato. La expectativa era total y absoluta.

—¡Atraparon a los ladrones! ¡Y gracias a ustedes!

—¡Y a usted, Efraín! —acotó Alejo.

—Cuenta, cuenta —dijo Lorenzo.

—El nombre y la dirección correspondía a un taller de herrería. Solo que además de trabajos normales, se dedicaban a otro tipo de trabajos...

—Quitaban la aldaba, sacaban el molde, la copiaban y se la vendían a los turistas ricos —dijo Alejo.

—¡Exacto! —exclamó el abuelo— ¡Serás un excelente detective! ¡O un excelente escritor! —concluyó.

—Como Gabo... susurró Alejo.

—Y además, vamos a salir en *El Universal*. Esta tarde nos hacen una entrevista —agregó Efraín.

—¡Iuju! —exclamaron todos.

"Por algo se empieza" —pensó Alejo, que se moría de ganas de seguir con la lectura de *Cien años de soledad*.

Después de leer: comprensión lectora

1. Responde verdadero o falso a las siguientes afirmaciones y corrige las falsas.

F	**1.** Las gemelas se quedaron en Madrid en Semana Santa. Las gemelas viajaron a Buenos Aires.
	2. Diego nació en España.
	3. Diego y las gemelas han formado un grupo de rock.
	4. Bogotá está a 800 metros de altura.
	5. En Bogotá todos se sintieron mareados.
	6. Los abuelos de Diego viven en el centro de Cartagena.
	7. Elsa y Julián se quedaron en casa de los abuelos de Diego.
	8. Cartagena está rodeada de una muralla.
	9. Alejo no sabía quién era Gabriel García Márquez.
	10. Alejo empezó a leer *El amor en los tiempos del cólera*.
	11. Alejo empezó a fotografiar las aldabas para hacerle un regalo a Efraín.
	12. En Cartagena es peligroso andar solo por la calle.

☐ **13.** Alejo llevaba una cámara digital.

....

☐ **14.** En Cartagena hubo una aldaba de oro.

....

☐ **15.** Los animales de las aldabas tenían un significado para los ladrones.

....

☐ **16.** Martín colaboró en la investigación.

....

☐ **17.** Los ladrones perseguían a los chicos.

....

☐ **18.** La policía sabía del robo de las aldabas.

....

☐ **19.** Los tornillos fueron fundamentales para la investigación.

....

☐ **20.** El mercado de Bazurto está en el casco antiguo.

....

☐ **21.** Los chicos saldrán por TV.

....

Gramática y vocabulario

1. Señala cuáles de estas palabras son colombianismos.

☐ colectivo	☐ pelado
☐ buseta	☐ paella
☐ arepa	☐ bacano
☐ mate	☐ alfajor
☐ subte	☐ dulce de leche

2. **Completa las siguientes oraciones con los verbos correspondientes en pretérito indefinido.**

1. En Bogotá los chicos .... (conocer) a los hijos de Gerardo.
2. Efraín los .... (llevar) a dar un paseo por la ciudad.
3. Marta y los chicos .... (ir) a la playa.
4. Los abuelos de Diego .... (ser) muy amables.
5. Ángela y Alejo .... (querer) incluir a Roberta y Diego en la investigación.
6. El primer día, Diego no .... (poder) acompañar a sus amigos en el paseo.

3. **Detecta errores en esta lista de verbos en pretérito imperfecto y corrígelos.**

- cantabo ➔ ....
- sabía ➔ ....
- estábamos ➔ ....
- podiais ➔ ....
- querías ➔ ....
- erais ➔ ....
- comiba ➔ ....
- tomaban ➔ ....
- leíban ➔ ....
- empezábamos ➔ ....

4. **Una de estas palabras no pertenece a la serie. Márcala con un círculo.**

1. avión - viaje - aeropuerto - maletas - pasaporte - muralla.
2. playa - olas - bañador - carpa - locutorio - sol.
3. puerta - aldaba - tornillo - collar - destornillador.
4. arepas - ordenador - ajiaco - plátano - jugos.

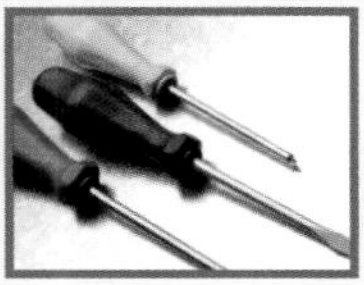

5. **Solo uno de estos dos verbos es correcto. Márcalo con un círculo y escríbelo.**

1. Cuando .... (llegaron/llegaban) a Cartagena, ya .... (era/fue) de noche.
2. Efraín le .... (prestó/prestaba) un libro a Alejo.
3. Elsa y Julián .... (viajaron/viajaban) a Colombia porque .... (tuvieron/tenían) un trabajo.
4. Gerardo .... (invitó/invitaba) a los chicos a Bogotá.
5. Efraín .... (tuvo/tenía) una biblioteca enorme.
6. Los ladrones .... (copiaron/copiaban) las aldabas.
7. El abuelo y los chicos .... (encontraron/encontraban) los tornillos en el mercado.
8. Ángela .... (se compró/se compraba) un collar de semillas.

Expresión escrita

1. **Describe tu ciudad o tu pueblo. ¿Cómo es? ¿Qué hay? ¿Te gusta?**

2. **Imagina que tienes que hacer un folleto turístico de Cartagena. Escribe el texto e incluye las información necesaria.**

Expresión oral

1. **Elige una de las palabras de la lista y defínela sin nombrarla. Tus compañeros deberán adivinarla.**

mareo ■ guayabera ■ archivo ■ huracán ■ carro ■ hamaca ■ caballito de mar

2. **¿Bogotá o Cartagena? ¿Cuál de las dos ciudades te gustaría conocer? Explica por qué.**

Me gustaría conocer Bogotá porque...

Me gustaría conocer Cartagena de Indias porque...

3. **¿A dónde has viajado últimamente? Cuéntale a tus compañeros cómo fue el último viaje que hiciste, con quién, qué actividades realizaste, etc. Toma notas del viaje de tu compañero.**

Aguapanela	Viene de "agua de panela". La panela es un derivado de la caña de azúcar. Se usa para hacer infusiones.
Ajiaco	Plato típico de Bogotá.
Alcalde/alcaldesa	Máxima autoridad que gobierna una ciudad.
Aldaba	Pieza metálica que se pone en una puerta para llamar con ella.
Arepas	Panecillos hechos de harina de maíz blanco.
Aretes	En España se llaman "pendientes" y se llevan en las orejas. Sobre todo, las mujeres.
Asunto	En un mensaje de correo electrónico, es el título o el tema.
Bacano/a	Palabra que se usa en Colombia para decir que algo es muy positivo.
Benidorm	Ciudad de la costa española, famosa por sus altos edificios.
Bocagrande	Zona turística por excelencia. Hay hoteles de lujo y todo tipo de diversiones.
Botero, Fernando	Pintor colombiano contemporáneo. Es famoso por pintar a personajes gordos.
Buseta	En Colombia, autobús pequeño.
Carpa	Estructura metálica con tela por encima para protegerse del sol.
Casco antiguo	Centro histórico.
Che	Expresión típicamente argentina.
Cien años de Soledad	Obra cumbre de Gabriel García Márquez, publicada en 1967, que le valió el Premio Nobel de Literatura en 1982.
Coletazo	Última parte o manifestación de algo.
Cumbia	Ritmo típicamente colombiano, mezcla de la tradición indígena, africana y española.
De civil	Con ropa normal, sin el uniforme.
El Universal	Uno de los periódicos de Cartagena de Indias.
Esperame	Imperativo del pronombre "vos". Espérame es la forma con "tú".
Estar en su salsa	Expresión que se usa para indicar que alguien se siente muy a gusto.
Estrenar	Usar algo por primera vez. Se dice también de las películas y las obras de teatro el primer día que se presentan.
Guapísimo/a	Expresión coloquial para decir "muy bonita".
Guayabera	Camisa masculina, típica de la zona. Suele ser de colores claros y puede llevar bordados u otros adornos.
Hipocampo	Sinónimo de "caballito de mar".
Islas del Rosario	Conjunto de islas que están en los alrededores de Cartagena. Es una excursión clásica.
¡Iuju!	Onomatopeya que se usa para expresar alegría y celebrar algo.

La Agencia Española de Cooperación Internacional	Órgano que depende del Ministerio de Relaciones Exteriores; se creó en noviembre de 1988 como órgano de gestión de la política española de cooperación internacional para el desarrollo.
La comida es la cena	En Colombia, al mediodía se almuerza, y por la noche, se come. O sea, "almuerzo" corresponde a "comida" en el España y "comida", a "cena."
Liadísimo/a	Palabra coloquial que quiere decir "muy ocupado".
Liga	Se refiere a la competición nacional de fútbol.
Llave	En algunos países se dice como en inglés: *pen drive*.
Locutorio	Lugar donde se puede llamar por teléfono. Casi todos tienen también ordenadores con conexión a Internet.
Mami	Suele usarse en toda la región del Caribe para tratar a una mujer.
Mareado/a	Malestar físico. Suele ir acompañado de náuseas y sensación de pérdida de equilibrio.
Me acompañás	Presente con el pronombre "vos".
Me da pesar	En Colombia quiere decir "lo siento mucho".
Mercado de Bazurto	Mercado central de Cartagena. Está fuera de la ciudad amurallada.
Museo del Oro	Allí se encuentra una de las más importantes colecciones de piezas de oro del mundo prehispánico.
No se preocupe	En Colombia el pronombre "usted" se usa para tratar a miembros de la familia, o para relaciones de confianza.
Ojo de venado	Semilla marrón, muy común en la región. Se dice que son "los ojos de las plantas".
Oxidarse	Efecto del hierro en contacto con el aire.
Palenque de San Basilio	Pueblo a 70 km de Cartagena.
Papelera	Representada en el ordenador con la imagen de una papelera, es el sitio donde van los archivos eliminados.
Patacón	Plátano frito, con sal.
Pelado/a	En Colombia, un "pelado" quiere decir "niño".
Rascacielos	Edificio muy alto.
Ratico	En Colombia suelen usarse diminutivos terminados en "ico", como ratico, momentico, etc.
Ratón	En muchos países se llama *mouse*.
Reyes Magos	En España los regalos de Navidad los traen Los Reyes Magos, no Papá Noel.
Ron	Bebida alcohólica típica de la zona.
Sombrero vueltiao	Sombrero tradicional de la costa colombiana.
Tornillo	Pieza metálica con rosca que sirve para unir o sostener dos elementos.
Trato hecho	Fórmula que se usa para cerrar un trato.
Vallenato	Ritmo típico de la zona de Valledupar. Se toca con un acordeón, entre otros instrumentos.

Antes de empezar a leer

1. 1. Argentina; 2. Chile; 3. Colombia; 4. Perú.
2. Ecuador: Quito y Guayaquil; Chile: Valparaíso; Colombia: Medellín, Bogotá, Cali y Cartagena de Indias; Argentina: Córdoba y Mendoza; Uruguay: Montevideo.
3. b. Ingrid Betancourt; e. Fernando Botero; g. Gabriel García Márquez.
4. a. V; b. F; c. V; d. V; e. V; f. F; g. F; h. V.
5.

B	I	M	E	T	O	C	V	I	A	D	U
I	R	E	S	M	E	R	A	L	D	A	S
O	Q	U	E	S	A	D	I	L	L	A	S
D	I	C	A	F	É	P	U	N	T	O	S
I	L	V	A	L	L	E	N	A	T	O	C
V	Z	A	R	O	N	U	N	C	A	T	O
E	B	R	U	R	O	X	A	C	E	R	G
R	S	U	R	E	C	A	M	A	S	T	A
S	A	M	B	S	Y	A	S	R	I	L	E
I	E	S	T	C	U	M	B	I	A	O	L
D	I	A	M	A	N	T	E	B	E	S	L
A	B	S	O	L	U	T	A	E	S	S	O
D	I	N	O	S	A	U	R	I	O	U	S

6. a. V; b. F; c. F; d. F; e. V.

Párate un momento

1. Capítulo 1: c; Capítulo 2: b; Capítulo 3: a; Capítulo 4: c; Capítulo 5: b.
2. 1. b; 2. a; 3. b; 4. a.

Después de leer: comprensión lectora

1. 2- F (Diego nació en Colombia); 3- V; 4- F (Bogotá está a 2600 metros de altura); 5- V; 6- V; 7- F (Elsa y Julián se fueron a trabajar a un pueblo); 8- V; 9- V; 10- F (Alejo empezó a leer *Cien años de soledad*); 11- V; 12- F (Cartagena es una ciudad tranquila); 13- V; 14- V; 15- F (Resultó ser una pista falsa); 16- V; 17- F (Era la policía quien observaba a los chicos); 18- V; 19- V; 20- F (El mercado de Bazurto está fuera de la ciudad amurallada); 21- F (Los chicos saldrán en un periódico).

Gramática y vocabulario

1. buseta, arepa, pelado, bacano.
2. 1. conocieron; 2. llevó; 3. fueron; 4. fueron; 5. quisieron; 6. pudo.
3. cantaba; podíais; comía; leían.
4. 1. muralla; 2. locutorio; 3. collar; 4. ordenador.
5. 1. llegaron – era; 2. prestó; 3. viajaron – tenían; 4. invitó; 5. tenía; 6. copiaban; 7. encontraron; 8. se compró.

Colombia

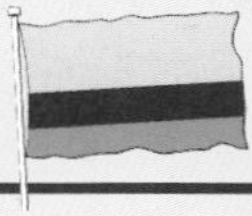

La República de Colombia es, por su extensión, el cuarto país más grande de América del Sur, con una superficie de 2 070 408 km^2, incluidas las islas de San Andrés y Providencia. Limita al este con Venezuela y Brasil, al sur con Perú y Ecuador, y al noroeste con Panamá. Cuenta con unos 44 millones de habitantes, con una fuerte presencia de comunidades indígenas.

Colombia está dividida en 32 departamentos y un distrito capital, Bogotá, que tiene casi 7 millones de habitantes. Otras ciudades importantes son Medellín y Cali.

Gonzalo Jiménez de Quesada fundó, en 1538, el Nuevo Reino de Granada, en el territorio de la actual Colombia.
En 1810 declaró su independencia de España, y en 1819 Simón Bolívar, héroe de la Independencia, se convirtió en el primer presidente del país.

Por su latitud, en la zona del Ecuador, Colombia tiene un clima tropical, pero la presencia de montañas hace que muchas zonas sean frías. Hay dos estaciones secas y dos de lluvias.

Ciudad Perdida

Un caso curioso es el de la Sierra Nevada de Santa Marta, cadena montañosa de la costa norte del país. Su pico más alto alcanza los 5775 metros. En sus cumbres hay nieves eternas, mientras que en la base tiene un clima cálido y tropical. En 1976 se descubrió Ciudad Perdida, enclave arqueológico que data del 800 d.C. , hoy protegido dentro del Parque Nacional Sierra Nevada de Santa Marta, que es la formación montañosa litoral más alta del mundo y es Patrimonio de la Humanidad.

El Parque Arqueológico San Agustín, a 520 km de Bogotá, es uno de los conjuntos precolombinos más importantes del continente. Se trata de un centro ceremonial donde los antiguos habitantes enterraban a los muertos. Por eso cuenta con muchos Parques Nacionales y áreas protegidas.

El café colombiano es famoso en todo el mundo y su producción se concentra sobre todo en la región denominada Eje cafetero, ubicada en el centro del país. Además, Colombia es un importante exportador de productos agrícolas tales como: banano, azúcar, aceite de palma y flores, como las orquídeas, que es la flor nacional.
Colombia destaca además por la producción de carbón, petróleo y esmeraldas.

En Colombia hay un importante patrimonio musical, con ritmos como la cumbia, la salsa y el vallenato.
Pero la figura internacionalmente más famosa es la cantante Shakira, sin olvidar a Juanes, quien ha liderado una importante campaña mundial contra la erradicación de las minas antipersonales.

En lo referente a la literatura, no podemos dejar de citar a Gabriel García Márquez, que obtuvo el Premio Nobel en 1982 por *Cien años de soledad*. Álvaro Mutis es también otro escritor colombiano de renombre mundial.

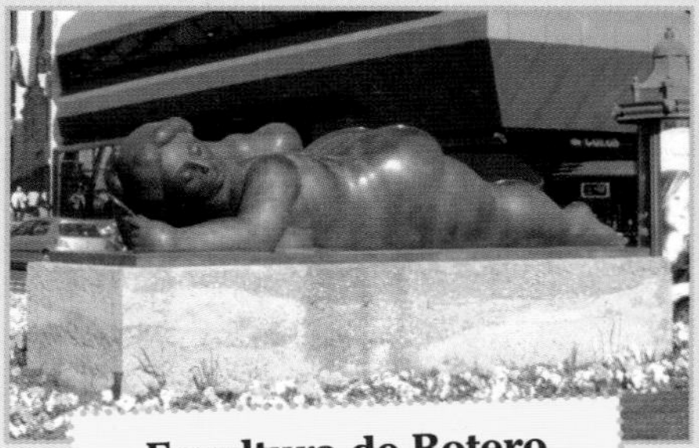

Escultura de Botero

Fernando Botero es quizás el pintor y escultor más conocido, famoso por sus figuras de gordos.

El deporte más importante en Colombia es el fútbol, aunque muchos consideran el tejo como el deporte nacional. El tejo es un deporte autóctono, muy difundido en el centro del país. En la costa norte, además del fútbol, es muy importante el béisbol, deporte que cuenta con representantes en las grandes ligas de los Estados Unidos, como Edgar Rentería.

Colombia figura dentro de la máxima categoría del automovilismo mundial gracias a Juan Pablo Montoya.

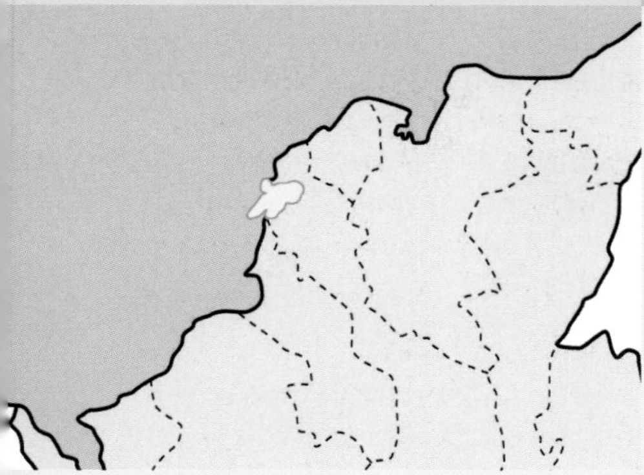

Cartagena de Indias

Ubicada a orillas del Mar Caribe, es la quinta ciudad del país en orden de importancia, pero la primera para el turismo.

En 1984 la UNESCO la declaró Patrimonio Histórico y Cultural de la Humanidad.

Fue fundada en 1533 por Pedro de Heredia y durante la época colonial fue una de las ciudades más importantes del continente, dado que de allí salían las mayores riquezas hacia España.

Cartagena de Indias

Muralla de Cartagena

Fue también el mayor punto de comercio de esclavos traídos de África. Fue asaltada varias veces por piratas y tropas inglesas, francesas y holandesas. Por eso el rey de España mandó construir una muralla para defenderla.

Cartagena es además una maravillosa ciudad colonial, de casas bajas con rejas y balcones de madera. Muchos edificios e iglesias que parecen de piedra, están construidos con coral blanco.

Monasterio de San Pedro Claver

Cartagena cuenta con 14 construcciones religiosas, entre las que destacan la Catedral, el Convento e Iglesia de Santo Domingo, la Iglesia y Monasterio de San Pedro Claver, entre otras.

Fuera de la ciudad amurallada se encuentra el Castillo de San Felipe de Barajas (1536-1657), que protegió a la ciudad de diversos ataques de piratas. En el interior hay galerías, trampas y túneles.

Los mejores ejemplos de edificios públicos son la Aduana, donde actualmente funciona la Alcaldía, y el Palacio de la Inquisición.

Fortaleza de San Felipe

La Bahía de Cartagena está rodeada de islas y lagunas. Una de las excursiones clásicas es la de las Islas del Rosario, una serie de 27 islas coralinas que son Parque Nacional. Para ir a las islas se pasa por el Fuerte de San Fernando y Fuerte de San José de Bochica.

Otra de las atracciones de Cartagena son sus playas. Bocagrande y Laguito son las más visitadas por los turistas.

A unos 70 km de la ciudad se encuentra Palenque de San Basilio. Fue fundada por esclavos rebeldes en el siglo XV, liderados por Benkos Biohó. El hecho de haber permanecido aislada permitió a sus habitantes mantener la mayoría de las tradiciones culturales africanas (música, medicina, ritos fúnebres, organización social). Además, allí se habla una lengua de origen africano: el palenquero. Se considera que es el primer pueblo libre de América. Sus calles de tierra, su música y la calidez de su gente nos hace sentirnos en otra época.